Penny-an-Acre Empire in the West

Penny-an-Acre Empire in the West

Collected and Edited by

Edgar I. Stewart

University of Oklahoma Press : *Norman*

By Edgar I. Stewart

Custer's Luck (Norman, 1955)
The Field Diary of Lieutenant Edward S. Godfrey (editor, with Jane R. Stewart) (Portland, 1957)
The Columbia River, by Ross Cox (editor, with Jane R. Stewart) (Norman, 1957)
Life and Adventures of Frank Grouard, by Joe De Barthe (editor) (Norman, 1958)
The March of the Montana Column: A Prelude to the Custer Disaster, by Lt. James H. Bradley (editor) (Norman, 1958)
My Life on the Plains; or Personal Experiences with Indians, by George Armstrong Custer (editor) (Norman, 1962)
Penny-an-Acre Empire in the West (Norman, 1968)

Library of Congress Catalog Card Number: 67–24618

Copyright 1968 by the University of Oklahoma Press, Publishing Division of the University. Composed and printed at Norman, Oklahoma, U.S.A., by the University of Oklahoma Press. First edition.

To the Memory of
PROFESSOR EUGENE I. McCORMAC
Greatest of Teachers and Best of Friends

Preface

The legend of the Great American Desert is one that has long persisted in American history. The idea that the region lying between the Missouri River and the Rocky Mountains was a barren and inhospitable area unfit alike for cultivation and for a civilized existence has persisted since the early days of the Republic, and is held in some places even today. It was widely believed that west of the one hundredth meridian there was little besides sagebrush and cactus, few inhabitants except prairie dogs and wild Indians, and it was firmly held that this meridian marked a barrier to settlement that was as real as the shore of the ocean.

Although the idea was held by many and was put forward by a number of writers, the classic expression of the theory was the pamphlet written by General William Babcock Hazen entitled *Our Barren Lands*. This pamphlet, which has long been out of print and is quite expensive when procurable, was the result of an earlier letter to the New York *Tribune* which produced a number of indignant letters in reply, especially one from no less a personage than General George Armstrong Custer. In this book I have reprinted the principal items emanating from the pens of the two adversaries as well as other pertinent materials which throw light upon the matter. While Hazen and Custer were old antagonists and seem to have entertained a strong mutual dislike for each other, the matter involved a number of other persons and factors. Although theoretically including the entire region of the Great Plains, in practice the dispute centered largely on the route of the

Northern Pacific Railroad west of the Missouri River and especially the valley of the Yellowstone River. As such it was almost a
matter of economic life and death to the developing towns along
the projected line of the railroad.

I have not attempted to survey the reports of explorers, army
officers, fur traders, missionaries and other travelers on the value
of the trans-Missouri region. While it was these reports that had
led originally to the belief in the existence of the Great American
Desert, even to summarize them would require a volume in itself.

Since no attempt is being made to produce facsimiles of the
various documents in this volume, I have taken a few editorial
liberties, such as the deletion of newspaper subheads and the
imposition of a kind of uniformity in letter headings and signa-
tures. The text, however, remains intact.

In a work such as this, one incurs many obligations, particularly so when the research has been continued intermittently over
a period of several years, and as new materials are constantly
being brought to one's attention. I am very greatly indebted to
Archibald Hanna and his staff of able assistants of the Western
American Collection at Yale University. Joseph O'Donnell, ar-
chivist at the United States Military Academy has checked several
items in the military records of both General Hazen and General
Custer for me. Edith Shaw of the Eastern Washington State College Library, Mary Dempsey of the Montana Historical Society,
and Margaret Rose, formerly with the North Dakota Historical
Society, have rendered that gracious and competent assistance
that is the trade-mark of the professional reference librarian and
that scholars, regrettably, too often take for granted. Michael
Brooke and Thomas F. Deahl of the Minnesota Historical Society,
and Walter Gustafson and William Mackenzie of the advertising
and publicity department of the Northern Pacific Railroad have
answered innumerable questions and given full co-operation in
every way. Laura A. Engstrom of the State Historical Society of
Colorado has supplied information about the career of Nathan C.
Meeker in Colorado, and Edward N. Holden has furnished information about James J. H. Gregory, the seed king of Marblehead,

Massachusetts. Senator Henry Jackson and his able staff have graciously secured all sorts of assorted information from various governmental agencies. My greatest debt, as usual, is to my wife, who has done most of the secretarial work and borne patiently with an author's idiosyncracies. To all of these I am deeply and sincerely grateful. None is responsible for statements of fact or interpretation nor for the errors that undoubtedly exist. These are ascribable solely to myself.

EDGAR I. STEWART

Cheney, Washington
September 1, 1967

Contents

Penny-an-Acre Empire in the West

1. Introduction

In January, 1875, Brevet Major General William B. Hazen, then holding the rank of colonel of the Sixth United States Infantry and commanding the post at Fort Buford, Dakota Territory, wrote a small pamphlet entitled *Our Barren Lands,* in which he declared that the great expanse of territory lying between the Missouri River and the Sierra Nevada mountains, and extending from the Río Grande to the Canadian border, was largely useless and not worth "a penny an acre." This pamphlet is of interest not only for the point of view which it so ably presents, but also because it represents almost the final expression of one position in an altercation between two of the most controversial figures of the United States Army during the post–Civil War period, Generals Hazen and George Armstrong Custer. The reputation of the latter is well known. Of General Hazen, the *Army and Navy Journal* said editorially at the time of his death: "No one in the Service had a more unfortunate faculty for involving himself in controversies, and it has not been easy in all cases to determine to what traits his difficulties were chargeable. His history shows that he was a capable soldier in spite of the criticisms to which particular episodes in it are subjected."[1] Thus, the backgrounds of both of the protagonists and of the pamphlet itself are not without interest and are necessary for an understanding of its importance as a historical document.

William Babcock Hazen was born at West Hartford, Windsor

[1] *Army and Navy Journal,* Jan. 22, 1887.

County, Vermont, on September 30, 1830, but at an early age moved with his parents to Hiram, Ohio. Here he grew to manhood, and here he came in contact with a number of persons, including James A. Garfield, who were later to be of importance on the national scene. In 1851 he received an appointment to the United States Military Academy at West Point, from which he was graduated four years later. His record as a cadet was rather mediocre, his order of general merit being in the lowest 50 per cent of the class. Drawing and philosophy were the only subjects in which he ranked above average. In his last year, during the course of which he received 163 demerits, he showed a striking deficiency in the military subjects. In a class of thirty-six, he was thirtieth in infantry tactics and twenty-sixth in both cavalry and artillery tactics. He graduated twenty-eighth with an appointment as brevet second lieutenant of infantry.[2] On the fourth of September, 1855, he was commissioned in the Fourth Infantry and served at Fort Lane, Fort Yamhill, and other posts in Oregon Territory until 1858. It was apparently during this period that he performed a feat rather remarkable in the army of that day. Most young officers coming on duty could expect to be assigned the responsibility of post commissary and quartermaster, and to learn the duties of the position often caused them a stoppage of pay, sometimes amounting to several hundred dollars. It was said of Lieutenant Hazen that he was the only officer to perform that duty when young in the service and to have no stoppages against him.[3]

In 1858, Lieutenant Hazen was transferred to the Southwest, where he won considerable official praise for the vigor and success of his actions against the Apache and Kickapoo Indians on the Nueces River. In November, 1859, he was seriously wounded in action against the Comanche Indians, a wound that was partially

---

[2] Dumas Malone, ed., *Dictionary of American Biography*, VIII, 478–79 (hereinafter cited as *Dictionary of American Biography*). This particular article was by Frederic Logan Paxson. In 1879, Hazen was described as "short, thick-set, with a typical French military cut of countenance." *Army and Navy Journal*, April 19, 1879. Details of Hazen's academic record at the Military Academy were furnished by Joseph O'Donnell, Archives and History Division at that institution.

[3] *Army and Navy Journal*, May 11, 1869.

to disable him for the remainder of his life. He was on sick leave as a result of wounds until February 21, 1861, when he took station at West Point as assistant professor of infantry tactics. In April he was promoted to first lieutenant and about six weeks later to captain in the Eighth Infantry. It was during this tour of duty at the Military Academy that he had his first encounter with Custer.

Custer, who was also from Ohio, had been appointed to the Academy in 1857. His academic record was the reverse of brilliant, and he seems to have excelled mainly in the accumulation of demerits. At this distance in time it is difficult to see how he escaped dismissal, and when he graduated in June, 1861, it was at the very bottom of his class. The Civil War was already in progress, and it may very well have been that the military authorities, realizing that the government had an investment in him and knowing that someone would be needed to drill the recruits, decided to give him a commission regardless of his shortcomings. Five days after graduation, he incurred official displeasure by failing to stop a fight between two cadets, which as an officer it was his duty to do. Rather, he encouraged it, insisting only that it be a fair contest. For this he was placed in arrest and court-martialed under charges preferred by Captain Hazen, the officer of the day. Custer, who seems to have been badly frightened, pleaded guilty and escaped with nothing more than a reprimand, the leniency of his sentence being due, at least in part, to favorable testimony from Captain Hazen, although Custer seems to have been unaware of the fact, since he said afterward that he never knew his sentence.[4] Had he known that Hazen had befriended him in his hour of need, his attitude might have been different, but on the other hand, his attitude toward Hazen may have arisen from the fact that the latter had befriended him. In some ways Custer seems to have been one of those individuals who could forget and forgive an injury but could not forgive a gracious gesture.

[4] Jay Monaghan, *Custer* (Boston, Little, Brown and Co., 1959), 43, has a very good account of this incident. Frederick Whittaker, *Popular Life of Gen. George A. Custer* (New York, Sheldon and Co., 1876), 43–46, gives the story in Custer's own words.

Both men went on to win honor and distinction in the Civil War; if Custer's career was the more flamboyant and spectacular, Hazen's was equally substantial. In September, 1861, Hazen was granted a leave of absence from the regular army to take command of the Forty-first Ohio Volunteers, a regiment that he had personally recruited. His service during the war was entirely in the western theater, culminating when he was with Sherman on the famous "March to the Sea." Custer, in the meantime, was with the Army of the Potomac. In the Grand Review in Washington at the end of the war, Custer rode at the head of the Third Cavalry division while Hazen was in command of the Fifteenth Army Corps.

With the shake-up of the army that followed the end of hostilities, both men reverted to the rank of captain. Both names were on the list of major generals ordered mustered out by General Order No. 158, Office of the Adjutant General, December 28, 1865, a list that included the names of Alfred Pleasanton, David S. Stanley, Andrew J. Smith, John Gibbon, and George Crook besides many others. Custer became a captain in the Fifth Cavalry, Hazen in the Eighth Infantry,[5] but the army was being reorganized and enlarged, and Custer was soon appointed lieutenant colonel of the newly created Seventh Cavalry, a regiment specifically organized for service against the Indians of the Great Plains. At almost the same time Hazen was named colonel of the Thirty-eighth Infantry, although he was then serving as acting inspector general on the staff of Brigadier General Philip St. George Cooke, commanding the Department of the Platte. In August he was sent to inspect the forts along the Bozeman Road and the upper Missouri River, visiting Fort Reno, Fort Phil Kearny, and Fort C. F. Smith before going on to Fort Benton. He described Fort Phil Kearny, soon to become famous as the locale of the Fetterman Fight, as one of the strongest that he had seen. The only post that exceeded it, in his opinion, was one built by the Hudson's Bay Company in British America. At Fort Kearny he had contributed to the weakening of the post by adding an officer and twenty-six mounted men to his

[5] *Army and Navy Journal*, Jan. 20, 1866.

escort before proceeding northward to Fort C. F. Smith, where he arrived on the third of September. Although General Cooke had suggested that it be abandoned, Hazen disagreed, and while recognizing the isolation of the post, agreed with Colonel Henry Carrington in his contention that it should be retained. Hazen expressed the opinion that travel over the Bozeman Road was safe and that there was little danger to parties that were well organized and did not straggle. From Fort C. F. Smith he proceeded north, down the Big Horn River to the Yellowstone and then across to Fort Benton. On this trip he passed through a good part of the region that he was later to write about so unfavorably.

At the end of this tour of inspection Hazen had written:

> After leaving Omaha the soil of the Platte Valley is highly productive for nearly two hundred miles yielding abundantly with the ordinary methods of American farming. At about that point or near old Fort Kearney, the soil becomes thin and weak and the atmosphere dry and continues so all the way to the Rocky Mountains, and west of them in Montana, Idaho and Utah, so far as I have seen.
>
> Of this entire country one-half may be considered of no value, the other half, for pastoral purposes, of about one-tenth the value of good grazing land in the northern states. Of this last half, on an average of about one acre in one thousand, can be made abundantly productive by irrigation and in no other way. These last points are found near springs under the mountains, or the immediate borders of most of the streams, and in the valleys of the Sun, Jefferson, Madison and Gallatin rivers. Each of these streams have fine rich valleys of from one to five miles in breadth, and from fifty to one hundred miles in length, all of which can be irrigated and cultivated. In the Great Salt Lake Basin along the base of the Wasatch mountains, and in the narrow valleys of the western slope of these mountains is good cultivable land, with abundant springs for irrigation. This section is about five hundred and fifty miles in length, and if all of the good land could be placed in one piece, it would have a breadth for the entire length of not more than ten miles. These lands are nearly all occupied by the Mormons, making a population of about one hundred thousand.
>
> Three-fourths of all the country passed over is made up of mountain ranges. Wild grasses of various qualities grow thinly over nearly all of it. Scattering cottonwood trees occasionally thickening into

groves, border the streams, and on the sides of some of the mountains pine timber grows of a very good quality.

Whatever mineral wealth the country may have can only be known when it is developed. It has large amounts of coal and some iron. Its precious metals, as at present produced, are damaging to the country at large, as they draw here ten times as much capital and labor as finds profitable employment.

The country has little value and can never be sold by government at more than nominal rates. It will in time be settled by a scanty pastoral population. No amount of railroad schemes of colonization, or government encouragement can ever make more of it.[6]

From this statement it is apparent that Hazen's opinion of the region west of the Missouri River was deep-seated and long standing, and that his later written communications were not the result of temporary exasperation.

The next few years were spent on various assignments, including a trip to Europe, although technically Hazen was still in command of his regiment. On the seventh of March, 1868, he joined the regiment at Fort Craig, New Mexico, but remained there only until the twenty-eighth of August, when he was assigned by General Sherman as military superintendent of the southern Indians with headquarters at Fort Cobb, Indian Territory. This was to bring him again into contact and conflict with Custer.

The colonel of the newly created Seventh Cavalry, which was activated at Fort Riley, Kansas, was Andrew Jackson Smith, a hard-bitten veteran of the Mexican War who, like Custer, had been a major general during the Civil War and during the fifties had seen considerable service on the western frontier. But he was now perfectly willing to leave to his subordinate the task of pounding the new regiment into shape. This was a task which Custer found far from congenial, especially in view of the fact that many of the raw and undisciplined troopers with whom he had to work had been drawn from the very dregs of society. Custer was a hard taskmaster, in addition to being something of a martinet, and

---

[6] "Inspection by Generals Rusling and Hazen," 30 Cong., 2 sess., *House Executive Document No. 45*. Although not in the title, this was "Tour of Inspection from the Missouri to the Pacific in 1866."

from the beginning desertion constituted a serious problem in the regiment. The penalty for this was not at all severe, and in many cases the deserters were such poor soldiers as not to be worth the expense and trouble of apprehension. As a result the regiment took shape slowly, but by the spring of 1867 it was sufficiently established as a military organization to constitute a part of the force which General Hancock led against the tribes of the Southern Plains.

This expedition, one of the most widely advertised efforts to chastise the hostile tribesmen, proved to be a dismal failure. But it was crucial for Custer. Desertions continued on a wholesale scale, even while the regiment was in the field, and in an effort to avert what he apparently considered to be nothing less than mutiny, Custer ordered the shooting down of deserters without trial. When the regiment returned to Fort Wallace, located near the site of the present town of Wallace, Kansas, Custer absented himself without leave from his command, going first to Fort Harker, where he reported and talked briefly to Colonel Smith, and then, apparently on the assumption that he had Colonel Smith's permission, on to Fort Riley. For this and for the shooting down of the deserters, Custer was court-martialed, convicted, and sentenced to suspension from rank and pay for one year. The leniency of the sentence, especially in view of the gravity of the charges and of the evidence against him, is difficult to explain. The presumption is almost inescapable that it was due to factors not mentioned in the written record of the proceedings. The Hancock expedition, of which so much had been expected, had proved to be a fiasco, and Custer was a convenient scapegoat. Also there was the possibility that the court felt that in his treatment of deserters, Custer had merely applied a drastic remedy to an equally drastic situation. So, after spending considerable time at Fort Leavenworth, where he occupied quarters considerately turned over to him by General Sheridan, Custer went to Monroe, Michigan, to spend the remaining months of his suspension.[7]

[7] Although Custer put on a brave front and claimed that this enforced leisure would give him the opportunity to do some long-deferred writing and also stated

9

Indian hostilities continued, and since General Alfred Sully, now in command of the campaign on the southern plains, had proved inept, General Sheridan finally intervened. He requested and obtained the remission of the remainder of Custer's sentence, and Custer lost no time in rejoining his command. He reached Fort Hays on the thirtieth of September to find his regiment encamped on Bluff Creek, a tributary of the Arkansas, and almost in a state of siege. Such a condition of affairs was not at all congenial to the Custer temperament, and he immediately began organizing his command for the purpose of carrying the war to the enemy. On the twenty-third of November, with eleven companies of his regiment—Troop L was stationed at Fort Lyon, Colorado—Custer moved out from Camp Supply, located near the confluence of Wolf and Beaver creeks about one mile above the point where they unite to form the North Fork of the Canadian River, on the campaign which was to culminate in the battle of the Washita four days later.

In the meantime, Hazen had assumed his duties as superintendent of the Southern Indian district. In this capacity he had charge of all the Indians in the region south of Kansas and east of New Mexico not actually under the charge of the Department of the Interior nor claimed on account of their hostile character as subject to the commander of the military district in which they happened to be. Some of these Indians, notably the Arapahos and Cheyennes, had already commenced hostilities; but others, such as the Kiowas and Comanches, professed to be peaceful, and since it was desirable that these tribes be kept from joining the hostiles, Hazen, together with Sheridan, met the Kiowas and Comanches in council at Fort Larned.[8] It was arranged for these Indians to go to Fort Cobb, located on the Washita River, with Hazen and remain near there. But since sufficient supplies were not then available at Fort Larned, it was agreed that the Indians were to

---

that he planned to spend some time abroad, there is no doubt that he was deeply hurt. See the dispatch from Fort Leavenworth, signed "Russell," in the New York *Times*, Sunday, Dec. 7, 1867.

[8] Fort Larned was located near the present town of Larned, Kansas.

be allowed to hunt buffalo for a week and then return to the post, secure their rations, and set out for Fort Cobb with Hazen and an escort of troops. But the Kiowas did not return to Fort Larned. Their explanation was that the buffalo hunt had carried them farther to the south than had been expected and that they disliked traveling in the company of soldiers, so they proceeded directly to Fort Cobb, only to find that Hazen had not yet arrived. Professing to believe that his absence indicated that the arrangements had been canceled, they moved to the vicinity of the Antelope Hills and prepared, as was their custom, to go into winter camp. While there, certain bands admittedly engaged in minor depredations against the Ute Indians as well as against settlers on the Texas frontier.

Hazen waited at Fort Larned a few days beyond the appointed time, but when the Indians failed to arrive set out for Fort Cobb. The smallness of his escort and the necessity of avoiding the area of hostilities made it necessary for him to make a wide detour to the east, and his arrival at Fort Cobb on the eighth of November was about two weeks behind the schedule agreed upon. Here he found the Comanches to the number of about seven hundred encamped. They had come straight through from Fort Larned. Also present were about seventeen hundred Caddos, Wichitas, and affiliated bands. Within the next few weeks most of the Kiowas, including the bands of Kicking Bird and Satanta, came in. They had definitely been engaged in depredations against the settlers. Thus, by November 20, all of the principal chiefs with their bands were gathered on the reservation, their camps extending along the Washita River for some twenty miles above and below Fort Cobb, this wide dispersion being made necessary by the amount of grazing land demanded by the Indian pony herds.

It was at sunrise on the twenty-seventh that Custer struck the camp of Black Kettle, located on the Washita River about one hundred miles above Fort Cobb. As the battle progressed, it was noted that supposedly hostile Indians from other camps located farther down the river, of whose existence Custer had been unaware, since no reconnaissance had been made, were observing

11

the battle from the bluffs along the river. Custer, having destroyed Black Kettle's village and fearing a concerted attack against his column, decided to withdraw. Knowing that a movement away from Indians was almost certain death, the troops feigned a movement downstream, and then turning abruptly began the return march toward Camp Supply. The withdrawal was rather precipitate and the troops left without having ascertained what had become of Major Joel Elliott and a small detachment of troopers who had ridden off in pursuit of a group of Indians. Later, when the badly mutilated and frozen bodies of these troopers were found, it was to lead to the accusation that Custer had deliberately abandoned a part of his command, a charge that deepened and intensified the factionalism that already existed within the ranks of the Seventh Cavalry.

A few days after returning to Camp Supply, the regiment, reinforced by twelve companies of the Nineteenth Kansas Volunteer Cavalry under the command of Colonel Samuel J. Crawford, again moved south. This time the command was accompanied by General Sheridan. The battleground of the Washita was visited and the bodies of Major Elliott and his troopers recovered and buried. After marching for seven days below the battlefield, and passing the sites of a number of recently abandoned Indian villages, one of which was said to have been the camp of Satanta, the notorious Kiowa chieftain, the command was confronted by a large group of apparent hostiles. The troops deployed for battle, but before an attack could be launched a courier arrived with a message from Hazen stating that these Indians, as well as the others between that point and Fort Cobb, were peaceable. Although Custer later declared that he was convinced that the Indians had come out to attack his command, and had been deterred only by finding the force arrayed against them much greater than had been expected, there was nothing to do but to accept Hazen's word. In a series of articles written for the *Galaxy* and later published in book form under the title *My Life on the Plains*, Custer described this incident, and stated his conclusion that Hazen had been deceived. Custer wrote:

12

In the example to which I refer, the high character and distinction as well as the deservedly national reputation achieved by the official then in charge of the Indians against whom we were operating will at once absolve me from the imputation of intentionally reflecting upon the integrity of his action in the matter. The only point to occasion is how an officer possessing the knowledge of the Indian character, derived from an extensive experience on the frontier, which General Hazen could justly lay claim to, should be so far misled as to give the certificate of good conduct.[9]

This called forth a reply from Hazen in which he strongly defended the course of action that he had followed. This reply, which was published in the form of a pamphlet in 1875, makes the controversy over the battle of the Washita contemporary with the one on the value of the lands west of the Missouri River.

At this distance in time there can be but little doubt that Custer was correct in his opinion that Hazen had been deceived, and that had he (Custer) been allowed to attack the Indians, a great deal of future trouble would have been avoided. That Sheridan shared his opinion is beyond question. A few weeks after this incident, Sheridan decided on the establishment of Fort Sill on Cache Creek near the eastern end of the Wichita Mountains as a permanent base for operations against the Indians of the Southwest. In 1872, General Sheridan wrote an exasperated reply to a criticism by Hazen of Indian operations, in which he accused Hazen of being too easily deceived by the Indians on this occasion.

On July 1, 1869, Hazen was transferred to the Sixth Infantry, serving with it at Fort Gibson, Indian Territory, and also discharging the duties of superintendent of Indian affairs, Southern Superintendency, serving until August 20, 1870, when he was granted a leave of absence for the purpose of visiting the theater of military occupations during the Franco-Prussian War. He was at the headquarters of the German Army and at Versailles. He also observed the siege of Paris before returning to the United

---

[9] George Armstrong Custer, *My Life on the Plains; Or Personal Experiences with Indians*, with an introduction by Edgar I. Stewart (Norman, University of Oklahoma Press, 1962), 291. General Hazen's reply to these charges is published as an appendix in the same volume.

13

States in 1871 and rejoining his regiment. He returned a short time after Custer's regiment, the Seventh Cavalry, had been transferred from the Department of the Missouri to the Department of the South, for duty in the states of the former Confederacy. Headquarters of the regiment were at Taylor Barracks, Louisville, Kentucky.

At the time there was considerable criticism of the traders licensed to do business at the various army posts. Up until 1870 the appointment and control of the post traders lay with the army and were the subject of open competition before a board of officers; but in June of that year a law was passed which took the post traderships out of the domain of public competition and placed them in the field of private favor. Under the circumstances the traders enjoyed almost a monopoly of the trade of officers and enlisted men alike. An editorial in the semiofficial *Army and Navy Journal* spoke of the post trader as "the alpha of prices and the omega of goods," and declared that it was "incomprehensible how so self-evident a swindle" had been allowed to build itself into an institution at all of the United States military posts. The editorial continued: "What then is this power, laughing at the press, law, and public opinion, that thus openly sucks the lifeblood of the soldiers? What is this monstrous rascality that our military authorities, composed of educated gentlemen and honorable men, have so blindly permitted to fasten upon the rank and file of our army?"[10] Later in the year, a letter from Fort Laramie listed as one of the principal causes of desertion "the extortionate prices charged enlisted men by the post-traders for every article they buy" and then went on to declare that the traders were not satisfied with a reasonable gain but insisted on realizing from 75 to 100 per cent profit on their goods.[11]

An explanation of the rapacity of the post traders was not long in coming. Early in 1872, Hazen, in an inspection at Fort Sill, had heard some of these complaints and had learned that the post trader there, Caleb P. Marsh, was paying tribute to someone in

[10] *Army and Navy Journal*, March 18, 1871.
[11] *Ibid.*, Jan. 20, 1872.

the East for the right to hold the post. As soon as he was reasonably sure of his facts, he wrote to James A. Garfield, then chairman of the House Committee on Military Affairs, to whom he referred as "my old friend and school-mate," calling his attention to the situation. Later, on invitation, Hazen appeared before the committee to testify about the staff organization of the French and German armies and was also questioned on the subject of post traders. To these questions he had remonstrated on the ground that his testimony might be considered unfriendly to the Secretary of War, but had been assured by the chairman, Mr. Coburn, that it would be considered confidential. However, Mr. Smalley, the secretary or clerk of the committee was also a reporter for the New York *Tribune*—an interesting example of an early case of a conflict of interest—and Hazen's testimony was openly published. Mr. Coburn later claimed that, although the evils of the system of post traderships were obvious, no one dreamed that the Secretary of War was making money out of the appointment of the traders. There were, however, plenty of persons who had a very good idea that such was the case. Later, Mr. Smalley was dismissed from his position with the committee, not for publishing the testimony of General Hazen, but, in the words of Mr. Coburn, "because he was totally unfitted for the position as clerk, and disagreed politically with a majority of the committee."[12]

In his article Smalley stated flatly that the trader at Fort Sill paid twelve thousand dollars a year in quarterly installments for the post to John S. Evans. Later Marsh was to testify under oath that he called the *Tribune* article to the attention of Secretary of War Belknap, and inquired about who could have written or inspired it. He received the answer that the Secretary believed it to be the work of Hazen. Secretary Belknap then brought the article to the attention of President Grant and was assured that he (Grant) did not believe a word of it.[13] There the matter was allowed to rest, leaving it a matter of veracity between the Secretary of War and the colonel of the Sixth Infantry. Secretary

[12] New York *Times*, April 5, 1876.
[13] *Ibid.*, July 11, 1876.

15

Belknap issued an order which he said would correct the abuse, but it was not enforced and things continued the same as before. Only a few weeks after Hazen's appearance before the committee, his regiment, the Sixth Infantry, was ordered transferred to Fort Buford. There were those who felt that he was being punished—exiled as it were—for daring to speak out against a favorite of the administration. Thus on Hazen's return from Mexico City in 1876, the New York *Tribune*, commenting on his return to his old command in Dakota, observed: "It is not supposed, however, that he can be kept there much longer. He was exiled for four years because of his indiscretion in exposing the post traderships business in 1872."[14] The Cincinnati *Commercial* declared flatly that it was his testimony in 1872 that had led to his transfer "from Fort Hayes [*sic*] to Fort Buford."[15] Custer, in testifying before the Clymer Committee in 1876, declared that Hazen for daring to make a communication relative to the Fort Sill business had been "exiled" to Fort Buford, which he characterized as "a lonely and forlorn post approximately one thousand miles to the west of St. Paul,"[16] and he ventured the prediction that similar testimony by any other officer would probably result in that officer's being exiled to an equally undesirable post.

However, it is by no means certain that Secretary Belknap was responsible for this transfer, and there is the definite possibility that it was nothing more than coincidence, although there is also the possibility that General Sheridan's animosity to Hazen may have been a factor in the selection of the Sixth Infantry for transfer. In the spring of 1872 the virtual certainty that the Indians of Montana would make war upon the Northern Pacific Railroad as soon as the line crossed the Missouri River led the War Department to the serious consideration of the necessity of strengthening the western forts which were in the area of probable hostilities. General Philip H. Sheridan, commanding the Division of the Missouri, reported that all trustworthy information indicated that

[14] *Army and Navy Journal*, May 6, 1876, quoting from the New York *Tribune*.
[15] As quoted in the New York *Times*, March 6, 1876.
[16] Edgar I. Stewart, *Custer's Luck* (Norman, University of Oklahoma Press, 1955), 131.

some two thousand hostile warriors, said to include representatives of all the various bands of the Sioux Nation, were collected at a point about 120 miles southwest of Fort Berthold. They had already torn up the stakes that the previous surveyors for the railroad had put down, and, led by such well-known chiefs as Sitting Bull, Black Moon, and Four Horns, were said to be planning an all-out attack on the railroad crews west of the Missouri River.

This had not been exactly startling information as far as General Sheridan was concerned. He had been conscious of the danger for some time, and in his *Report* of the year before had declared his intention of strengthening the forts in Montana and along the Missouri River. Increasing the garrison at Fort Buford also had a high priority. At that time this post was occupied by three companies of the Seventh Infantry with a total of 9 officers and 152 enlisted men under the command of Lieutenant Colonel C. C. Gilbert. These three companies were now to be moved farther west, proceeding by steamer up the Missouri River to Fort Benton, the highest point to which steamers could go, and from there they would march overland to Fort Shaw, located on the Sun River. Replacing them at Fort Buford would be six companies of the Sixth Infantry.[17]

When the report that Hazen and his regiment had been ordered to Fort Buford as an act of personal vengeance came to the attention of General Belknap, he issued a prompt and vigorous denial. In a letter addressed to General Sheridan he requested information about the reasons for ordering the transfer of the Sixth Infantry from the Department of the Missouri to the Department of Dakota. To this Sheridan replied that he had made out a full statement of the factors in the transfer and that he had "yet to learn" that Secretary Belknap had anything to do with the order. He added that he was "reluctant to believe that Colonel Hazen would have started or countenanced such false rumors as to the motives for the movement." The *Army and Navy Journal* added editorially that while a great deal had been seen of Hazen when he

[17] *Army and Navy Journal,* June 1, 1872.

was in New York, he had never been heard to hint at such a reason for his transfer. It added that it did not believe that he was responsible for the rumors and ended by observing that there were numerous papers and memoranda dealing with the subject that led to the conclusion that the transfer was "in the ordinary course of detail," and that the Secretary of War "had nothing to do with the matter besides authorizing the transfer of a regiment without indicating which one."[18]

One other reason for ordering the transfer has been alleged. As a result of his observations and experiences in Europe during the Franco-Prussian War, Hazen had written a book entitled *The School and the Army in Germany and France with a Diary of Siege Life at Versailles,* which was published by Harper and Brothers during the summer of 1872. The exact date of publication is uncertain, but on May 18, 1872, the *Army and Navy Journal* reported the book in press and added that "it will be looked for with interest." The *Journal* then went on to say: "It gives his views on army matters, some of our military peculiarities being criticized with the frankness characteristic of the author."[19] In this volume Hazen made several criticisms of the American military system together with unflattering comparisons with that of Prussia. One chapter, especially, is said to have given offense to Generals Sherman and Sheridan and to have been a factor in the decision to order the Sixth Infantry to Fort Buford. There is always the possibility that one or both of the men may have seen an advance copy, but other than the probability of the book's having had any influence is remote since the transfer was ordered before it appeared.

In any event, on the twenty-third of April, 1872, the Sixth Infantry was ordered transferred from various stations in Kansas and Indian Territory to the Department of Dakota. Prior to the transfer the regiment was distributed as follows: Headquarters

[18] *Ibid.,* May 13, 1876. The transfer seems to have been ordered by General John Pope, commanding the Department of the Missouri.

[19] *Army and Navy Journal,* May 18, 1872.

and Companies A, G, and I were at Fort Hays, Kansas; Companies B, C, H, and K were at Camp Supply, Indian Territory; Companies E and F were at Fort Dodge; and Company D at Fort Larned, Kansas. Under the new orders, Headquarters and Companies A, D, E, F, G, and I were to take station at Fort Buford; Companies B and C, under the command of Lieutenant Colonel Carlin, who had not yet joined the regiment, were to be stationed at the new post being constructed at the Northern Pacific Railway crossing of the Missouri River. This post was subsequently named Fort McKeen, the name later being changed to Fort Abraham Lincoln. The remaining two companies, H and K, were to constitute the garrison at Fort Stevenson, located eighty-nine miles above Bismarck on the north bank of the Missouri River near the present town of Garrison, North Dakota. Apart from the greater isolation of Fort Buford, there was little to choose between the two areas, Kansas and Dakota.

En route to his new post of duty, General Hazen became engaged in another controversy. He learned from newspaper accounts of the murder by Kiowa Indians of sixteen persons near Howard Wells, Texas. This massacre caused a great deal of excitement and there was considerable comment in the press. It awakened bitter memories on the part of General Hazen, since he had suffered his painful wound near there at the hands of these same Indians. In an outspoken letter to the New York *Tribune*, written at Sioux City, Iowa, May 21, 1872, and later reprinted in the *Army and Navy Journal*, he declared that the marauders were probably Indians from the Fort Sill Reservation. He went on to say that the worst feature of the whole affair was in the newspaper accounts which made the mistake of "attempting to charge it to the Indians from Mexico, and to Mexicans and negroes, thus excusing ourselves from performance of a duty which we have long evaded." Stating that he had served two years along this line before the war and knew "perfectly the habits of the Indians who have always made the Wells a point of attack," and that for a year after the war he had been in charge of the Indians who made the

19

raids, he asserted that the full facts were known to the agents of the United States government, but despite reports and complaints, no action had ever been taken.[20]

This was hitting directly at General Sheridan, commanding the Division of the Missouri, and he immediately wrote an exasperated reply. After first endorsing General Augur's remarks that the Kiowas were "without a single trait or sentiment that Christianity or any other ennobling principle" could use "to improve or elevate them," he declared that the tribe needed punishment of the severest kind, and that the army was prepared to administer it to them whenever the proper authorities should so order. He then continued:

> Had it not been for Colonel Hazen, who represented that these Indians were friendly when I followed their trail without missing it for a moment from the "battle" of the "Washita" until I overtook them, the Texas front would be in a better condition than now, and we would be free from embarrassment. He seems to have forgotten in his recent newspaper communication when he censures the government for not chastising these Indians that when I had my sabres drawn to do it, he pronounced them, in the name of the Peace Commissioners, friendly. . . . The Government will not be able for a much longer time to avoid the demands of progress and settlement, and must insist upon the measures which will render every portion of our extensive frontier safe for a citizen to travel over or occupy.[21]

This, then, was the situation when General Hazen, with one company of infantry, one hundred recruits, and the regimental band, arrived at Fort Buford in the latter part of June, thus completing the garrison of the post. The effect of the entire situation upon a person of Hazen's irascible and belligerent disposition may very well be imagined. He was sick, hurt, and angry, and in a mood to strike out at anything that annoyed him.

Fort Buford, the successor to Fort Union, was named for Major General John Buford, the dashing cavalry leader who had won fame and distinction in the Civil War. It was located on the left

[20] *Ibid.*, June 1, 1872.
[21] *Ibid.*, June 29, 1872.

bank of the Missouri River, a short distance below its confluence with the Yellowstone. The military reservation had been established in 1864 by General Alfred Sully, who had realized the inadequacy of Fort Union, but it was not until June two years later that the work of construction had been begun by a detachment of the Thirteenth Infantry under the command of Brevet Colonel John Rankin. Its establishment had constituted both a challenge to the Indians and an invitation to attack from the very beginning, and in the spring of 1867 the fort had been the subject of a sensational report that it had been captured and the entire garrison massacred. The story was later demonstrated to be false —it was apparently the concoction of someone's overpowered imagination—but not until after a good two months had elapsed. During that time, however, the report of pillage and massacre gained wide circulation, and as a result of the sensational hoax, the majority of the American reading public had learned the location of Fort Buford.

In the summer of 1867 the garrison was increased to five companies, and this made necessary the erection of a new post. The new buildings were built largely of adobe and were surrounded by a stockade twelve feet in height. These quarters proved to be largely unsatisfactory and uncomfortable; they were hastily constructed, the adobe bricks had not been given adequate time to dry, and little attention was given to such factors as ventilation and cleanliness. It was the belief of many officers that a stockade was unnecessary except at the very smallest posts, since its existence gave the Indians the idea that the soldiers were afraid of them, so in 1871 the stockade was removed and two sets of officers' quarters, a hospital, guardhouse, and storehouse were erected outside of the original enclosure.

Indian opposition, however, did not cease, and during all of this time it was never safe for anyone to go more than five hundred yards from the stockade line without an escort. Until May, 1870, the fort had been garrisoned by companies of the Thirteenth Infantry, the total force consisting of less than one hundred men; but in that month the Thirteenth and Seventh Infantry regiments exchanged stations, and Companies D, F, and I of the latter regiment, took over at Fort Buford. The next month, General Sheridan, returning from an inspection trip to the western forts, was en route down the Missouri River by steamer. Because of low water he was forced to leave the river about one hundred miles above Fort Buford and to proceed overland to that post with only a small escort. His trail was followed by about three hundred Indians who on the day after his arrival attacked the post. They first struck a party of woodchoppers, a short distance from the fort, wounding four of the men, and made an attack on the post itself, where a lively fight took place.[22]

Probably the worst feature of the situation at Fort Buford was its almost complete isolation from civilization for the greater part of the year. Although it was only three days by steamer above Bismarck, the post was in communication with the outside world only when the river was open, which was generally from late May to early October. During the winter months communication was kept open a part of the time by a system of overland couriers and mail carriers. To facilitate their operations and to keep the couriers from losing their way during the winter storms, the route between Fort Buford and Fort Stevenson was, in 1870, ordered marked by a series of mounds. These were made of sod, were circular in form and six feet in height. At the base they were four feet in diameter, narrowing to one foot at the summit, and were constructed of sods one foot square. Where practicable they were placed on knolls and other commanding points, and always so arranged and at such distances from each other that from any one, two others (one in front and the other in the rear) were always visible. Mail communication during the winter months was very irregular, as travel was attended with great danger from Indians as well as from the extreme cold and the sudden unpredictable storms. Mail twice a month was the best that could be hoped for, and during the most severe part of the winter, the interval would frequently be protracted to a month. During the winter it took an

[22] *Ibid.*, July 9, 1870.

average of three weeks for a letter to travel from Fort Buford to department headquarters in St. Paul.

In 1872 the War Department had made an allocation of funds for construction and enlargement at Fort Buford. The original intention apparently had been to station an entire regiment of infantry at that post, but when a reduction in the size of the contemplated garrison was decided upon, the sum of forty thousand dollars was ordered diverted and used for the construction of quarters and barracks for the troops at the new post being built at the Northern Pacific crossing of the Missouri River. Despite this reduction in funds sixteen sets of officers' quarters were constructed at Fort Buford in 1872, and in the years following a number of additional improvements were made.

As late as 1875 conditions were still far from satisfactory; the barracks consisted of seven adobe buildings with gravel roofs which had been built in 1867. The walls were seventeen inches thick but were out of line and in addition were cracked and crumbling. This made it almost impossible to keep the interior of the buildings clean. The ventilation was also poor, and in winter the heating problem was serious, since all the heat came from wood-burning stoves. The scarcity of water in the winter months made it difficult for the men to keep themselves decently clean, or even to wash face and hands. This shortage of water also presented a serious problem for the hospital.

The river at Fort Buford averaged about half a mile in width in its usual channel but had a flood plain varying in width from about forty rods to several miles. This was covered with water during the occasional floods which occurred every few years. The *mauvaises terres* or "Bad Lands," which were described as a succession of barren hills or buttes averaging from two to three hundred feet in height, extended back five or six miles from the flood plain. Beyond them was a rolling prairie. The entire region was described as badly watered and not arable, although it was believed that some crops could be grown with irrigation.[23]

[23] *Report of the Hygiene of the United States Army, with a Description of*

When the Sixth Infantry was ordered to Fort Buford, the Northern Pacific Railroad was building west. The company's charter, granted in 1864, had given it the right to construct a railroad and telegraph line across the continent from Lake Superior to Puget Sound by the most eligible route within the territory of the United States north of the forty-fifth parallel. It might be noted in passing that the main trunk line was to be built via the Columbia River to near its mouth and then north to Puget Sound, but that a branch line was to be constructed "to Puget Sound across the Cascade mountains, from some convenient point" on the main trunk line. This planned branch in practice came to be the main line of the railroad across the present state of Washington. The company was granted a right-of-way through the public domain to the extent of two hundred feet on each side of the track and the right to take timber, stone, and other building materials from the lands adjacent to the track. Moreover, for each mile of track constructed, the company was granted twenty alternate sections of the public lands (640 acres to the section) on each side of the line of the road in the territories through which the railroad ran and ten alternate sections on each side of the line in the states. This was the equivalent of 25,600 acres per mile in the territories, and 12,800 acres per mile in the states. The total land grant to the company thus exceeded 50,000,000 acres, an "imperial landed domain" larger than all of the six New England states combined and nearly seven times as large as Belgium.

By 1860 belief in the existence of the Great American Desert had become almost an article of faith with the American people, and in the years following the close of the Civil War, that conviction had deepened and intensified. The lands granted to the Northern Pacific, especially those west of the Missouri River, lay right in the heart of this imperial domain of sagebrush and cactus. To encourage the sale and settlement of these lands, the company organized a department of emigration, and a determined effort was made to attract settlers, both from the more thickly settled

---

Military Posts, Circular No. 8, War Department, Surgeon General's Office, May 1, 1875, 399–401; *Army and Navy Journal*, July 17, 1875.

portions of the United States and from European countries. Since the income from the sale of lands would be insufficient to pay the costs of construction, the company also had recourse to the sale of bonds, known as "seven-thirties" from the fact that the yearly interest on a hundred-dollar bond amounted to $7.30. For the sale of these securities it enlisted the services of Jay Cooke and Company as financial agents.

To facilitate the sale of land and bonds and also to convince the investing public that the bonds constituted an attractive investment, Jay Cooke and Company issued a number of brochures or pamphlets describing the territory through which the Northern Pacific was to be constructed.[24] These pamphlets were frankly and quite obviously propaganda. They stated that "successful agriculture and the sustenance of a dense population," were dependent on three conditions: (1) a climate warm enough to ripen crops and secure the comfort of man and beast; (2) a soil of reasonable natural fertility; and (3) sufficient moisture to render that soil productive. As might be expected, the region to be traversed by the railroad was declared to excel in all these respects and to be much superior to the territory included in the land grants of the other transcontinental railroads. Since the region did lie in the northern latitudes, recourse was had to the argument of isothermal lines which indicated that the country had a much milder climate than might have been expected from its geographical position in respect to latitude, although even this was said to be within the parallels "which in Europe, Asia and America, embrace the most enlightened, creative, conquering and progressive populations." The matter of temperature was summed up with the declaration that "Minnesota has the average temperature of Northern New York, without the discomfort and chill; Dakota, that of Iowa, with a drier and more invigorating air; Montana, that of Ohio without its dampness and changeableness; Washington and Oregon have

---

[24] These two pamphlets, neither of which bears any indication of authorship, were entitled *The Northern Pacific Railroad's Land Grant and the Future Business of the Road*, and *The Northern Pacific Railroad; Its Route, Resources, Progress and Business. The New Northwest and Its Great Thoroughfare*. Both were issued by Jay Cooke and Company.

the climate of Virginia, with more rain and cooler summer nights."

As for moisture, the region "tributary to the Northern Pacific Railroad, and embracing its land grant," was declared to have "an adequate supply of atmospheric moisture for all purposes of agriculture and stock-raising." This was said to be beyond question and the proof "abundant and conclusive," although it was admitted that there were exceptions. It was also emphasized that the great point of difficulty with the central region traversed by the Union Pacific was the aridity, but even in those detached regions along the Northern Pacific where irrigation was necessary, the grazing was said to be good. As a whole the land grant of the Northern Pacific was abundantly irrigated and "the wonderful network of living brooks, lakes, streams, and navigable rivers, with which this region is supplied is perhaps its most striking feature."

In regard to the fertility of the soil, there was no question; it was uniformly good, and there were no "alkali plains, sand, and sagebrush" along this route, and forty bushels of wheat to the acre were said to be not unusual in the Yellowstone Valley. The exact locality in which this wheat had been raised was not stated, and perhaps it was just as well since there was not a settlement at this time between Bismarck and Fort Ellis. In the valley of the Yellowstone proper were the cabins of a few settlers who maintained a precarious tenure at the sufferance of the Sioux, and who were more interested in trading whisky with the Indians than in the peaceful pursuits of agriculture. The pamphlet continued:

> That the climate of that New Northwest, which is now opening to settlement, travel and trade, is such as to make a congenial home for the migrating millions of central and northern Europe, and the crowded portions of our own land, there is no doubt. Thus its soil, its resources of minerals and timber, its matchless water courses, and its accessibility to the commerce and the markets of the world, also adapt it to be the residence of a numerous and thrifty population, is equally unquestionable.

The pamphlet then presented the opinions of experts, people

who were said to be in a position to judge the value of the land in question, and their opinions were unanimously favorable, as might have been expected. Lord Selkirk, who in 1805 had attempted a settlement in the Red River Valley near Pembina, was quoted as having claimed that his tract would support a population of thirty million people. But the greatest reliance was placed on the testimony of Mr. Lorin Blodget, who was regarded as the highest scientific authority on climatology in the United States.

Mr. Blodget had attended Geneva (now Hobart) College in Geneva, New York, but did not graduate. After teaching country school for several years, he became a volunteer meteorological observer for the Smithsonian Institution, and was soon placed in charge of the research on climatology. This led to the publication in 1857 of his *The Climatology of the United States,* the first book of any importance on the climate of any portion of the Americas, in which he made a full comparison of the climates of this country with those of Europe and Asia at the same latitudes. "It was based on all the appropriate meteorological data that he could obtain" and was so carefully and thoroughly done that "the subsequent myriads of observations have essentially but confirmed Blodget's major conclusions." Later, he was transferred to the War Department and employed in the Pacific Railroad Survey, having charge of the work of determining altitude and gradient by use of the barometer.[25]

In a letter dated February 24, 1871, and addressed to Jay Cooke and Company, he stated that he had reviewed in the proof sheets the statements made in the brochure regarding "the climate and cultivable capacity of the great region tributary to the Northern Pacific Railroad." He then added: "I have no hesitation in saying that the anticipations you have of the future of that great section fall far below, rather than exceed, the results that will be realized. Its advantages of climate and of soil alike are still imperfectly appreciated, even by those who have given most attention to their examination." He declared that, instead of the

---

[25] *Dictionary of American Biography,* II, 377. The article is by William Jackson Humphrey.

"arid spring and summer" that prevailed in the plains of lower latitude, the area adjacent to the Northern Pacific route would have "a fair and even an ample supply of rain at these critical seasons." His charts had been prepared in 1857 when no observations of rainfall existed in the area, and since "there was a constant exaggeration of the aridity of the plains generally pressed on the public by most writers and travellers," he felt that his rain maps for the spring and summer should be corrected by adding about two or three inches of rain for both spring and summer, or a total of five inches for the year. He then stated:

> From my earliest knowledge of that rich Northwest, derived from Sir George Simpson in 1851, and from all the scientific and other surveys subsequently conducted, I have been deeply impressed with the beauty, fertility and mildness of climate in this future Germany of the American continent. The line of the Northern Pacific Road was claimed by me, long before Governor Stevens' survey was organized, to be naturally the most favored in the passage of the Rocky Mountains, in exemption from heavy snows, and in the capacity for settlement along the entire line.[26]

The brochure then reprinted from the *New York Independent* of March 2, 1871, an article by Schuyler Colfax, vice-president of the United States, praising the route of the railroad as well as the region it traversed. He argued that development was the great duty of the American people after the trials through which the nation had recently passed and detailed the exceptional advantages of the Northern Pacific. He then mentioned that while the land grant was probably sufficient for the completion of the road, nevertheless "millions of private means are already invested in it." He declared that the bonds which were based on the land grant "and a mortgage on the Road itself," yielding about 8 per cent a year in currency, ranked "with the best class of railroad securities."

Other brochures were issued, containing many of the same arguments and using much the same material. Another expert who

[26] This letter is cited in *The Northern Pacific Railroad; Its Route, Resources, Progress and Business.*

endorsed the construction, the business, and the future of the road was Professor Robert von Schlagintweit,[27] a German physical scientist who had made extended travels in the United States, and who admitted that he had not "by personal inspection, made the acquaintance of the regions to be traversed by the Northern Pacific Railroad," yet was of the opinion that he could issue a confirmation of the statements in the pamphlet.

In 1873 the construction of the Northern Pacific reached Bismarck and stopped there, not to be resumed for several years. This halt was due to the failure of Jay Cooke and Company, which precipitated a nationwide panic or depression and led to considerable controversy about whether the Northern Pacific would ever resume construction. It was also during the summer of 1873 that George A. Custer, with ten troops of the Seventh Cavalry as a part of a larger expedition under the command of Colonel David Stanley, explored the basin of the Yellowstone River and adjacent territory and acquired the information upon which his letter in reply to that of General Hazen would be based. This expedition, after traveling from Fort Lincoln across to the Yellowstone and establishing a base camp near present Glendive, Montana, moved up the river to the neighborhood of present Billings, having several brushes and one pitched battle with the Sioux. From Pompey's Pillar, Custer went north to the Great Bend of the Musselshell and from there moved eastward in returning to the base camp, across some of the most arid and desolate country in North America.

In the same year, before its failure, Jay Cooke and Company issued another pamphlet promoting the sale of the Northern Pacific Railroad bonds, in which much the same material was presented as in the previous pamphlets but with some additions. This publication was entitled *The Northern Pacific Railroad: Its Land Grant, Resources, Traffic and Tributary Country. The Valley Route to the Pacific.* It opened by listing the public reasons which not only justified but required "the building of a railroad

[27] The translation of his letter was published in *The Northern Pacific Railroad's Land Grant and the Future Business of the Road.* In it he said that it was written in reply to an inquiry from the German representative of Jay Cooke and Company and of the Northern Pacific Railroad.

across the continent near the 46th parallel." These reasons, some of which were developed in considerable detail, included:

1. It would open up one of the most interesting and valuable sections of the continent, which included a great part of the remaining unoccupied public domain. Its resources should be developed and utilized for the benefit of the rest of the country.

2. The construction of such a railroad would give a definite money value where none now existed for every acre of land in the area, thus adding to the wealth of the nation.

3. The region through which the road was to run was practically destitute of railroads which were important politically as well as commercially and industrially. The railroad would give the "New Northwest" more direct contact with the rest of the nation.

4. It would bring about "the prompt, thorough, economical and humane settlement of the Indian problem in the Northwest." In support of this argument, the pamphlet quoted the report of the Commissioner of Indian Affairs to the effect that construction of the Northern Pacific would solve the Indian problem in the region between the line of the Union Pacific Railroad and the Canadian border. It would render the Sioux "as incapable of resistance to the Government as are the Indians of New York or Massachusetts," and would save up to seven million dollars a year in reduced garrisons, avoidance of Indian wars and the cheapening of government transportation.

5. Public considerations were also said to demand private construction of the road. Arguing that outright construction by the government would constitute a wise economy, it was said that private building was justified as a national improvement and a legitimate commercial enterprise, since upon completion the railroad would have between fifty and sixty million acres in its land grant.

In describing the country to be traversed by the railroad, this brochure, after noting that the route proposed had the lowest altitude of any of the projected transcontinental railroads, spoke

30

of the region to be crossed as a vast plain, "partly timbered but mostly prairie," and a plain which had a varied surface through which flowed several rivers and many smaller streams. The route, after crossing the Red River at Fargo, would run almost due west across the "the rolling prairies of Eastern Dakota" and then follow the valley of Apple Creek to its junction with the Missouri, cross that river at Fort Abraham Lincoln near the confluence of the Heart River, ascend the valley of the latter stream to near its source, and then cross to the Yellowstone, striking it near the mouth of Powder River. Actually the railroad crossed the Missouri near the mouth of Burnt Creek some six miles north of Apple Creek. This change in plan was probably due to two factors: (1) all of the land near the mouth of the latter stream had fallen into the hands of speculators, and (2) the Northern Pacific engineers discovered that the more northern line was preferable to the one earlier selected. Once across the Missouri, the railroad ran directly westward, crossing a small divide, and followed Glendive Creek to the Yellowstone and then ascended the valley of this river. The original plan had been to cross the Yellowstone, the line then to run northwestward to the Belt Mountains, which would be crossed by a suitable pass, and then, after crossing the valleys of the Gallatin, Madison, and Jefferson rivers, to cross the Rocky Mountains at Flathead Pass.

Continuing exploration by the engineers revealed an even better route, and as a result the Northern Pacific ascended the Yellowstone to near the mouth of the Shields River, the only considerable northern affluent of the Yellowstone, near the present city of Livingston, then crossed the Gallatin Range, one of the outlying ramparts of the Rockies at Bozeman Pass. It turned north along the Gallatin River to where that stream unites with the Jefferson and Madison to form the Missouri, and down the latter to the head of the Prickly Pear Valley and the settlement of Helena, then across the Rocky Mountains by way of McDonald Pass, and down the Little Blackfoot River to the Deer Lodge Valley. Later another line crossed from Bozeman Pass to the Jefferson River and up that stream, and crossed the Rockies at

Pipestone Pass into Deer Lodge Valley, where it connected with the line built earlier. From Missoula it followed the Bitterroot and Clark's Fork to Lake Pend d'Oreille, then dropped to the south and across the great grass plain of eastern Washington to the junction of the Snake and Columbia rivers, where it turned northeast and crossed the Cascades to Puget Sound. The original intention had been for the line to run from the junction with the Snake, down the Columbia River through the Cascade Range, which was then also known as the Sierra, with a branch terminating at Portland, and the main trunk line extending north to the main terminal city on Puget Sound. Actually the road along the Columbia River was not built until later and then as a joint project of the Northern Pacific and Great Northern, and the line across the Cascade Mountains, intended as a branch line, became the main line of the railroad.

This brochure attempted to meet certain criticisms of earlier efforts. It stated that no claim was made that the winters of Minnesota or Dakota were "mild or attractive to those who dislike crisp, sharp cold at the proper season," but maintained that with proper provision against storms and exposure, the winter months were not only "endurable but enjoyable." Although the cold as indicated by the thermometer might be intense for certain weeks, the atmosphere was dry and exhilarating. For a period of 396 days in the Prickly Pear Valley, there were only five on which the thermometer stood below zero at noon, while the average summer temperature was about seventy degrees, or the same as that of central Pennsylvania. The growing season, between frost and frost, was about 150 days. Of the area spanned by the railroad it was said that "on the whole and making liberal allowance for exceptional waste tracts," it was "a region of singular fertility of soil and salubrity of climate."

Whether Hazen read these pamphlets is not certain, but it is a fair assumption that he did. And his reaction to them can easily be imagined, since he apparently already had very well-formed opinions of the value of the region west of the Missouri River. But the catalytic agent, the spark that apparently fired the powder magazine, was an article appearing in *Harper's New Monthly Magazine* for December, 1873, written by T. B. Maury and entitled "Poetry and Philosophy of Indian Summer,"[28] in which the author spoke of Indian Summer as the fifth season of the year and as one not unknown in the high latitudes of both hemispheres. Again recourse was had to the argument of isothermal lines and the line of equal winter temperature contrasted with the degrees of latitude. St. Joseph, Missouri, was declared to have the same winter climate as along the Clark's Fork of the Columbia, the upper Missouri, and the Yellowstone rivers. A quotation from Lieutenant Mullan, who had built a military road from Fort Walla Walla, Washington Territory, to Fort Benton, Montana Territory states:

> In other words in the longitude from St. Joseph to the Rocky Mountains it [the isothermal line] has gained six degrees of latitude. . . . This is as true as it is strange, and shows unerringly that there exists in this zone an atmospheric river of heat flowing through this region, and this affects the kingdom of natural history, botany and climatology to such an extent that herein we find mild winters and vigorous grasses even in mid-winter that enable stock to be grazed on the open hills, and give a facility for travel during the severest seasons of the year.

Then Maury went on to assert that while the winter of 1871–72 had been one of unprecedented severity in the United States, in the extreme Northwest it was much less severe than farther south, and that while the Union Pacific and Central Pacific were overwhelmed with ice and snow, the valleys of the Yellowstone and Missouri rivers had had a comparatively light snowfall, and "the thermometric depression indicated much milder weather than in Wyoming, Colorado, or Utah."

Speaking of the "vast and splendid domain" lying west of the ninety-eighth meridian and north of the forty-third degree of latitude, he quoted Mr. Lorin Blodget as asserting that this area

[28] Although Hazen refers to him simply as Captain Maury, this was Professor Thompson B. Maury of the Signal Office. He was a popular writer of the day, especially on scientific subjects.

was "not inferior in size to the whole United States east of the Mississippi" and was "perfectly adapted to the fullest occupation of cultivated nations . . . . The buffalo winters on the Upper Athabasca at least as safely as at St. Paul, Minnesota." Mr. Blodget was quoted further:

> Buffaloes are far more abundant in the northern plains than on the plains which stretch from the Platte southward to the Llano Estacado of Texas, and remain through the winter at their extreme border, taking shelter in the belts of woodland of the Upper Athabasca and Peace rivers. All the grains of the cool temperate zone are produced abundantly; Indian corn may be grown on both branches of the Saskatchewan, and the grass of the plains is singularly abundant and rich. The parallel in regard to the advancement of American States here may be drawn with the period of the trans-Alpine Roman expansion, when Gaul, Scandinavia and Britain were regarded as inhospitable regions, fit only for barbarian occupation. The cultivable surface of the district (bordering the Pacific Ocean) can not be much less than 300,000 square miles. Of the plains and their woodland borders, the valuable surface measures fully 500,000 square miles.

The Northern Pacific Railroad had not been mentioned, nor had its bonds and its land grant, but to General Hazen the inference was apparent, and his letter to the New York *Tribune* followed.

2. Worthless Railroad Land

THE NORTHERN PACIFIC RAILROAD COUNTRY
VIEWS OF
Major-General Hazen[1]
A Region of Extreme Cold in Winter and Drouth in
Summer—Storms in which Men and Beasts Perish—
The Soil can only be Cultivated by Irrigation—The
Land Not Worth a Penny an Acre.

To the Editor of the Tribune

SIR:—For two years I have been an observer of the effort upon
the part of the Northern Pacific Railroad Company to make the
world believe this section to be a valuable agricultural one, and,
with many others, I have kept silent although knowing the falsity
of their representations, while they have pretty fully carried their
point in establishing a popular belief favorable to their wishes.

When reading such statements of its fertility as appear in the
article entitled "Poetry and Philosophy of Indian Summer" in
that most estimable periodical, *Harper's Monthly*, of December,
1873—in which are repeated most of the shameless falsehoods
so lavishly published in the last two years, as advertisements in
the interests of that Company, and perhaps written by the same
pen—a feeling of shame and indignation arises that any of our
countrymen, especially when as highly favored with the popular
good-will and benefits, should deliberately indulge in such wicked
deceptions.

[1] Colonel Hazen's Letter was published in the New York *Tribune*, Feb. 27, 1874.

The theoretical isothermals of Captain Maury and Mr. Blodgett [*sic*], which have given rise to so much speculation, and are used so extravagantly by those who have a use for them, although true along the Pacific coast, are not found to be true, by actual experience and observation in this middle region.

My post of duty is at the mouth of the Yellowstone, at the intersection of 104 meridian west with the 48th parallel north, in the midst of this so-called "northern tropical belt," and while nature stares me in the face with its stubborn contradictions, I shall put them on paper. I shall just give a table of temperatures and rainfall taken from accurate daily observations at this post since 1866:

TABLE OF TEMPERATURES AND RAINFALL AT FORT BUFORD, D. T., FROM THE 1ST OF AUGUST, 1866, TO THE 31ST OF DECEMBER, 1873

	JANUARY			FEBRUARY			MARCH		
	Warm-est Day	Cold-est Day	Month-ly Mean	Warm-est Day	Cold-est Day	Month-ly Mean	Warm-est Day	Cold-est Day	Month-ly Mean
1866	—	—	——	—	—	——	—	—	——
1867	52	–25	9.11	51	–29	8.77	55	–39	4.53
1868	28	–30	1.01	44	–23	11.38	78	10	33.94
1869	43	–60	16.19	40	–13	17.96	62	–17	21.40
1870	43	–23	6.82	43	–35	15.25	49	–16	13.93
1871	36	–29	7.56	38	–29	10.27	67	6	26.68
1872	41	–37	18.45	47	–28	14.86	46	–18	22.37
1873	45	–35	2.15	40	2	6.18	53	–8	25.13
Mean monthly temperature in 8 years		8.75			12.09				21.14

	APRIL			MAY			JUNE		
	Warm-est Day	Cold-est Day	Month-ly Mean	Warm-est Day	Cold-est Day	Month-ly Mean	Warm-est Day	Cold-est Day	Month-ly Mean
1866	—	—	——	—	—	——	—	—	——
1867	72	14	44.23	80	31	53.26	96	44	64.23
1868	83	22	45.42	89	40	60.82	96	51	71.09
1869	70	13	42.24	87	39	58.34	95	49	64.04
1870	85	14	50.30	90	41	58.95	102	48	71.48
1871	69	18	39.36	95	34	61.71	89	51	68.00
1872	72	20	37.96	90	29	51.16	92	47	65.80

36

| 1873 | 69 | 7 | 37.29 | 74 | 15 | 50.40 | 90 | 48 | 65.85 |

Mean monthly
temperature
in 8 years   42.40   56.38   67.21

| | JULY | | | AUGUST | | | SEPTEMBER | | |
	Warm-est Day	Cold-est Day	Month-ly Mean	Warm-est Day	Cold-est Day	Month-ly Mean	Warm-est Day	Cold-est Day	Month-ly Mean
1866	—	—	—	94	49	63.94	97	35	56.01
1867	94	52	72.74	100	36	74.02	88	34	57.94
1868	106	56	75.75	99	47	67.25	71	19	48.84
1869	96	51	69.19	99	46	67.99	90	32	55.13
1870	95	60	73.36	93	39	61.53	88	31	60.32
1871	93	50	73.38	97	43	66.56	84	31	57.03
1872	101	50	73.22	96	37	77.38	93	30	53.37
1873	100	48	68.77	102	35	62.92	84	16	45.82

Mean monthly
temperature
in 8 years   72.30   67.70   54.31

TABLE OF TEMPERATURES AND RAINFALL AT FORT BUFORD, D. T., FROM THE 1ST OF AUGUST, 1866, TO THE 31ST OF DECEMBER, 1873

| | OCTOBER | | | NOVEMBER | | | DECEMBER | | |
	Warm-est Day	Cold-est Day	Month-ly Mean	Warm-est Day	Cold-est Day	Month-ly Mean	Warm-est Day	Cold-est Day	Month-ly Mean
1866	96	9	45.17	60	7	34.86	60	−24	16.65
1867	76	17	46.30	55	6	30.61	40	−17	9.33
1868	78	20	42.19	67	−3	27.30	51	−22	15.48
1869	75	4	38.19	73	−9	26.25	40	−18	18.58
1870	71	12	39.10	55	18	33.45	46	−29	9.58
1871	72	10	42.15	51	−33	14.00	44	−35	2.43
1872	80	19	41.83	45	−28	18.38	48	−35	0.87
1873	80	5	36.83	60	−2	28.20	43	−27	5.57

Mean monthly
temperature
in 8 years   41.42   26.63   9.81

Annual Rainfall

| 1866 | 1.40 | 1871 | 10.42 |
| 1867 | 6.58 | 1872 | 19.99 |

37

1868	11.50	1873	21.11
1869	9.74	Average	12.64
1870	9.19		

I certify that the above is a correct transcript from the hospital records.

J. V. D. MIDDLETON, *Asst. Surgeon, U. S. A.*

A true copy. J. F. MUNSON, *Lieut. 6th Inf. Adjt.*

Fort Buford, D. T., Jan. 3, 1873

The excessive cold of winter is here shown, the monthly mean being worthy of special notice, while the annual variation of temperature is from 130 to 138 degrees. June, July and August were the only months in the last twelve in which we have not had snow storms, or the temperature down to 15 degrees. I have before me the meteorological reports from the other military posts in the region and they do not differ widely from this.

The humidity as seen is insufficient for any general agriculture, such agriculture requiring in countries remote from the sea from 40 to 50 inches. To the average here given, however, may be added about four inches that fall in snow.

The Indian Summers here are beautiful beyond description, that of the past Autumn rivaling the wildest flights of the imagination, and lasting until the 25th of November without doubt extending to the country of Saskatchewan. But ten days afterward, December 5, the thermometer stood at 27° below zero. The storms in Minnesota and Dakota last Winter and Spring in which hundreds of people lost their lives are fresh in the memories of all. This entire northwestern country is subject to these terrific Winter storms which animal life cannot withstand unless thoroughly protected. I have seen an area of country 20 miles across strewn with the carcasses of buffalo that must have perished in one of these storms. Not a Winter has passed since this post was established in 1866 but some poor soldier of its garrison has lost life or limb from freezing.

I have under my command 30 Indian scouts, among whom there are several northern Assiniboines, whose country and range extend well into the British Possessions on both branches of the Saskatchewan. I have made the most particular inquiries about the Saskatchewan country of all these people, as well as of half-breeds who have been in the employ of the Hudson Bay Company, and officers of the army who have been longest in this country. They agree in the following description: That in general appearance it resembles Minnesota, being a level upland prairie, with numerous lakes and a good soil. It is a more desirable country than that along the upper Missouri in these respects, but is colder, and has a shorter and dryer season. They raise wheat, oats, barley and native corn if the season is wet enough, but the crops often fail for want of moisture.

The past season, as seen by the meteorological report, has been exceptionally rainy and favorable for agriculture here, and the post has with great care, and by utilizing all available season, made an extensive garden with the following results. The garden is situated immediately on the river bank about two feet above high water. Potatoes, native corn, cabbage, early-sown turnips, early peas, early beans, beets, carrots, parsnips, salsify, cucumbers, lettuce, radishes and asparagus have grown abundantly and matured. Melons, pumpkins and squashes have not matured. Tomatoes did not turn red; American corn (early) reached to roasting ears. Onions, with wheat and oats, matured at Fort Berthold, D. T., 150 miles below on the Missouri River. I am told by those who have been here a long time that this may be taken as a standard of what may be expected the most favorable seasons on the immediate bottoms of the streams. The native Indian corn matures in about ten weeks from planting. It puts out its ears about six to eight inches from the ground, and has a soft white grain without any flinty portion and weighs about two-thirds as much as other corn.

My own quarters are situated on the second bench of the banks of the Missouri, about 50 feet above that stream, and 600 yards away from it. And to raise a flower garden 10 feet by 40 the past two years, has required a daily sprinkling of three barrels of water, for which we were repaid by about three weeks of flowers.

39

The site of this post is supposed to be exceptionally fruitful, but I have before me a letter from Mr. Joseph Anderson of St. Paul, Minn., who was the hay contractor at this post in 1872. His letter states that, in order to find places to cut the hay required by his contract that season, some 900 tons, he was compelled to search over a space of country on the north side of the river some twenty-five miles in extent in each direction from the post, or some 2,400 square miles, and that there was none thick enough to cut for as great a distance beyond.

Respecting the agricultural value of this country, after leaving the excellent wheat-growing valley of the Red River of the North, following westward 1,600 miles to the Sierras, excepting the very limited bottoms of the small streams, as well as those of the Missouri and Yellowstone, from a few yards in breadth to an occasional water-washed valley of one or two miles, and the narrow valleys of the streams of Montana already settled, and a small area of timbered country in north-west Idaho (probably one-fiftieth of the whole), this country will not produce the fruits and cereals of the East, for want of moisture, and can in no way be artificially irrigated, and will not, in our day and generation, sell for one penny an acre, except through fraud or ignorance; and most of the land here excepted will have to be irrigated artificially. I write this knowing full well it will meet with contradiction, but the contradiction will be a falsehood. The country between the one hundredth meridian and the Sierras—the Rio Grande to the British possessions—will never develop into populous States because of the want of moisture. Its counterpart is found in the plains of Northern Asia and not in Western Europe. We look in vain for those expected agricultural settlements along the Kansas and Union Pacific Railroads, between these two lines, and for 20 years hence the search will be quite as fruitless. We have in Nevada and New Mexico, fair samples of what these populations will be.

My statement is made from the practical experience and observation of 18 years of military service as an officer of the army, much of which has been upon the frontier, and having passed the remainder of my life as a farmer. For confirmation of what I have here said I respectfully refer the reader to Gen. G. K. Warren[2] of the Engineer Corps of the army, who made a scientific exploration of this country extending through several years and has given us our only accurate map of it, or to Prof. Hayden,[3] for the past several years engaged upon a similar work. The testimony of Gov. Stevens,[4] Gen. Fremont,[5] and Lieut. Mullens[6] is that of enthusiastic travellers and discoverers, whose descriptions are not fully borne out by more prolonged and intimate knowledge of the country.

Herr Haas, the agent of the Berlin and Vienna banks, sent out to examine the country, could easily say the country is good, so long as he advised his people to invest no money in it, and it is doubtful if that remark was based upon a sufficiently authoritative

[2] Lieutenant Gouverneur K. Warren had made several explorations in the region west of the Missouri River. Although he felt that much of the country was irreclaimable desert—he compared the edge of the desert to the shore of the ocean—he was impressed by the great numbers of wild game that roamed over the country. His *Preliminary Report of the Explorations in Nebraska and Dakota in the Years 1855–'56–'57* was published at Washington in 1875.

[3] Ferdinand Vandiveer Hayden, although a Doctor of Medicine, is best known for his work in geology and topography. In 1856 and 1857, he had been with Lieutenant Warren in the exploration of the Missouri and Yellowstone rivers and the Black Hills; in 1859 he was with Captain W. F. Raynolds on the Yellowstone, and after service in the Civil War, he continued his topographical work with surveys of Nebraska, Colorado, Idaho, Montana, Wyoming, and Utah. He had a very high opinion of certain parts of the West, but was more reserved about others. One of his assistants, however, noted that in agricultural matters old concepts familiar in the East would have to be abandoned and new ones adopted and followed.

[4] Isaac Ingalls Stevens, appointed first governor of Washington Territory, had also been appointed director of the exploration of the extreme northern route for the proposed transcontinental railroad. His report, "Narrative and Final Report of Explorations for a Route for a Pacific Railroad . . . from St. Paul to Puget Sound," in *Explorations and Surveys . . . for a Railroad Route from the Mississippi River to the Pacific Ocean* (Washington, Government Printing Office, 1855), XII, had been favorable to the country through which he had passed on his journey to Washington Territory.

[5] John Charles Frémont, the famous explorer of the American West in the period prior to the Civil War.

[6] The reference is to Lieutenant John Mullan who had been with the Stevens party. Later, he was in charge of the construction of a military road connecting Fort Walla Walla on the Columbia River with Fort Benton on the Missouri. His *Report on the Construction of a Military Road from Fort Walla Walla to Fort Benton* was published in 1863.

investigation of the country to merit the credence given it. Certainly it is incorrect. And especially valueless is the testimony of men of distinction of our own country who are not practical agriculturists, but have taken journeys in the fruitful months of the year to the Red River of the North, to the rich valleys of Montana, or to the enchanting scenery of Puget Sound, except upon those particular points.

I am prepared to substantiate all I have here said, so far as such matters are susceptible of proof, but from their nature many things herein referred to must, to many people, wait the action of the great solvent—Time.

I have no personal feelings in this matter since, rather on the contrary, the railroads in these Western countries ameliorate the condition of troops serving here; but I would prefer to see these roads based upon honesty and the needs of the country, commensurate with their cost. Nor can I see much difference between the man who, in business, draws a check upon a bank where he has no money, and selling bonds secured by lands that have no value.

I will say to those holding the bonds of the Northern Pacific Railroad that by changing them into good lands now owned by the road in the valley of the Red River of the North and East of that point is the only means of ever saving themselves from total loss.

W. B. HAZEN

Fort Buford, D. T., Jan. 1, 1874

3. Hazen's Horoscope

General Hazen did not have long to wait for a reaction to his article. On Saturday, February 14, 1874, the Minneapolis *Tribune* in a half-serious, half-bantering account, summarized his arguments and presented a refutation. This account follows.

Fancying that the Northern Pacific Railroad is wounded, the whole flock pounces upon it—like the rest of the flock upon a wounded falcon. The last assailant is General W. B. Hazen, stationed at Fort Buford, Dakota. It is not certain that General Hazen's design is a sinister one, so we shall not call his motives in question; he is stationed at a detached outpost and has, very likely, without any prejudice to the Northern Pacific, been misled by too hastily drawing general conclusions from particular facts. He says the friends of the N. P. R. R. Co. "have pretty fully carried their point in establishing a popular belief favorable to their wishes," but he thinks the solemn truth ought to be told which will explode all the pretensions of this Northwest, and completely counteract the insane tendency of so many people to buy its corner lots.

To effect this tremendous result the ammunition he uses is confined to two charges: 1st, that Fort Buford is cold, 2nd, that Fort Buford is dry. The table of temperature and rainfall which he presents does pretty effectually establish these facts—that it is both cold and dry at Fort Buford. So much may be admitted without hesitation. Indeed, we supposed so much was generally known.

When General Hazen sticks to his tables he does extremely well, and there is no doubt they are mainly correct. It is only when he attempts to draw deductions from the tables that he fails. The mathematics seem to bewilder him as sadly as they did at West Point.[1]

He gives the monthly record for seven years at the Fort; and a recapitulation of his tables shows that the monthly mean of temperature has been as follows for the whole time, the result being given in degrees and minutes.

AVERAGE TEMPERATURE

January	8.75	July	72.30
February	12.00	August	67.50
March	21.14	September	54.21
April	42.40	October	41.42
May	56.38	November	34.63
June	67.21	December	9.81.

These are, of course, all above zero. The average of rainfall for the seven years was 12.64.

We might rest the claim of the Northern Pacific here, and claim that the table is a complete vindication of all its friends have claimed, were it not for the wild utterances in which General Hazen indulges his imagination. For instance, he says "the annual variation of temperature is from 130° to 138°," and therefore, he assumes it is bad for cropping. But the range of temperature in New York and New England is very nearly as great—not more than 10° less—whereas the annual range in Spain is not more than 15°, and in Southern California not more than 10°. Are the climates of Santa Barbara and Barcelona therefore more fructifying and more attractive than that of Albany? Does not the extreme range of our temperature rather show an adaptability of the seasons to each other, in such a way that July shall offset January? It will be noticed in the table given above, that the range in the *annual mean* between January and June for seven years is only

[1] In both the first and second years at the Military Academy, Hazen had ranked number thirty-eight in a class of sixty in mathematics.

63.45, considerably less than half of the extreme range of certain years.

Again we quote: "June, July and August were the only months in the last twelve in which we have not had snow storms, or the temperature down to 15°." The full table does indeed show this surprising result for 1873 at Fort Buford (if we add September as another exception, per table). But why does not General Hazen, being a fair-minded man and a gentleman, state that *this was the only year of which it was true?* Indeed, it was the only year in which it came anywhere near being true. The table above, giving the monthly mean for seven years, shows that there were only three months in which the *average* temperature was below 15° below zero. Excepting last year, the coldest day in May during the seven was 29° above zero. Excepting last year, the coldest day in September during the seven years was 30° above zero. During several of the years, the "coldest day" in April and October was considerably above the minimum 15°.

Hazen continues, speaking of the rainfall: "The humidity as seen, is insufficient for any general agriculture, such agriculture requiring in countries remote from the sea from forty to fifty inches. To the average as here given, however, may be added about four inches that fall as snow."

That particular section of Dakota in which Fort Buford is situated, being almost treeless is, of course, quite arid. But this cannot be said of any very large portion. And the attempt to blast the prospects of the Northern Pacific, by the peculiarities of one short bit of the line, is laughable, and if the author of the attempt was not General Hazen it would be regarded as malignant. What does he think of the sage-brush and alkaline plains of the Union Pacific stretching across several territories? What does he think of the vast unwatered basins of Utah? What of the rainless regions of California? The line of the Northern Pacific is ten times as well watered as the line of the Central and Union Pacific, as every well-informed man knows. And General Hazen is a well-informed man.

The complainant did not succeed in making a very good garden at Fort Buford. This is probably because he is better at drilling

45

recruits than at drilling peas; better at raising deductions than tomatoes. Every year the Northern Pacific sends down to our fair, magnificent specimens of crops of all kinds,—wheat, corn, oats, potatoes, squashes, melons, tomatoes, even fruits. A fact is more potent than an inference. The one mammoth pumpkin from the "lands that have no value," exhibited at the State Fair in 1872, is enough to shield the road from the whole of Hazen's artillery. The best wheat on this continent is from north of Minneapolis, and its prolific belt extends 600 miles north of Fort Buford, far beyond the Saskatchewan—a splendid empire from which a score of populous States will yet be carved. General Hazen makes, by implication, the crazy statement that oats will not mature at Fort Buford. Does he not know that they will mature on the north side of Hudson's Bay? A hypothesis cannot hold its own against a demonstration; and these scientific theories and fancies will be covered up by the annual harvest, as a flock of sheep are swept away and buried by a Nebraska snow-storm.

4. Rosser Interview

On Tuesday, February 17, the Minneapolis Daily *Tribune* followed up this rather moderate summary of General Hazen's letter with an editorial in a more critical vein. This read:

Elsewhere we print an important interview of a *Tribune* representative with General Rosser, concerning the recent letter of General Hazen on the climate and soil of Dakota and the prospects of the Northern Pacific railroad. It is needless to say that General Rosser knows ten times as much about the region alluded to as does Hazen. Indeed the latter seems to be familiar only with the climate of the Fort Buford kitchen garden, which formed the basis of his Munchausen inferences.

In printing a resume of General Hazen's letter the other day, we assumed that he was personally honest in making his extraordinary statements, and was moved only by a sincere desire to expose fraud and enlighten the benighted world. What was our surprise and mortification on being informed yesterday, on high authority that, when going to Fort Buford, he applied to the officers of the Northern Pacific for a pass for himself and *twelve hundred pounds of baggage.* [Italics in the original.] As he was an army officer on a good salary, the Company could not see why it should cart half a ton of baggage for him, and gracefully declined. It is unlikely that so slight a disappointment could have turned the pen of this good soldier to gall, but it is perhaps worth mentioning.

Thomas Lafayette Rosser (1836–1910) was born in Virginia, but at the age of thirteen he moved with his family to Texas. This action was apparently due to financial reverses and conditions apparently did not improve greatly in the new location. In 1856 he was appointed to the United States Military Academy at West Point, but at the outbreak of the Civil War resigned to cast his fortunes with the Confederacy. Before the end of the conflict he had received the rank of major general and had won a reputation as "a gifted cavalry leader of the audacious school." In the course of the war he became a perennial rival of George Armstrong Custer, whom he had known at the Academy, and something of a professional feud developed between them. By a bold maneuver he escaped the surrender at Appomattox but was captured shortly afterward at Hanover Court House.

He found it difficult to support his family in Virginia after the war and entered the employ of the Lake Superior and Mississippi Railroad, later transferring to the Northern Pacific. Because of his ability and energy, he soon became one of its leading engineers. In 1871 he was in charge of the party that surveyed a route from the Missouri River near Fort Rice westward to the confluence of the Yellowstone and Powder rivers. He was also in charge of the surveys of 1872 and 1873, and during this last-named expedition, which was escorted by ten troops of Custer's regiment, the Seventh United States Cavalry, he renewed his friendship with his old classmate and military rival.

After the disaster at the Little Big Horn River, Rosser engaged in a public controversy with Major Marcus A. Reno regarding whether the latter had fully complied with the spirit of Custer's orders and implied that Major Reno had been responsible for the disaster. General Rosser also won some notoriety by offering to raise a regiment of his old Confederate comrades for the purpose of making war on the Sioux and avenging Custer. It is quite possible that his criticisms had a great deal to do with the growing public opinion that came to hold Reno responsible for Custer's defeat and led to a court of inquiry into Major Reno's conduct at the Little Big Horn.

Later General Rosser superintended construction of the Northern Pacific from Bismarck, North Dakota, west to Livingston, Montana, on one occasion taking the construction materials and other supplies across the Missouri River on a track laid on the ice. After the ice became too thin to sustain the weight of the locomotive, the cars were hauled across by horses. But while the exploit won worldwide attention, it was more spectacular than effective since it did not perform the work for which it was expressly designed. By the time of the spring breakup there was not material enough across the river to build more than twenty miles of track. In 1881, General Rosser became chief engineer for the Canadian Pacific Railroad, serving until 1886, when he retired to live at Rugby, an estate which he had purchased near Charlottesville, Virginia. In 1898 he was commissioned a brigadier general in the United States Army by President McKinley and served during the Spanish-American War. Later he was appointed postmaster at Charlottesville, a post that he held at the time of his death.[1]

In 1874 he was living at Minneapolis, and because of his three expeditions into the western country and his known favorable opinion of the country to be traversed by the Northern Pacific Railroad, he was asked for his views concerning the opinions expressed by General Hazen. The details of his interview with a *Tribune* reporter were chronicled as follows.

The reporter found General Rosser in his library at home, and the conversation which ensued was about as follows:

Reporter.—General, have you read the letter of General Hazen in the New York *Tribune* concerning the Northern Pacific Railroad?

General Rosser.—Yes, I have read that remarkable document.

Reporter.—What could have prompted General Hazen to write such a letter?

General Rosser.—General Hazen is a very peculiar man; vain, ostentatious and fond of notoriety, and consequently scribbles a

[1] *Dictionary of American Biography*, XVI, 181–82. The article is by Joseph Mills Hanson.

49

great deal for the papers. Sometimes his theme is the wanton and cruel waste of the buffalo on the plains by reckless hunters,[2] sometimes this desire is indulged in at the expense of the staff corps of the army.[3] He has written a book, and now like the visitor to the sick lion, he feels that the Northern Pacific is sick, and he must give it a kick.

Reporter.—General Hazen writes from Fort Buford. Where is that point?

General Rosser.—Fort Buford is 400 miles (by river) above Bismarck where the Northern Pacific crosses and leaves the Missouri River. This post, he tells us, is on the 48th parallel, and his statistics are collected there. The Northern Pacific Railroad lies wholly south of the 47th parallel through the Territory of Dakota, and only reaches the 47th parallel at one point in Montana.

Reporter.—What opportunity has General Hazen had for learning so much about this northern country?

General Rosser.—This letter of General Hazen's surprises me for I know that he has never seen an acre of the country traversed by the Northern Pacific Railroad between the Missouri and the Yellowstone rivers, and I believe he has never seen the valley of the Yellowstone except at one point where he crossed it *en route* from some point south to Fort Benton, and this was high in Montana. Consequently he knows nothing personally concerning the lands which he so flippantly charges the railroad company with fraudulently misrepresenting.

Reporter.—What do other prominent army officers say concerning the agricultural prospects of the country?

General Rosser.—Generals Stanley[4] and Custer, who are quite as distinguished in their profession as General Hazen, and I dare

[2] In a letter to the New York *Times* from Fort Hays, Kansas, General Hazen had not only deplored the senseless slaughter of the buffalo, but declared that the argument that the buffalo should be killed to deprive the Indians of a food supply was a fallacy, as the Indians were becoming harmless "under a rule of justice," New York *Times*, Jan. 26, 1872.

[3] In his book, General Hazen had been very critical of the staff organization of the United States Army.

[4] David S. Stanley, who had commanded the Yellowstone expeditions of both 1872 and 1873.

50

say equally experienced in agriculture, pronounce that portion of Dakota west of the Missouri River better than that portion east of it, and so far as the eastern portion is concerned we have the verdict of thousands who have crossed it since the road has been in operation, establishing its fertility and susceptibility of agricultural development far above the attacks of the gallant commander of Fort Buford.

Reporter.—General Hazen speaks particularly of the scarcity of hay in Dakota and vicinity. What have been your experiences in procuring hay along the line of the road?

General Rosser.—As evidence of the unfairness or ignorance of General Hazen, I will state that from the bottom lands of the Missouri and Heart rivers in a range of five miles from Fort Abraham Lincoln, where the Northern Pacific crosses the Missouri River, 2,500 tons of excellent hay were cut by machinery last summer and fall, and the post supplied under contract of $12 per ton, and the fortunate contractor got it cut and cared for at $4 per ton. Thousands of tons were put up in the vicinity of Bismarck in the summer of 1872, while our road was being built, for $5 per ton. In the valley of the Heart River along the line of our road west of the Missouri River, I have seen hundreds of acres of good grass that would at least yield three tons per acre, yet because there is no hay at Fort Buford, or perhaps because his contractor wants an excuse for asking a good price for putting it up, General Hazen desires to create the impression in the minds of his readers that there is no hay on the Missouri River 400 miles south of him.

Reporter.—For confirmation of his slanders, General Hazen refers to General G. K. Warren, of the Engineer Corps, and his report on that country. What do you think that amounts to?

General Rosser.—General Hazen [*sic*] made a boat survey of the Yellowstone and Missouri rivers, and those explorations were confined to the immediate vicinity of those rivers, and his information consequently is very limited.[5]

[5] Here General Rosser is unfair to Warren, who as a lieutenant of the Topographical Corps of Engineers had made a number of explorations in the Trans-Mississippi West. Among other expeditions, he ascended the Yellowstone River from its mouth to a point opposite its confluence with Powder River.

Reporter.—General Hazen does refer to the testimony of Governor Stevens and General Fremont on this matter. What do you think is the animus of that?

General Rosser.—He asks us to reject the testimony of Governor Stevens, General Fremont and Lieutenant Mullen, who not only examined the valleys, but the hills and country generally, with reference to its susceptibility of cultivation, because their statements are favorable to the road.

Reporter.—Are there any particularly favorable sections of country which General Hazen has neglected to mention?

General Rosser.—If General Hazen has ever seen this country he so pitilessly disparages, and is a fair man, and if his intentions are pure and honest, I can't see how it is that he fails to mention the beautiful and fertile region extending along the Sweet Briar[6] and Heart rivers, each side of the line of the Northern Pacific Railroad, and the vast district of excellent coal through which this road runs from Heart River to the upper waters of the Yellowstone. Indeed, General Hazen attacks the Northern Pacific Railroad at such "long range" that I am satisfied that his ammunition is needlessly wasted.

Reporter.—What do you know of the truth of the representations of the Northern Pacific Railroad Company concerning their lands?

General Rosser.—All the surveys west of the Missouri River, through Dakota, into eastern Montana, have been made under my direction, and the statements made by the officers of the road were based on my official reports and those of other engineers, and all they have said officially, so far as I know, is *strictly the truth.* [Italics in the original.]

Reporter.—What are the facts concerning the freezing of soldiers? Are they warmly enough clothed?

General Rosser.—General Hazen fails to tell us that. United States soldiers serving on the 48th parallel are clad in precisely the same manner as those serving in Texas, Florida and Louisiana.

---

[6] A northern tributary of the Heart River, which in turn enters the Missouri from the west, a short distance below and across from the present city of Bismarck.

Reporter.—How do the Indians stand this fearful climate? *General Rosser.*—The Indians live in a state of hostility to the government along the line of the Northern Pacific Railroad in Dakota and Montana, and subsist on the abundance of game which the country supports during winter; and their ponies have nothing in the way of food provided in summer for winter use, but live upon the pickings of the Hazen desert.

Reporter.—How was the weather at Bismarck and beyond during the last winter?

General Rosser.—The river broke up on the 18th of March last spring, some weeks before the Mississippi did. The employees of the road were running hand cars from Jamestown to Bismarck, a distance of 115 miles through prairies during the whole of the winter and were not interrupted at all. At no time last winter was there sleighing between those places while there was an unusual amount of snow in Southern Minnesota. In the light of the facts, I am of the opinion that Hazen's attack is malicious to say the least.

Reporter.—General Hazen says that in order to be able to produce anything, these lands must be artificially irrigated. What is your opinion on that subject?

General Rosser.—I know that in the vicinity of Bismarck last year, that oats matured on a piece of ground that was not watered nor manured. The oats were planted upon a spoil bank which is clay dug up out of a ditch. The oats produced were of the best kind. I also saw trees several hundred feet above the river and flatlands, which had plenty of rain to nurture them and were doing well. During the three years in which I have been engaged in travelling across this country, I have noticed an abundance of water for agricultural and other purposes. In 1872 I had a beautiful garden in Second Cheyenne in Dakota,[7] 60 miles west of the Red River. There are patches all along the line which have been cultivated and have yielded vegetables and fruit in abundance.

Reporter.—What do you think of Hazen's statement that the lands will not sell for a penny an acre?

---

[7] This was the second crossing of the Cheyenne River, the first crossing being just west of Fargo, North Dakota.

General Rosser.—I think that is all folly. As an evidence that it will sell and for good prices too, large numbers of people are occupying it now and contending for the possession of every inch of the ground. The army officers are all taking claims through Dakota, and show by their actions their appreciation of its worth. There are flourishing settlements at the crossing of the James River, at Cheyenne, at Crystal Springs and numerous other points.

Reporter.—Hazen refers to the report of Herr Haas, who was sent out by the Vienna banks to investigate the country and calls it incorrect?

General Rosser.—Yes, I noticed that, but then Haas had no motive in making the statements that he did, as Hazen evidently has in what he says. Haas is a practical man. I was with him when he went across the country and he expressed himself as charmed with it as were all of the commission who accompanied him. All that they objected to was the manner in which the road was managed. If Hazen cared at all for the interests of the bond-holders, he would not make such recklessly untrue statements as he does, and thus I am led to believe that he wrote what he did either from hearsay or he has done it with malicious intentions. He has taken the statements of some of those interested for the basis of some of his assertions. I think that he has either been hired to write that letter or he did it, as I said before, to make himself notorious.

The interview then terminated and the reporter bade the General "Good-morning."

5. Maginnis Letter

General Hazen's letter was printed in the New York *Tribune* for February 7, 1874. A week later the *Tribune* published a reply to the Hazen communication written by Mr. Martin Maginnis, territorial delegate from Montana, then residing in Washington, D. C.

Martin Maginnis, of Irish descent, one of the staunchest boosters of Montana, was born on the twenty-seventh of October, 1841, in Wayne County, New York. His family moved around a great deal, going first to Illinois and later to Minnesota, where he attended Hamline University for a time. With the coming of the Civil War he enlisted in the United States Army, and at the end of the conflict was mustered out with the rank of major.

In 1866 he organized and led a group of about 150 men to Montana, where they engaged in mining. About a year later he joined with another man in editing the *Daily Rocky Mountain Gazette*, which later became the *Helena Independent*, and which was established for the purpose of advancing the interests of the Democratic party in the territory. In 1872 he was elected territorial delegate to Congress, where he served six continuous terms. His principal activity was in serving the interests of Montana and its settlers. He was interested in everything that would speed up the settlement of the area and also contribute to the well-being of its settlers. So, when General Hazen leveled his charges regarding the worthlessness of the lands west of the Missouri River, it was expected that Major Maginnis would come to the defense of the territory he represented in Congress. He apparently felt that construction of the Northern Pacific was essential to the prosperity of Montana, and when the road was under fire because of the failure of Jay Cooke and Company, he was a zealous defender of its charter. He was an interested witness, and his letter defending the region west of the Missouri and answering the assertion that they were "barren lands" was that of a partisan advocate.[1]

To the Editor of the New York Tribune
SIR:—While most of the army officers since the commencement of the Government have been among the first to appreciate the capabilities of the ever Westward-moving frontier along which they have been stationed, it is a strange fact that in every successive age of our country's progress there have been a few officers who could see no good in the new country in which they were doing duty, and who condemned every step of that progress as a foolish stride into a worthless, a sickly, or uninhabitable land. These statements were not often born of malice or mendacity, but generally were conceived in the peculiar fancies of dissatisfied men who regarded their term of service on the frontier as an exile from the joys of civilization, and who naturally hated the country the defense of which required them to be absent from the easy life and social enjoyment of garrisoned towns or the forts which guard our Eastern cities. As these maledictions have successfully been uttered over every spot in the new, wealthy and blooming States of Ohio, Indiana, Illinois, Wisconsin and Minnesota, it is not strange that these dismal croakings, although forever refuted by the successful march of emigration and empire, should still faintly echo from the new frontier which now faces our new Northwest, and that we should still find one of the germs alive in the person of General Wm B. Hazen, commandant of the melancholy, Sioux-surrounded and Sitting-Bull-besieged Fort Buford, on the plateau which divides the most northerly portion of the Missouri River from the Saskatchewan, in the middle of the wind-swept plains and the

[1] *Dictionary of American Biography*, XII, 199. The article is by Paul Crisler Phillips.

centre of the arid belt. If he had confined his remarks in a late number of the *Tribune* to the vicinity of his unhappy domicile, neither to which nor to any place in the vicinity of which does anybody propose to build a railroad, he might peacefully vent his spleen, nourished as it is by exclusion from an Eastern home, where wealth might make life enjoyable, and deepened by the disgust which he feels at having General Crook[2] put over his head for heroism and activity among the Apaches, which General Hazen might with credit to himself imitate among the Sioux.

But our doughty warrior, who has not been over successful in smiting the heathen with the sword, appeals to the pen as a mightier weapon with which he can demolish the whole country, from the Red River west to the Pacific—Indians, whites and all— and more especially slay those who are endeavoring to develop its capabilities by the construction of the Northern Pacific Railroad. So far as General Hazen's letter in the *Tribune* is concerned we might refute it from the facts recorded in its files by its faithful correspondent, Richardson, who also could scarcely in his book find words to express his admiration of the larger part of the country which Colonel Hazen condemns as a whole; or from the correspondence and the book of Colonel Alex. K. McClure of Philadelphia, or from the reports of the Governors and Surveyors-General of Montana, Washington and Idaho Territories, or the records of the Land Office in Washington City, or from the tax lists of the Territories named, or from the census returns; but as this martial asseverator announces in advance that all who dare to contradict him are liars, perhaps we had better *leave out all the testimony of civilians,* and merely quote military witnesses in rebuttal. Leaving out Stevens whom he classes as an enthusiast unworthy the attention of any sober-minded man, let us refer to the opinions of U. S. Grant, and of Phil. Sheridan; of General Hancock, late commander of that department; of General John Gibbon, District Commander of Montana; and of General Sully,

2 General George Crook, one of the greatest Indian fighters, had been assigned as lieutenant colonel of the Twenty-third Infantry following the close of the Civil War. In October, 1873, he was commissioned a brigadier general, thus being promoted over the head of Hazen and a number of others.

late Superintendent of Indian Affairs, and of Generals Ingalls and Hardee,[3] all of whom have placed themselves on record in direct and positive opposition to the statements now made by the infallible Hazen. True, these gentlemen travelled over and knew the country, which General Hazen does not; for he admits even his ignorance of the vicinity of his own fort by quoting as authority the letter of a hay contractor, who plays on the General the nearly worn out frontier trick of complaining of the scarcity of hay in order to enhance the value of what he delivers at the post. So far as Montana, which he is pleased to include in his denunciations, is concerned, any contradiction of his grotesquely absurd statements is unneeded by the informed.

A Territory that has in the ten years of its existence produced $160,000,000 in gold, nearly enough to redeem one-half of all our greenbacks; that has paid into the National Treasury nearly three-quarters of a million in Internal Revenue taxes; that has a taxable property of $15,000,000 in goods, houses, lands and cattle—the mining property is not taxed—where in the year just passed 620,000 acres of the public domain are reported by the Governor, from the Land Office records, as having been taken up; where 150,000 head of horses, cattle and mules, and 20,000 sheep are now in the middle of this winter, as they have been for winters past, roaming in fatness on her hills, unsheltered, unhoused and unfed, save as they shelter and feed themselves on their ample winter grazing ranges—this cannot be the arid country in summer or the frigid country in winter which General Hazen misrepresents it to be. The reader has only to look at the reports of the Surveyors-General to see that we have an area of cultivable land that is scarcely encroached on—land that yields for its average crops from 25 to 35 bushels of wheat to the acre, and whose premium crops at our Agricultural Fair have to go over 100 bushels to the

---

[3] Maginnis is here indulging in the common practice of "name dropping." But in 1869, General Hancock in replying to a toast had referred to Montana as "a country rich in resources" (Helena *Weekly Herald*, July 1, 1869), and a year later General Sheridan, in expressing his surprise at the resources of Montana Territory, said that he had expected to find the mineral resources "but not the rich agricultural lands" (*Rocky Mountain Gazette*, Helena, M. T., May 17, 1870).

acre to win the prizes; where 600 bushels of potatoes and 100 bushels of oats are no uncommon yield, and where we raise rye and barley [which] at the World's Fair in Vienna surpassed everything on exhibition there. He can find, too, that of all the lands not arable the greater portion is of the finest summer and winter pasture, and the residue covered with timber and veined with valuable mines. Let him look at the books of our transportation companies, and he will find that we annually import and export enough to pay for the maintenance and operation of a railroad in this one Territory alone, though her mines of gold and silver are as yet scarcely scratched, and her coal, lead, iron and copper totally untouched. What will she do when her magnificent resources are developed?

As to her climate the meteorological record kept at Fort Benton and at Deer Lodge for 20 years has again and again been published in the government reports, and as it shows a more favorable winter average than that of Philadelphia, the people of New York can scarcely put it down as unendurably cold, while those who have the happiness to reside there, though they are gathered from all quarters of the Union and of the globe, claim preference for it over the climate of any State east of the mountains from Maine to the Gulf.

These facts being true of Montana are indisputably true of Idaho and Washington Territories, the former, like Montana, a mining Territory, the latter more exclusively devoted to agriculture and lumbering, and either of them superior in climate and natural resources to any State east of the Alleghanies. They will be able when developed and populated to support not only one but many railroads, but one at least is needed for their development and population.

The fiscal agents of the Northern Pacific Railroad, miscalculating their ability, and disappointed in their reasonable expectations of European support, failed to complete a project too great for individual enterprise, and which only needed to be completed to become a magnificent success. Their failure was the signal for a financial revulsion, produced by a variety of causes. In that

59

crash, industries were paralyzed and fortunes lost; but none lost more magnificent fortunes than the unfortunate projectors. Over this crash the country feels bitter, and is ready to applaud anybody who may kick the scapegoat of all our financial sins; but all this clamor weighs not against the intrinsic merits of the project itself, nor does it suddenly change the character of the country over which the road was to pass. Even by the agents of the European company that country was recognized to be as good or better than reported. There can be no just reason why under any circumstances any portion of our national domain should be unjustly depreciated or undervalued, and no motive therefor excepting in the jealousies of competing cities along the lines of competing routes. New York is too great to share in these. She is the metropolis of the whole country, and her press should see to it that no portion of that country is falsely disparaged, and that no great enterprise is libeled down.

MARTIN MAGINNIS, Delegate from Montana
Washington, D. C., February 19, 1874

On this letter the New York *Tribune* commented editorially:

Major Martin Maginnis, Delegate from Montana, sends us through the office of the Northern Pacific Railroad Company an answer to General Hazen's letter printed in last Saturday's *Tribune*. We are happy to give a fair hearing on both sides, and we therefore publish the reply, although it is neither good-tempered nor conclusive. Major Maginnis, having been in the army himself, ought to know better than to asperse the military record of one of our most gallant and distinguished officers in the service, merely for the alleged offense of slandering the thermometer. General Hazen's statements as to the climate of that portion of the Northern Pacific route of which he writes are not random rhetorical assertions, but the transcript of a series of careful, scientific observations, and we cannot see that the Delegate from Montana has weakened their force in the slightest particular.

It should be borne in mind that what Major Maginnis says of

the crops of Montana may be quite true, and yet it may be equally beyond dispute that the railroad lands in Northern Montana and Dakota are just what General Hazen declares them to be—cold, and dry, and unsuitable for agricultural settlements. The fertility of the wheat region of the Red River of the North, and of the bottom lands along the Missouri, the Yellowstone, and some other streams, is well known; but it is not of these that General Hazen speaks.—*New York Tribune*, 14 ult. (February 1874).[4]

In the same issue and on the same page of the *Tribune* in which the letter from Martin Maginnis appeared were printed editorial comments in support of General Hazen from other newspapers. The first was the Cleveland *Herald*, which, under the heading of "An Interesting Communication," had remarked:

The communication of General Hazen to the New-York *Tribune*, transferred to our columns, concerning the climate and soil of the territory traversed by the Northern Pacific Railroad line, will be read with interest, especially in Northern Ohio, where General Hazen is so well known personally. The General is a man of positive opinions, and expresses those opinions with blunt directness, without stopping to consider whether they will prove palatable or not. He should be well qualified to know whereof he speaks, having been bred a farmer, and for several years past having had abundant opportunities for testing by actual experience the qualities of the soil and climate of the northern frontier in the neighborhood of the 100th meridian. Recollections of the cold he has suffered in winter, and his struggles to raise a few flowers and a bunch or two of radishes in the short Summers, cause him to speak his mind with perhaps even more than his usual bluntness.

The second comment, from the Providence *Press*, was entitled "Not a Good Showing." It read:

General W. B. Hazen, U. S. Commandant at Fort Buford, Dakota, who distinguished himself in the war and is well known in

4 Cited in the Helena *Weekly Herald*, March 12, 1874.

the army, writes to the *Tribune* a fearful exposé of some of the statements of Jay Cooke's advertising agents relating to the fertility of the regions through which they are building the Northern Pacific Railroad. He affirms his ability to substantiate all of his assertions, but if any one doubts let him go and see for himself. Altogether it is not a good showing for Carleton and Wilkeson, who have written the thing up for Cooke.

The third comment, from the Cincinnati *Commercial*, was entitled "A Needed Public Service" and was somewhat lavish in its praise of what General Hazen had done.

General W. B. Hazen has performed an important and much needed public service in writing the letter to the New-York *Tribune* about the worthless Northern Pacific Railroad lands, which we reproduce elsewhere. It is positive that General Hazen has no interest in the matter save that of serving the people by giving them honest information. His facts gathered largely from personal observation are overwhelming. The exposure of the false pretensions of the demagogues and speculators, and able editors, interested in Jay Cooke's isothermal scheme, is interesting.

6. A Question of Fact

Another person entered the controversy, when, on the thirteenth of March, 1874, the Helena *Daily Herald* published a
"card" from Colonel Thomas P. Roberts, entitled "A Question of
Fact." It was admittedly in reply to the statements of General
Hazen, and while written by an employee of the Northern Pacific
Railroad, was also the work of a person who had spent considerable time in the region of which he wrote, and who had a knowledge, gained at first hand, of the conditions that existed there.

Colonel Roberts was a civil engineer hired in 1872 by the
Northern Pacific Railroad to study the portion of the Missouri
River above Bismarck with the object of determining the practicability of steamboat navigation of the upper river in conjunction
with the railroad. His researches were painstaking and thorough.
He even worked out plans for a railroad around the Great Falls
of the Missouri to operate in connection with boats both below
and above that point. His official report was published by the War
Department in 1875 under the title, *Report of a Reconnaissance of
the Missouri River in 1872*. A somewhat informal article dealing
with his trip down the Missouri from the Three Forks to the Great
Falls was published in Volume I of *Contributions to the Historical
Society of Montana* (pp. 234–67), under the title "The Upper
Missouri River; from a Reconnaissance Made in 1872."

The painstaking thoroughness with which he carried out his
assignment is shown in the voyage down the upper Missouri.
Embarking at the Three Forks on July 27, his party arrived at

63

the mouth of Sun River on August 6. They had found the upper Missouri to be navigable, and described the Missouri Valley below the point where they emerged from the mountains as "one of the best grazing and agricultural districts in this mountainous Territory."

A QUESTION OF FACT

The Northern Pacific Railroad Lands—A Card from Colonel T. P. Roberts, in Reply to Statements of General W. B. Hazen.

At the request of acquaintances and friends, upon my return on different occasions from the far North-west, from along the route of the Northern Pacific Railroad, I wrote articles descriptive of those regions, confining myself mostly to the agricultural resources of the country, upon the merits of which, perhaps, more than anything else, depends the success of the railroad.

During two years that I was engaged on the surveys of the road, I travelled East and West through Montana Territory in a number of directions, from a point nearly 200 miles west of the Rocky Mountains to the Missouri river, and from the southern border north to Fort Benton, latitude 47 degrees 50 minutes north. On the occasion of my second visit to the Territory, I travelled up the Missouri river from Sioux City, Iowa, via Fort Buford, to Fort Benton, a distance of 2,000 miles, taking thirty-six days, which trip enabled me to collect much information regarding Dakota in general. As late as last November I made a third trip, going to Minnesota and Dakota, passing over the line of the completed road from near Duluth to Bismarck, opposite Fort Lincoln on the Missouri, which point is about four hundred miles below Fort Buford, at the mouth of the Yellowstone.

A fair statement of facts regarding the agricultural, grazing and lumber resources of different parts of the route of the Northern Pacific Railroad, which I made, appeared somewhat marvelous to some, but I brought evidences of the truth in specimens of grain, which have not been equalled for quality, so far as I know, at any State fair or exhibitions anywhere. Samples of cereals, several bushels of each, which I forwarded to New York, I understood received the premium at the American Institute fair, over Minnesota, California, and all other grain, and afterwards received the first premium at the Vienna Exposition, over the far-famed grain from Russia and Poland.

I do not desire to again particularize those features of Montana. That Territory stands like an oasis in the desert, compared with her sisters South. Her sparkling brooks, abounding with fish; her grass-covered hills and timbered mountains, with that abundance of game and herds of cattle, in the settled parts, speak the language of *facts* which no fancied theory from those who have never been there dare dispute. Winter and Summer the grazing is alike good; and although it may not be the "Banana Zone," as the Cincinnati *Commercial* derisively calls it, the climate is far superior to, and more healthful than Ohio or Pennsylvania. The bane of the valleys of the Little Miami, Wabash and Maumee—fever and ague—is entirely lacking in Montana. Ploughing is usually done in the latter part of January and early part of February, and in the latter part of February and first of March the grain is planted—before a plough is usually sunk in the Miami valley north of Cincinnati.

The Missouri river at Fort Benton breaks up in the spring at least one month earlier than it does at Sioux City, two thousand miles below. In the Spring of 1872 it broke up at Fort Benton the same day that it did at St. Louis, ten and a half degrees farther south. This is not one of "Jay Cooke's lies," but comes direct from the United States signal observer at Fort Benton. About 20,000 intelligent white people reside in Montana, and they support telegraph lines and daily newspapers. I have yet to hear from one of her citizens an authoritative denial of any of the reports published by officers of the Northern Pacific Railroad regarding the region in question.

Several years have elapsed since the road was begun, and nothing appeared to dispute the statements concerning the land, productions, climate, etc., until recently General W. B. Hazen the commandant of Fort Buford, Dakota, writes to the New York *Tribune* a sweeping condemnation of the road, and likens the selling of bonds, with such a basis as these lands, to a fraud, and says that all who dispute *his* statements are falsifiers.

Fort Buford, undoubtedly, is a poor place to live, but still, I think General Hazen has not done it justice. The winds are famous in that part of Dakota, as I experienced myself, and the Winters, doubtless, very severe *at times*, though the general average of temperature, by General Hazen's own statements, is about the same as that of Philadelphia. It matters not how low the thermometer may go in Winter, if the Summers are sufficiently warm to produce paying crops, agriculturists will be content to settle. General Hazen reports a failure in the garden at his post, but adds, further, that "onions, with wheat and oats, matured at Fort Berthold, 150 [miles] below, on the Missouri river." Why did he not go on and state that not only his post, but even Fort Berthold, was considerably north of the Northern Pacific Railroad? But he prefers not to mention that fact, but have it appear, as it has in the press, that he is on the line of the road, and knows all about it. By river, Fort Buford is over 400 miles above the Northern Pacific Railroad, and at the nearest point the surveyed lines are nowhere less than 130 miles *south* of that point. It is a curious idea that some entertain, that the isothermal lines, with their kinks and bends towards the north-west, were placed on the maps at the instigation of Jay Cooke. The mean Summer and Winter temperatures were collated by the military authorities from years of observation at the several posts, and the lines were drawn in the first instance in Washington some years ago and have the sanction of Lorin Blodgett, (*sic*) the greatest climatologist of the country. General Hazen, therefore, when he disputes their correctness, quarrels with his own figures, and the figures of the whole of the army surgeons in the country.

Further on, he presumes to condemn Montana and Idaho Territories, and portions of the road many hundreds of miles away

66

from his quarters, of which, doubtless, he has not the slightest personal knowledge. Had Columbus landed on the Jersey coast in mosquito time, he, no doubt, would have published America as one great sandy desert, utterly worthless. Thus, General Hazen says: "Respecting the agricultural value of this country, after leaving the excellent wheat-growing valley of the Red-river of the North, following westward 1,600 miles to the Sierras, excepting the very limited bottoms of the small streams, as well as those of the Missouri and Yellowstone, from a very few yards in breadth to an occasional water-washed valley of one or two miles, and the narrow valleys of Montana already settled, and a small area of timbered country in north-west Idaho (probably one-fiftieth portion of the whole), this country will not produce the fruits and cereals of the East, for want of sufficient moisture, and can in no way be irrigated; and most of the land here excepted will have to be irrigated artificially. I write this knowing full well it will meet with contradiction, but the contradiction will be a falsehood."

Certainly such statements, so much at variance with the truth, will meet with contradiction. Not a twentieth nor a one-hundredth part of the arable land in Montana is settled; and where irrigation is required to start crops, water in superabundance can be found and utilized at little cost, owing to the favorable "lay of the country." I made special inquiry into the subject of areas of arable land, and gauged the volume of the principal streams on both sides of the main range, and satisfied myself fully in regard to this matter.

My conclusions were, that the valleys within sixty miles of the proposed route of the railroad through Montana would produce at a much lower average yield per acre than that now produced in the Gallatin or Prickly Pear Valley, at least 125,000,000 bushels of wheat per annum—equal to the product of any state in the Union, though it is the grazing and mineral resources of that Territory that is claimed to afford the best and most certain prospect for business on the railroad.

There is little to note in passing along the river in the neighborhood of Fort Buford. Still I find in my notes some things perhaps worth mentioning as disputing General Hazen's statements regarding the grazing in that vicinity.

May 23, 7:30 P.M.—Passed Fort Buford, three and a half miles below the mouth of the Yellowstone, on the left bank. Quite a village, quarters, etc., well built, timber used said to be cottonwood, but well painted and neat looking. This upper river cottonwood seems to be more serviceable timber than that along the lower Ohio. The Yellowstone and Missouri unite in the middle of the valley; the neck or point between them for a few acres in extent is open, back of which is a belt of young willow. About a half mile above the mouth of the Yellowstone, we had a beautiful sunset view of its valley, for many miles. *The immediate valley is a beautiful bottom covered with luxuriant grass*, sloping from the low rolling hills on the left bank to a dense timber growth, which works in a general way, the course of the Yellowstone. Its valley is about four miles wide from hill to hill," etc., etc.

We had in sight at least twenty square miles of the "luxurient [*sic*] grass," none of which was more than six or eight miles from Fort Buford. At 20 square miles there would be 12,800 acres, which, at half a ton to the acre (to be reasonable), there was certainly not less than 6,400 tons of hay to be had for the cutting. At the time of my visit the grass was about ten inches high, beautifully green, not having attained its full growth. General Hazen was certainly never at the spot, or he would not have credited the story of the contractor, who reported the utmost difficulty in providing nine hundred tons of hay for the post, *after examining 2,400 (?) square miles of territory* in the neighborhood. My journal on the following morning, passing the mouth of the Big Muddy a few miles above mentions "excellent grazing" and further on "grass northward as far as the eye can reach," etc., etc.

All the buffalo we saw were quite fat, and they were returning from the north in British America, where they winter in vast numbers. At the mouth of the Muscleshell, the deepest snow had been only seven inches, horses and cattle had grazed out the winter previous—1871–2. General Hazen disposes of all the military officers who write contrary to him as "enthusiasts" though some he mentions had much more extended experience in the regions in question.

THOMAS P. ROBERTS

Pittsburgh, February 25, 1874

On Thursday, March 19, 1874, the Minneapolis *Tribune* printed under the heading of "Brazen Hazen," excerpts from a letter written by a gentleman from Cincinnati who had recently been in Bismarck, Dakota Territory, and who wrote that "the crusade against this great enterprise Northern Pacific is sufficiently explained by their refusal to carry his baggage for nothing." He continued: "This Hazen letter is a very brazen letter and reveals here and there the animus of the writer. He asserts the land to be not worth a *penny an acre* and closes up his budget of spite by advising the bondholders to buy it at four or five dollars an acre as a means of saving themselves. He has invoked the wind and the weather and has ransacked heaven and earth for material to ruin a great national enterprise. His zeal in the dirty work has outstripped his judgment and prostrated his veracity as the unsightly gaps in his net work abundantly show."

7. Milnor Roberts Letter

William Milnor Roberts, more generally known as Milnor Roberts, was born February 12, 1810, at Philadelphia of Welsh-Quaker descent. In 1825 at the age of fifteen he joined an engineering group engaged in the construction of canals and roads, and by 1831 had risen to a position where he was the senior assistant engineer for the survey of the proposed Allegheny Portage Railroad. At the age of twenty-five he was chief engineer for the Lancaster and Harrisburg Railroad. He also turned his attention to bridge construction and to canal work, especially the enlargement of the Erie Canal, but in 1849 returned to railroad engineering work and was instrumental in bringing about the adoption by the nation's railroads of standard gauge. He was then engaged for a number of years in railroad construction work in Brazil and after his return in 1866 spent some time in improvement of river navigation and in the building of the Eads bridge across the Mississippi at St. Louis. Late in 1869 he was appointed chief engineer for the Northern Pacific Railroad, a position that he held for ten years. Thereafter he returned to Brazil, where he died of typhus in 1881.[1]

During his decade of service with the Northern Pacific, he traveled over most, if not all, of the proposed route, and became an authority on the region through which the road was to be constructed. His position as one of the outstanding civil engineers of the day gave authority to his statements, and his writings were

[1] *Dictionary of American Biography*, XVI, 19 (article by Carl W. Mitman).

widely used in support of the practicability of the road. There was scarcely a brochure or pamphlet issued by the company which did not contain a letter or at least a statement by W. Milnor Roberts, so that when General Hazen's letter appeared, it was only natural that Mr. Roberts should prepare a reply.

In an article entitled "Hazing Hazen," the *Minneapolis Daily Tribune*, on March 10, 1874, presented a summary of a letter written by "General" Roberts,[2] in which, as the newspaper said, he also took "a hand at Hazen." The article then went on to remark that the number of volunteer champions who had defended the Northern Pacific Railroad against the attack of General Hazen had performed so ably that the company could well have afforded to pay the General for his letter. It continued: "His attack was so evidently malicious, and displayed such a contempt for the intelligence of the country, that men have come to the defense who would otherwise have never been tempted to say a word about the land on the 46th parallel." The article then quoted extensively from General Roberts together with its own comments, but it did not reprint his letter.[3]

To the Editor of the Tribune

SIR:—General Hazen's letter to the *Tribune*, dated at Fort Buford, Dakota Territory, January 1, although probably not so intended, conveys to strangers some erroneous impressions concerning the route and characteristics of the country through which the Northern Pacific Railroad will pass, and over which for 450 miles, between Lake Superior and the Missouri River, it is constructed. It certainly conveys the idea that the writer of the letter is living on or in the immediate vicinity of the line of the road, whereas Fort Buford is, by way of the Missouri River, 400 miles above the crossing of the railroad at Bismarck and Fort Abraham Lincoln, and in a materially different region.

2 The title of "General" seems to have been entirely honorary.

3 This communication, which I had difficulty in locating, was finally discovered in a pamphlet of newspaper clippings in the William Robertson Coe Collection in the Yale University Library.

The letter states that Fort Buford is in latitude 48° and longitude 104°. Fort Abraham Lincoln, at the railroad crossing, is about latitude 46½° and longitude 100°—1½° further south and 4° east. The first locations for the railroad across Dakota were made considerably further upstream, but still south of Fort Buford, passing as high as Devil's Lake, near Fort Totten, and thence to the Missouri. That route was discarded because of the inferior nature of the country, and because it increased the distance. The present line was selected because it passes through a much better region for settlement and is remarkably favorable and direct. It has been estimated by good practical farmers that there is not much more than 10 to 12 per cent of the land between the Red River of the North and the Missouri, 196 miles, along the line of the road, that is not arable. General Hazen testifies, in his letter, to the excellence of the land in the Red River Valley, although the letter does not clearly show what a valuable body of it belongs to the Railroad Company. He seems to make light of the fact, or ignores it, that the Company by their construction of their road to the Missouri River, have already secured 10,000,000 acres of land, a large proportion of which is not only capable of settlement, but is now rapidly being settled.

When a gentleman of the standing of General Hazen, who has a highly honorable record in the service of the country, makes a sweeping assertion which conveys to the public mind an impression that the bulk of the United States Territories between the Red River of the North and the Pacific Coast Range, 1,600 miles is "not worth a cent an acre," it may be well to study the matter a little more critically. General Hazen does not claim to have seen the country himself between the Missouri River and the Pacific Coast but refers to General G. K. Warren and Professor Hayden for confirmation of his opinion. He also refers to Governor Stevens, General Fremont, and Lieutenant Mullan, though in a rather singular way. He says: "The testimony of Governor Stevens, General Fremont, and Lieutenant Mullan is that of enthusiastic travellers and discoverers, whose descriptions are not fully borne out by more prolonged and intimate knowledge of the country." Probably General Hazen has not made himself familiar with the early history of this railroad route to the Pacific, or he would scarcely have penned that paragraph. Governor Stevens with the most perfect and extensive military and civil engineer corps ever organized in the United States, in 1853–54 made a most careful and elaborate survey of the country between the Mississippi and the Pacific Coast. His reports with the accompanying maps and profiles, bear evidence of the most thorough and conscientious investigation by himself and his able coadjutors among whom were Lieutenant Mullan and Captain de Lacy. Governor Stevens settled in the country, became Governor of Washington Territory, lived and died on the route of this road,[4] honored as a far-seeing, high-minded pioneer. Captain Mullan remained in the country in the service of the government for years, chiefly in Montana Territory, exploring, locating, and constructing military roads. His reports since show him to have been a practical and intelligent gentleman. Captain de Lacy also remained in Montana as a practical surveyor and engineer, and he has ever since lived in Montana Territory. He is a substantial citizen of acknowledged skill and sound judgment. These gentlemen were no "enthusiasts," but practical men of good sense. General Fremont's explorations were made many hundreds of miles south of the line of the Northern Pacific Railroad, and had not the slightest connection therewith. Governor Stevens' route was not by way of the Yellowstone but passed out along the valley of the Missouri River to the Rocky Mountains, and thence over into the present general route of the railroad. The explorations of General Warren were confined chiefly to the Atlantic Slope and between the Lower Missouri River and the Rocky Mountains. He passed over but a small portion of the present route of the railroad. General Reynolds [*sic*] and Captain Maynadier made a rapid reconnaissance of the Yellowstone River and wrote favorably of it as a railroad route. Professor Hayden has also passed along the Yellowstone River, studying the river in its geological aspects; and during the last three years the Railroad Company

4 Actually, Stevens was killed in action at the battle of Chantilly, September 1, 1862.

has had engineers with Government escorts carefully examining the Middle Yellowstone Valley and their reports prove it to be on the whole a very favorable route for the road, and possessing facilities for future settlement, both agriculturally and for mining.

Now General Hazen states the case thus:—

> Respecting the agricultural value of this country, after leaving the excellent wheat-growing valley of the Red River of the North, following westward 1,600 miles to the Sierras, excepting the very limited bottoms of the small streams, as well as those of the Missouri and Yellowstone, from a few yards in breadth to an occasional water-washed valley of one or two miles (there are bottoms or grass plains in the Yellowstone Valley 10 to 15 miles wide) and the narrow valleys of the streams of Montana already settled and a small area of timbered country in North-West Idaho (probably one-fiftieth of the whole), this country will not produce the fruits and cereals of the East for want of moisture, and can in no way be artificially irrigated, and will not, in our day and generation, sell for one penny an acre, except through fraud or ignorance; and most of the land here excepted will have to be irrigated artificially.

It is somewhat curious that the only portions of the country that the Company has ever claimed as desirable for agricultural purposes are the portions designated in General Hazen's letter. As to the great bulk of the region traversed by the road, they have stated that it has great value as a grazing region, from which a very large cattle transportation on the road will be derived, and that its other values will come from numerous mines of coal in Western Dakota and along the Yellowstone, an article daily more in demand along the Pacific coast; from mines of gold, silver, copper, and iron in Montana and Idaho; and from agriculture and timber lands in Washington Territory. The Company have always claimed, and it is susceptible of proof, that taking the entire line of the Northern Pacific road, its natural advantages and capabilities for settlement and for yielding railroad traffic are very superior to those along the route of the Union Pacific and Central Pacific Railroads.

The want of moisture in the climate west of the Missouri is not a discovery of General Hazen; it has been distinctly referred to in the published reports and letters from the Company's officers. Even if there were abundant moisture, it might be entirely safe to say that in our day and generation all this vast country will not be developed into populous States. A region in the interior of an immense country like the United States, say 1,400 by 400 miles containing 560,000 square miles—a territory large enough to cut into 12 States as large as New York—is not to be taken up and settled in our day and generation.

A very large portion of the territory of Pennsylvania by reason of mountains, is not adapted to agricultural purposes; yet settlements have taken place in the comparatively narrow valleys and lands, once regarded as worthless, "not worth a cent an acre," are now valued even more than the valleys for their abundant mineral wealth. There was a day when Pennsylvania might have been condemned on account of its large proportion of mountain regions, but that day has passed away.

General Hazen may feel justified in his own mind in voluntarily presenting to the public a letter calculated to lessen confidence in the Northern Pacific Railroad as a great national route between the East and the West; but when presenting it before the grand jury of public opinion it would have been at least kind, if not prudent, to have referred to some of its attractive as well as its repulsive features. Men are never wholly bad, and it can scarcely be possible that the United States is the owner of 500,000,000 acres of land worth in the future not one cent an acre. Do settlers take up or buy land which has no value? Is it likely that the Northern Pacific Railroad Company, any more than the Union Pacific Company, can sell the worthless portions? How could they, so long as they have good lands to sell? It may be an excellent move on the part of General Hazen to advise bondholders to buy lands from the Company along the Red River Valley. It is well to know that the Company had some good lands in Minnesota and Dakota. At the close of 1873, by the completion of 105 miles on the Pacific side in Washington Territory, the Company has also come into possession of 1,000,000 more acres of land. Is that worthless? It embraces one of the most valuable timber regions on the globe, in a climate of abundant moisture, without which forests do not appear to thrive, and a mild climate where out-door work is carried on all the year round, and where crops never fail.

It is 20 years since the first survey for the Northern Pacific Railroad was made. It was and it is a herculean undertaking—a work which has enlisted the skill and untiring energies of many good men, who have devoted years to its prosecution through all sorts of difficulties. Without Government aid (for surely the giving of 50,000,000 acres in alternate sections of "worthless land" could not be called aid), this Company has constructed 550 miles of railroad, which, in a few years, when the country along that portion of it is better settled, will pay from its local receipts. It must have a little time. It would be unreasonable to expect that the road should be put through an unsettled region today, and tomorrow pay ten per cent dividends. Meanwhile, even in its partly finished condition, it is of great service to the National Government by the convenience it affords for the speedy and more economical transportation of army supplies and soldiers to the frontier. Montana will get her supplies cheaper and quicker by this route than by any other, and all the upper forts along the Missouri and in Montana will be greatly accommodated. Experience shows that as the railroads are extended along the valleys of the sparsely settled Rocky Mountain region in Colorado and in Utah, the industries and settlements which sprung up along the lines of the roads, even where the adjacent land has little agricultural value astonish the most sanguine. The local business on the Central Pacific Railroad arising directly or indirectly from mining operations is enormous, and so it will be when the railroad is extended along the Yellowstone, to the Montana mining regions. General Hazen in his letter refers to the successful raising of wheat and oats at Fort Berthold, 150 miles by river below Fort Buford, from which point he was writing. Now the crossing of the Northern Pacific Railroad is 250 miles farther down the river, where the land is better and the climate milder. No officer of the Railroad Company has attempted to deceive the people respecting the climate of Dakota, but it is known that many immigrants from

Northern Europe prefer a cold, dry Winter Climate, as more nearly approximating that of their native land. People go out and see the land, and ascertain about the climate before they buy. On and east and west road, 2,000 miles long, extending across a continent, it is natural to suppose that great diversities of climate would be found. Such is the fact. The winters in Minnesota and Dakota are very severe, yet both are now rapidly filling with inhabitants. The winters in the same latitude in Central Montana are much milder; so that cattle are herded in the valleys and on the mountain slopes all Winter without shelter and with no food but the bunch grass of that region, and get fat. While the Territory of Dakota is almost treeless, the hill-slopes along the Yellowstone Valley have numerous forests of pine, and the valley of Clark's Fork of the Columbia presents magnificent forests which continue all around Lake Pend d'Oreille. Then come the treeless plains of the Columbia River, and then again the grand forests of the Cascade Mountains and a climate between that range and the Pacific Ocean almost tropical. No where perhaps on the continent, along any given parallel of latitude, could greater diversity of soil and climate be found. The Railroad Company has gone on in good faith and opened 550 miles of new country. If it proves to be what they believe it is, it will soon be peopled, and like other roads running to the Missouri River, contribute largely to the general prosperity. It has met with a present misfortune, but time will cure it.

W. MILNOR ROBERTS

New York, February 19, 1874

8. Custer Letter

Despite the great number of volunteers who had come to the defense of the Northern Pacific, the main work of rebuttal was apparently to be entrusted to George Armstrong Custer, like Hazen a brevet major general, and at the time of the Hazen letter, lieutenant colonel of the Seventh United States Cavalry, then serving at Fort Abraham Lincoln just across the river from Bismarck, Dakota Territory, at the place where the Northern Pacific was expected to cross the Missouri. His refutation was expected to be so complete and devastating as to silence forever the criticism of such carping malcontents as General Hazen.

On Thursday, March 12, 1874, the *Tribune* noted that Major General Custer "was preparing for publication an account of his last summer's expedition through Dakota," and that this statement would entirely contradict the assertions made by General Hazen regarding that section of the country. The newspaper declared that Custer had had abundant opportunity for observation since his troops were acting as the escort to the Northern Pacific surveying party, and Custer had been forced to take copious notes of the country through which they traveled. The newspaper then promised to bring before its readers "the substance of General Custer's letter."

As previously noted, Custer and Hazen were by no means unknown to each other and had clashed before. Following the encounter in which Hazen had prevented an attack by Custer's troops on a band of Kiowa Indians, the Seventh Cavalry had been

78

transferred to the Department of the South. But in 1873 the growing menace of the Sioux, as well as other tribes on the northern plains, and the necessity of affording protection to the surveying and construction crews of the Northern Pacific had led General Sheridan to order the regiment to Dakota Territory, where it was to be based at Fort Abraham Lincoln, which was to be built while the regiment was in the field. Here the Seventh was to win its reputation.

The regiment was transferred from various posts in the Department of the South to Sioux City by river steamer. Here two companies, D and I, were detached and put en route to Fort Snelling. During the next two summers, those of 1873 and 1874, they were, under the command of Major Marcus A. Reno, to constitute the escort to the party surveying the northern boundary from the Lake of the Woods westward to the Rocky Mountains. The remaining ten companies moved by rail from Sioux City to Yankton, Dakota Territory. Here they experienced one of the worst blizzards in the history of the region. In late spring, after the grass was sufficiently advanced to furnish adequate grazing for the animals, these ten companies marched overland to Fort Rice, from where they moved out shortly afterward as a part of the Stanley expedition accompanying the engineers who were surveying a route for the Northern Pacific Railroad westward from the Missouri River. They struck the Yellowstone River near the present site of Glendive, Montana, and marched up the stream as far as Pompey's Pillar, the most famous landmark on the river. During the march Custer with the cavalry had a couple of brushes with the Sioux and a brief tiff with General Stanley; but amicable relations were soon restored, and at the close of the expedition Custer, at Stanley's order, marched with the greater part of his regiment and a wagon train eastward from the Big Bend of the Musselshell to the Yellowstone, passing over some of the most difficult terrain in the United States without losing a wagon.

The country across which Custer had marched was described as "terrible" and "almost destitute of water and vegetation," and was said to be "with the exception of the valleys of the Musselshell an uninhabitable desert."[1] From the river, the command marched almost due eastward to Fort Abraham Lincoln, which had been built during the summer on the right bank of the Missouri a few miles below present Mandan, North Dakota, and at the place where the Northern Pacific Railroad was expected to cross the river. It was on the experiences of this expedition that Custer drew for the material used in his reply to Hazen's statements. When it was pointed out that some of Custer's statements were at variance with those of the correspondent for the New York *Tribune* who had accompanied the expedition, General Rosser explained that this correspondent did not accompany the engineers who were escorted by Custer's detachment, but, instead, had been with the main body of the troops who had followed the old, abandoned route south of the Heart River, and hence the press descriptions of the country traversed did not apply to the new route, which not only was superior but had the advantage of good water all the way from the Missouri to the Yellowstone.[2]

In 1874, Custer, with the same ten companies of his regiment and an infantry detachment, had explored the Black Hills and had written a somewhat rhapsodical account of the region, but this was after his letter in reply to Hazen. In this instance his opinion was largely shared by the correspondent of the *Tribune*.

On the same day that Custer's letter appeared, April 17, 1874, the Minneapolis *Tribune* editorially called attention to his article in the following language:

We print this morning an able and very interesting letter from Major General G. A. Custer, commanding Fort Abraham Lincoln, Dakota, descriptive of his observations in Dakota and Montana during the last year. It will be remembered that General Custer last year commanded the cavalry escort to the Yellowstone Surveying Expedition which was sent out to finally locate the route of the Northern Pacific Railroad through Dakota and Montana. His opportunities for observation could not have been excelled,

[1] *Army and Navy Journal*, Sept. 27, 1873.
[2] *Ibid.*, Aug. 23, 1873.

for while the surveying party moved slowly the cavalry was exploring and the writer of this knows from personal experience that when on the march, General Custer embraces every opportunity for seeing everything that is to be seen.

General Custer, in his letter, refutes in detail the wholesale condemnation of the lands and resources of the northwestern country which were contained in a letter written by General Hazen and published in the New York *Tribune* some months since. General Hazen writing from his post of observation over a hundred miles distant from any land owned by the Northern Pacific road, and without any knowledge of the lands that are contained in their grants, made the sweeping assertion that they were "not worth a penny an acre." The fact, as shown by General Custer, is that the section of country of which General Hazen has knowledge, in the vicinity of Fort Buford is comparatively worthless, and for that very reason the surveyors of the Northern Pacific refused to run the road anywhere near it, but selected a route farther south through a fine agricultural and grazing country.

To prove that these lands are valuable, General Custer does not rely upon his own observation but brings the experience of other army officers, surveyors, engineers, civilians and settlers to corroborate his own. He describes the areas of "Bad Lands" with fidelity, and deducting these from those that are arable, shows a larger percentage of excellent agricultural and grazing lands than will be found in many of the more eastern and mountainous States. He shows that, while the virgin lands of Dakota and Montana abound in a luxurious growth of grass, with sufficient wood and water, those portions which have been brought under cultivation yield abundantly of those crops which farmers rely on for their subsistence and profit. Wheat, oats, corn, rye, barley, potatoes, turnips, carrots, beets, cabbages, melons, peas, beans and vegetables of all kinds grow with as much vigor as they do at the east, produce more profitably and reach full maturity. Wheat was seen which yielded forty bushels to the acre, and corn, seventy-five bushels. Apples, pears, peaches, plums, and other fruits thrive well, while all fruits grow in abundance. Flowers, which General

81

Hazen was unable to cultivate at Fort Buford, are produced with little difficulty while wild flowers, rare and beautiful, are found in profusion.

The General also gives his experiences with the climate the past winter at Fort Lincoln where he went hunting very often, wearing neither overcoat nor gloves, and in December and January taking afternoon naps in the open air while waiting for his companions. In the same months the soldiers of the post performed their ordinary duties without overcoats, while mail carriers performed the journey from Fort Lincoln to Fargo—two hundred miles—without any interruption from either snow or extreme cold.

General Hazen's condemnation of the Northern Pacific lands— and of the Northwest generally—was made up of prejudice and rumors of an exceptional character, while General Custer speaks from personal observation and experience, and brings abundant corroboration for every assertion he makes. His letter is an able vindication of the country, and we trust his statements will be given as wide publicity as were the false and groundless misstatements of General Hazen.

Fort Abraham Lincoln, D. T.
April 9th, 1874

To the Editor of the Minneapolis Tribune:—

I had promised friends of mine when I first came to this part of the country to furnish them, at some future period, a statement, giving the results of my observation and experience with reference to the general character of the soil, climate, production, etc., pertaining to this section of the country.

As I was to enjoy unusual and superior facilities for determining the character of the country through which the Northern Pacific Railroad proposed to extend its route, my attention was invited more particularly to that portion of western Dakota and Montana, included or to be included in what is known as the Northern Pacific Railroad Land Grant. I had been deferring from one cause or another, the preparation of such a statement, until the recent appearance of the remarkable letter of General Hazen induced me to believe that no more fitting opportunity would probably occur for me to redeem my promise than the present. If any peculiar weight is to be attached by the public to statements herein set forth by me, it will be largely due to the belief that whatever opinions or facts are given, are those of a disinterested person. I will endeavor therefore in what follows to express what is clearly and positively the result of observation, of one who is engaged in the public service, and who so far as he is aware, is entirely free from personal feeling in the matter. I will not set out, by stating as General Hazen has, that whoever entertains and expresses opinions not in accordance with mine will be guilty of falsehood. Perhaps the General, before penning his sweeping letter, had been reading the advice of one of our prominent comic writers—"never kick a man who is down, unless you are sure he cannot get up again."[3] I have too high a regard for General Hazen to insinuate even that he would knowingly publish that which is not strictly founded on truth. Yet I propose to satisfactorily prove in this communication that General Hazen's statements are not only not founded on fact, but are exactly the reverse and were written in ignorance thereof.

I have passed and repassed over every mile of the route of the Northern Pacific Railroad, beginning at its eastern terminus near the 92nd, and extending to the 108th meridian. That portion referred to, lying west of the Missouri River, and east of the Mussel-shell River, I have ridden over on horseback, having accompanied the "Yellowstone Expedition" last season. I not only saw such portions of the route passed over by that expedition as might have been seen by any individual accompanying the troops, but scarcely a day was spent in marching that I did not diverge from the direct route, from five to fifteen miles, so that I believe I am safe in asserting that no individual connected with the "Yellowstone Expedition" whether civil or military, saw so much of the adjacent

---

[3] The source of this quotation has not been located. Inquiries sent to the New York Public Library, the Library of Congress, and *Notes and Queries* have alike failed to produce the answer.

country or became as familiar with it as myself. In writing, therefore, of the belt of country through which the Northern Pacific
Road passes, I rely upon my personal knowledge of a country
which I have seen, and with which I am familiar, and do not base
my statements upon such unreliable data as the idle and uncertain
opinions of Indian scouts in regard to the character of a portion of
British America, upwards of five hundred miles north of country
under consideration. This is but one of the modes General Hazen
has adopted in his letter to place the lands of the Northern Pacific
Railroad in a false light; and in so doing he misleads the public
and wantonly depreciates the value of property in which thousands
are interested.

Those who read General Hazen's letter will observe that he
takes the trouble to collect and publish certain portions of the
hospital records at Fort Buford, showing the temperature and
amount of rainfall at that point within certain periods. He then
calls upon his Indian scouts and half-breeds to inform him what
they know concerning a comparatively unknown portion of British
America. Fortified with these extremely reliable statistics General Hazen, after a period of incubation, which, according to his
letter, extended through two years, suddenly appears before the
public and announces that, because of certain meteorological
facts observable at Fort Buford on the extreme northern bend of
the Missouri River, and of the statements made to him by his
Indian scouts concerning the unknown and uncared for regions of
the Saskatchewan, therefore those portions of Dakota, Montana,
Idaho and Washington Territories, through which the route of
the Northern Pacific Railroad passes, are entirely worthless. If
General Hazen had informed his readers that Fort Buford, over
whose melancholy surroundings he is so eloquent, is located far
to the northward of the Northern Pacific Railroad, and at its
nearest point is over one hundred miles distant from the contemplated route of the latter; that the engineers of the Northern
Pacific Road had first examined the country in which General
Hazen is stationed, and about which he writes, and had pronounced it worthless and impracticable as a railroad line;[4] that

84

he had, so far as I believe, never been nearer to the lands or route of the Northern Pacific Railroad, extending from the Missouri to the Yellowstone rivers, than he was when he penned his remarkable letter, viz, over one hundred miles distant; and so far as his letter goes to prove had not even conversed with a single person who had seen those lands; if General Hazen had informed his readers of those facts they could have placed a truer estimate on the value of his opinions. What would be thought of a person who should attempt to form and publish an opinion of the rich, fertile soil composing the sugar and cotton lands of the Southern States, when such an opinion was only based upon an examination of the swamp lands of Florida or Louisiana or Mississippi? Yet a similar course has been pursued by General Hazen. The reader might well infer from his letter that the Northern Pacific Railroad company desired or intended to build their road near Fort Buford and along the valley of the Upper Missouri, when the fact is, that route was first explored, and pronounced undesirable for various reasons, some of which are stated by General Hazen. After repeated explorations by men experienced and distinguished as engineers, a route was selected which, while being more direct, possesses the great advantage of passing through a section of country not like that in which Fort Buford is located, and of which General Hazen really writes, but possessing the advantages of good soil, water and fuel.

One more reference to the remarkable letter of General Hazen —remarkable on account of its many and glaring inaccuracies of statements—and I will review the character of the country passed over by the Yellowstone expedition last summer, particularly that lying between the Missouri and Yellowstone rivers. The opening paragraph in that letter states that for two years General Hazen has observed "the effort of the Northern Pacific Railroad Company to make the world believe this section to be a valuable agricultural one," and that during all this time he has "kept silent although knowing the falsity of their representations." Finally

---

[4] It is worthy of note that today the main line of the Great Northern Railroad passes a few miles to the north of the site of Fort Buford.

after two years silent observation, and when apparently all the evil possible had been accomplished, "a feeling of shame and indignation arises," and no longer able to restrain his pent-up feelings he rushes forth "and while nature stares him in the face with its stubborn contradictions," he proceeds "to put them on paper." If the object in writing that letter as professed, was to warn the public against "such wicked deceptions" and to indicate to the bond holders "the only means of ever saving themselves from total loss," does it not occur to the reader that it would have appeared more consistent, more sincere and certainly more efficacious had the writer not "kept silent" so long; if he had not waited until the railroad company had "pretty fully carried their point in establishing a popular belief favorable to their wishes," but had at once published the "stubborn contradictions" which go to make up the letter which appeared in the New York *Tribune* of February 7. I am not familiar with the law; but it seems to me that I have read somewhere that he who is present at, or has a knowledge of, the commission of a crime, and takes no steps to prevent its commission, is regarded in somewhat the same light as the parties who commit the act. Waiting two years and until the act has practically been committed would hardly be deemed a prompt interference to prevent the commission of an alleged wrong. The letter referred to is unfortunate in its beginning, as the first sentence is lacking in the essential element—accuracy. The Northern Pacific Railroad, as far as my knowledge and impressions extend, have always represented that the lands included in their grant were classified as follows:

The agricultural lands which are peculiarly valuable as such are to be found east of the Missouri River, while the lands west of the Missouri are regarded as being valuable for purposes of grazing, and as a mineral region. To show that their statements were made with candor and fairness, I refer to the following extract from their printed description of the lands contained in the grant:

> The promoters of the Northern Pacific Railroad did not enter upon the work of construction until they had definitely ascertained, from thorough personal inspection, that the section of country to be

spanned by rail was, on the whole, and making liberal allowance for waste tracks, (*sic*) a region of singular fertility of soil and salubrity of climate. The fact being once established that a fair proportion of the land between Lake Superior and Puget Sound is well adapted to the production of cereals and vegetables, it became a certainty that the unexcelled grazing, the invaluable forests, the iron, the coal, and the deposits of gold, silver and copper which occupy much of the remainder—added to its favorable commercial position—rendered the region in question one of great attractiveness and natural wealth and assured its rapid settlement and solid growth.

The best agricultural lands embraced within the grant are situated between the Mississippi and the Missouri rivers, in western Minnesota and eastern Dakota (including the superb Red River valley, some eighty miles in width), in the valleys of the Yellowstone and its branches, and the tributaries of the Missouri in Montana, and the portions of Idaho, Washington and Oregon, bordering on the Columbia and its branches. Eastern Minnesota and western Washington, at the two extremes of the route, being mainly timbered, are not classed as agricultural sections, although there is very excellent farm land on both.

In a note at the bottom of the same page, it is stated that, in describing the grant "as a generally fertile and attractive region, due allowance is, of course, made for the unproductive and comparatively worthless sections which are necessarily embraced in any area of so great extent." It is to be remembered that in some of the oldest and richest agricultural States, considerably less than half the land is suitable for tillage, and practically a very moderate percentage of the whole has ever been turned by the plow. For example, the report of the United States census for 1870 shows the percentage of improved lands in each of the several States named to be as given in the following table, and to ascertain the percentage of area actually tilled or plowed, the following figures must be considerably reduced, by deducting grass lands, mountain pasturage, and other areas not properly classified as either tilled lands, forest or waste.

PROPORTION OF IMPROVED LAND

| Louisiana | 6½ |
| Alabama | 15½ |

North and South Carolina	16⅐
Virginia and West Virginia	27½
Average for southern states	17¼
New York	52
Pennsylvania	29½
Maine	14½

Let us compare these statements of the company, so far as they are intended to apply to the country between the Missouri and Yellowstone rivers, with the positive knowledge obtained last summer by the Yellowstone Expedition, which twice passed over the entire route of the Northern Pacific Railroad between those two rivers. Fortunately I am not compelled to rely upon memory alone, as I have before me my diary, in which is carefully recorded all the prominent incidents in each day's march; the exact number of miles passed over from day to day, with special remarks as to the character of the country, the quality and quantity of wood, water and grazing, as observed in our daily progress. I find from a careful reference to my diary that we left Fort Rice twenty-five miles below the point at which the Northern Pacific Railroad crosses the Missouri River, the 20th of June and began our march for the Yellowstone. The horses and mules accompanying the expedition numbered upwards of 3,000 while in addition we had about 600 head of beef cattle. The distance between the Missouri and Yellowstone rivers by our route is about 225 miles. The daily marches averaged perhaps fifteen miles. My diary shows that my command encamped every night, with a single exception, where wood, water and grass were to be had. The horses of my command were put out to graze every evening, their allowance of grain in consequence being reduced to less than one-third. The beef cattle subsisted entirely upon the grazing obtained by them after arriving in camp in the evening, and their condition was good.

Now to refer to the "exceptional waste tracts" which the railroad company admits are to be found here, as in all areas of so great extent. Of the entire area lying between the Missouri and

Yellowstone rivers, and included in the company's grant, there
are two strips of these "exceptional waste tracts." We encountered the first when we arrived within about eight miles of the
valley proper of the Little Missouri river, and there for the first
time we saw the famous "Bad Lands" which General Hazen would
have his readers believe is a fair sample of the lands through
which the Northern Pacific railroad is to pass. This strip of "bad
lands" being a portion of the "exceptional waste tracts" referred
to, no doubt, in the land circular of the company, follows the general direction of the Little Missouri river probably its entire
length, its average width does not exceed fifteen miles, half being
on one side of the river, and half on the other. This strip of "Bad
Lands" crosses the company's route and grant almost at right
angles in a north and south line. And so clearly is this line marked
which divides these "Bad Lands" from the adjacent country
through which they extend, that the effect upon the observer is
startling and wonderful. For upwards of a hundred and fifty
miles, after leaving the Missouri, we marched day after day over
a beautiful and rolling country, by a route, which, under ordinary
circumstances, would be entirely practicable for a lady's phaeton.
Up to the dividing line, which is as distinctly marked as the opening furrow through a beautiful meadow, we rode without obstacle
to where at our very feet, spread out before us, lay the wonderful,
awe-inspiring "Bad Lands" which, at first glance seemed im-
passable to man or beast. Yet we found a route for our immense
wagon train to pass through them without scarcely displacing a
shovelfull of earth except in repeated crossings of a water-course.

These "Bad Lands" although bounding the Little Missouri on
both sides, do not appropriate the immense valley through which
the river runs, but on the contrary, as I know from a personal
examination, the valley itself often expands to a width of several
miles on either side. I rode up and down the valley for many miles,
while hunting, and found not only one of the best timbered streams
in the west,[5] but possessing an immense area of rich bottom land,

---

[5] The Sioux knew the Little Missouri as the Thick Timber River, and it was one
of their favorite winter camping places.

89

covered at that time with a luxuriant growth of the finest pasturage and capable of sustaining a dense population. Deduct from the company's grant, the "Bad Lands" which border this rich valley of the Little Missouri, and allow that their width embraces about fifteen miles in the direction of the surveyed land of the railroad.

We then continued our march toward the Yellowstone over a country not quite so level as that lying between the two Missouri's, yet not sufficiently broken to render it undesirable from that cause. The grazing, wood and water were found in ample quantities to suit our purposes until we encountered the "exceptional waste tract"—the "Bad Lands" of the Yellowstone, and which, in character, dimensions, etc., do not vary much from those lying along the valley of the Little Missouri. These "Bad Lands" follow along the direction of the Yellowstone river until the latter reaches the Missouri at General Hazen's post of duty, at the intersection of the 104th meridian with the 48th parallel, and it may offer a partial explanation, perhaps, of General Hazen's statements, to assume that his personal knowledge of the country of which he writes, there being nothing in his letter to the contrary, is confined to that portion made up of these "bad lands" which entirely surround and hem in Fort Buford. For I do not presume that General Hazen has ever been ten miles from his Post in the direction of the Northern Pacific Railroad, at the nearest point of the latter. Deduct then this additional strip of "pine lands" which, as far as the company's "grant" is concerned, does not exceed fifteen miles in width, and does not include the valley proper or bottom lands of the Yellowstone; and all parties will admit that for purposes of agriculture or grazing the "Bad Lands" will never be worth "a penny an acre." But this does not irrevocably establish the fact that they may not be discovered valuable for other purposes. On the contrary I think that a great portion of the "Bad Lands" both of the Little Missouri embraced in the grant, and together only amounting to about thirty miles in width, will be found of peculiar value to the other portions.

I have seen—hundreds of men whom I can name, members of

the expedition, will support this statement—at a great many points both in the "Bad Lands" of the Little Missouri and in those of the Yellowstone, the exposed veins of coal which future development could and will render of incalculable value to the adjacent country. I have tested specimens of this coal, taken from the surface and found it to answer admirably to the purposes of fuel, although I saw none which would be suitable for smelting or manufacturing purposes. Yet it must be remembered, I selected loose specimens which had fallen from the exposed croppings of the veins.

After crossing the Yellowstone River, the expedition moved up the valley of the river, keeping in the "Bad Lands," or between them and the river, until we reached a point—Pompey's Pillar—near the intersection of the 108th meridian with the 48th parallel. We then left the Yellowstone River, and after passing through the narrow strip of "Bad Lands" west of that valley we bore off to the northwest until we reached the valley of the Musselshell River. Here I will note one fact connected with the Yellowstone Valley, a fact which can be attested by every member of the Yellowstone expedition. Each day as we ascended the river we found the water becoming clearer, and the stream itself more beautiful. Where we first struck it the water was almost as murky and uninviting in appearance as that of the Missouri—"Old Muddy," as the boatmen term the latter—while, at the point we left it, the water was observed to be clear and transparent, and abounding in the kinds of fish peculiar to mountain streams. The soil also improved as we ascended, while the timber and grass increased both in quantity and quality.

The Musselshell Valley was found to surpass in beauty our highest expectations. I find from reference to my diary such notes as the following: "Arrived at the Musselshell River which is indeed a beautiful stream of water." "There is an abundant growth of timber all along this stream." "Here, no doubt, is a good place for the trapper, or stock-raiser—rich pasturage for cattle." "Good grazing for our animals." "Caught three head of cattle, which are supposed to have stampeded from Colonel Baker's command last year.[6] They were in fine condition." (These cattle had wintered upon the natural grass.) Then in regard to our camps at various points as we moved down the Musselshell such notes as follows are to be continually found: "Halted in order to give the animals rest, this being a very good place for foraging." Sometimes, the extent of each day's march being regulated by the engineers, we were forced to occupy very inferior camps. At the same time we now know that there were excellent camps within three or four miles of the points we occupied. In some of the camps on the Musselshell river we found the grass not only of the finest quality but so high as to leave no part of our horses visible while grazing except their bodies.

In returning from the Musselshell River, which we left at a point known as the Great Bend, to the Yellowstone, my command, consisting of the cavalry, separated from the main portion of the Expedition, the latter heading in a southerly direction in order to strike our old trail up the valley of the Yellowstone, while the cavalry, accompanied by the engineers of the Northern Pacific Railroad, bore directly toward the point on the latter at which the Expedition crossed in going west. In doing this we were compelled to pass through a section of country entirely unknown to white men[7]—not even excepting General Hazen. This, and the restrictions upon our movements necessarily imposed by the fact that we regulated the direction and extent of each day's march by the progress of the survey then being made by the engineers, did not permit us to select the most available and convenient camps at all times; yet I find in my diary such references to the country as the following: Camp 55, "good water but little grazing." Camp 56, "excellent grazing—the best that can be found in this latitude"—

[6] In 1872, Colonel Eugene Baker had commanded the escort to a surveying party working down the Yellowstone River. Near the present site of Huntley, Montana, a short distance above Pompey's Pillar, they had been attacked by a large force of Sioux. During the battle a part of the cattle herd had been stampeded and were not recovered.

[7] This statement is not exactly true as Lieutenant John Mullins and a detachment of the Second Dragoons had marched from Fort Benton to Fort Union across the region lying between the Yellowstone and Missouri rivers.

"none better since we left Fort Rice:" "a beautiful lake in the center of camp." Camps 57, 58 and 59, while answering their purpose, were not particularly remarkable. Camp 60 is thus referred to: "Marched 26 miles; good grazing; a beautiful stream of water."

Our next camp was on the west bank of the Yellowstone, at a point which we had occupied in going west, at which time the grazing was quite indifferent, but on our return we found the grass abundant for all our wants. On the 12th of September my command having recrossed the Yellowstone, set out on its return march to the Missouri river, the engineers of the Northern Pacific Railroad accompanying us, it being their intention to shorten and correct certain portions of their former survey, so that this gave us an opportunity to see and judge of a different portion of the country from that we passed over in going west.

Being at that time in command of a large force of cavalry, interested not only in its immediate wants at that time, but anticipating that future exigencies of the service might require me to accompany troops through the same section of country, and having had no little experience on the plains, I naturally directed my attention to the character and natural products of the country, with particular reference to the points just stated, and I may here remark that, aside from defensive considerations, the same reasons which render a location desirable as a camp for cavalry, will render the same location desirable to the farmer or grazer, as it must possess the three requisites—water, grass and wood. Without going into detail and referring to each camp occupied by my command on its homeward march, in September last, I will make one statement which can be applied generally to the country between the Missouri and Yellowstone rivers, along the route of the Northern Pacific Railroad, embracing about 225 miles of territory. From this I will deduct the two narrow strips of "Bad Lands," the "exceptional waste tracts" running up and down the valley of the Little Missouri and the east side of the valley of the Yellowstone—in all say a belt twenty-five miles wide—deduct this, which, as I have before stated, will never be valuable or fit for agricultural

93

purposes; and the residue, taken as an immense area, constitutes as fine a grazing region as I have ever seen. We occupied but one camp which did not possess the three requisites of wood, water and grass in sufficient quantities.

Our marches averaged something like thirty miles per day—not from necessity but from choice. Sometimes it seemed almost as though we were passing through beautiful meadows; as far as the eye could reach, to the right and to the left of our route, it rested on an almost unbroken sea of green, luxuriant, wavering grass, from six inches to one foot in height. This was not only observable at rare moments, but almost entire days were sometimes spent in marching over such country. We found the water not only generally good, but abundant. A portion of the country was somewhat new to us, as we were returning by a different route from that we had passed over in going west. Should I be called upon in the future, in the corresponding season of the year, to march from here to the Yellowstone, in the vicinity of the same route, I feel confident that I would have no difficulty in finding an abundance of grass at almost every point, while ample quantities of both wood and water could be obtained, on an average every six miles. I regretted that the efficient and careful correspondent of the New York *Tribune* who had accompanied the expedition in its westward march over this country the early summer, did not, returning by steamer, from the Yellowstone,[8] and I so expressed myself to him upon meeting him after his return to this point. The season last year was considered by those familiar with the subject as at least one month later than usual, consequently when the expedition moved west from the Missouri River in June he did not find the grass so advanced and abundant as in September, so that opinions formed of the country for grazing purposes would be more just and accurate if based upon an examination made later in the season. And I feel confident that had the *Tribune* correspondent—who accompanied the expedition and whom I know

[8] The correspondent of the New York *Tribune*, Samuel J. Barrows, had left the expedition on its return to the Yellowstone River and had returned to Bismarck by boat. Thus he had not passed over the area between present Glendive, Montana, and Bismarck, North Dakota, on the return trip.

to be not only an exceedingly conscientious but painstaking writer —accompanied us on our return march and seen the country under favorable conditions strictly in accordance with what I have herein written.

It will be borne in mind by the reader that in stating what I have regarding the aspect of the country as seen by me in marching from the Yellowstone to the Missouri rivers, I am not testifying to facts observed only by myself, but I was accompanied by a large number of officers of the army, of superior intelligence and experience, by citizens of education and culture, distinguished in their profession as engineers, and by hundreds of men composing my command. My statements, therefore, do not depend for their accuracy upon my individual opinion alone; nor, as in the case of those put forth by General Hazen upon the random utterances of Indian scouts and half breeds concerning a remote portion of British America, hundreds of miles distant from the country about which we both write. Facts brought to light by the ill-fated North Pole expedition are almost as applicable to the question under consideration as the vague ideas and opinions which are endeavored to be put forth concerning the Saskatchewan country. When any person or company proposes to build a railroad or ship canal along the valley of the Saskatchewan, or when it is proposed to build a railroad within a hundred miles of General Hazen's post of duty, Fort Buford, it will be time enough for the General to produce the statements contained in his letter.

In returning to the Missouri we frequently crossed our old trail, and occasionally passed our old camps, made the latter part of June or early July. We had been absent from these old camps about two months and a half. I more than once noted that in places where we had fed our horses on the ground the scattered grains of oats had sprung up and matured finely. On one occasion I called the attention of my companions to this fact, and dismounted from my horse to pluck a few specimens of the oats there developed and ripe. The stalk, or straw, was fully four feet in height and the heads five inches in length, and well filled out. This was not on what is termed bottom land, but on a high point of the upland.

95

I have given my personal views of the character of the country between the Missouri River in Dakota and the Musselshell River in Montana lying along the line of the Northern Pacific Railroad. General Hazen has referred his readers to the reports of Professor Hayden in support of his opinions as to the value of the lands lying along the road for agricultural purposes. I intended to introduce witnesses in support of what I assert herein, and if I can employ General Hazen's own witness, not only to disprove his assertions but prove mine I accomplish two purposes. Let us read what the reports of Professor Hayden contain on this subject. Before me lies the official report of his "Survey of Montana and Adjacent Territory," published by the government in 1871. From Chapter IV, page 248 to 269, I find the following evidence as to the fertility and productiveness of the soil embraced in the land which General Hazen deliberately states "will not produce the fruits and cereals of the east for want of moisture." About 600 miles of the route of the Northern Pacific Railroad lies within the limits of Montana Territory. General Hazen would have his readers believe that the only surface capable of cultivation are "the very limited bottoms of the small streams," which he describes as "a few yards in breadth," or "an occasional water-washed valley of one or two miles." Professor Hayden's report states that "about two-fifths belong to the mountain region, three-fifths consisting of broad, open plains lying east of the Rocky Mountain range." The Northern Pacific Railroad route enters Montana from the Pacific slope near the north-western corner of the Territory, and runs within a few miles of the Kootenay River. Professor Hayden's report states that the country in the vicinity of the Kootenay River is composed of high, rolling prairies, through which the stream, here some two or three hundred yards in width, flows with a moderate current. "I am informed by Mr. Bonner that the immediate valley of this river is from five to fifteen miles wide and well grassed, affording excellent pasturage. Potatoes have been grown there for several years, the tubers being large and quality good, and although the cereals have not been tried, he thinks the climate would present no serious obstacle to their production."

Passing further east along near the line of the road and through the most mountainous portion of the territory, reference is made to "heavy timber" and a region "thickly timbered with pine, tamarack and fir." While north of the Flathead Lake there is a prairie "some thirty miles in length and fifteen to twenty miles wide." "Below the lake, Flathead River is from one hundred to one hundred and fifty yards in width, averaging two to three feet deep and descending at the rate of 10 feet to the mile, at one point having a fall of 12 to 15 feet." The proposed route of the railroad crosses this river not far from this point. It is admitted that this being the mountainous portion of the territory the arable lands are mostly in small detached areas. The report adds: "We are surprised at the extent of the farming operations carried on. All the grain and corn, potatoes and other vegetables, cattle and horses, butter and cheese needed for several hundred persons are produced here (Pend Oreille Mission) by the labor of Indians under the superintendency of the Brothers." This mission was established by Father DeSmet and I understand is the oldest in Montana.[9]

Jocko River runs through one of the prettiest valleys in this entire section. It contains about fifty square miles, most of which can be easily irrigated and which, if properly cultivated, will produce beautiful crops, the soil being quite fertile. Surrounded by lofty mountains which form its triangular walls, little rills flow into it from all sides, furnishing a never failing supply of pure, clear water. Last year the Indian agent, with but little help except that of the squaws (the Indian men generally being too lazy to work) raised over 1,000 bushels of potatoes, 1,500 bushels of wheat, 300 bushels of corn, etc., the corn as he reports yielding as much as 75 bushels to the acre. Upon many of the little streams which flow down from the mountains will be found small arable lands amply supplied with water for irrigation.

Continuing eastward along the route of the Northern Pacific road, we follow up the valley of the Bitter Root River, which

[9] St. Mary's Mission in the Bitterroot Valley, near present Stevensville, Montana, had been established by Father de Smet in 1841.

contains some of the finest agricultural lands in the Territory. The valley is about eighty miles in length and averages nine or ten miles in width. Professor Hayden's report says "it is all well adapted for agriculture, the soil being a rich, dark loam, mingled with sand and gravel; and where undisturbed by the farmer's implements, is covered with luxuriant grass, supplying most excellent pasturage." By proper efforts this entire valley can be brought under cultivation, affording a rich agricultural area of at least 400,000 acres.

The average mean temperature in this valley is given at about 47°. "But one of the best means of judging of the climate, so far as its bearing upon agriculture is concerned is a list of the productions." Not only can wheat, oats, barley, rye and the hardier vegetables be raised, but Indian corn of a tolerably good quality is grown here year after year; melons, tobacco and broom corn thrive, and such fruits as apples, pears, plums and cherries mature their fruit; muskmelons, squashes, tomatoes, beets, carrots and onions of excellent quality and large size have also been raised. These facts give undoubted evidence of the comparative mildness of this climate in the northern latitude.

Major Wheeler,[10] the United States Marshal of Montana, in 1871, speaking of the country and agricultural resources of that portion of the Territory here referred to, and directly through which the route of the Northern Pacific Railroad passes, says: "The large fields of wheat, corn and potatoes, the vegetable gardens and especially the flower gardens, excited our admiration. We saw fifty acres of wheat, averaging 40 bushels to the acre, and twenty acres of corn averaging 50 bushels, ripe and sound. Everything else was in the same ratio. I brought away specimens of corn, onions, melons, tobacco, broom corn and even peanuts, which for quality and size cannot be surpassed anywhere."

The flower garden was a gem of its kind, covering half an acre

---

[10] After service in the Civil War, William Wheeler, also known as Colonel Wheeler, had been appointed United States marshal for Montana. He served from 1869 to 1878. He became greatly interested in the territory and wrote a good deal concerning it. It was due to his enthusiasm and efforts that the Historical Society of Montana came into existence.

and containing over a hundred varieties. (How does this agree with General Hazen's experience, who produced three weeks of flowers, in a flower garden 10 feet by 40, by a daily sprinkling of three barrels of water for—as he says—two years! He must have drowned his flowers out.) Major Wheeler, continuing, says of an orchard of apple and plum trees of four years growth: They look very thrifty, varying from 6 to 9 feet in height. Frost has never injured a twig. Reference is also made to a field of timothy grass, from which twenty tons of excellent hay were cut, being a yield of two tons to the acre. Here were vegetables of the best quality, in the greatest profusion—water-melons, musk-melons, squashes, tomatoes, beets, carrots and onions of large growth.

In regard to the productions of this portion of the Territory the following statement is taken from the report and only includes "such things as will mature with ordinary care, not indicating those things which require extraordinary care and protection: wheat, oats, barley, rye, corn (of such varieties as are ordinarily raised in western New York), potatoes, (remarkably large and of a superior quality), onions, turnips, peas, beans, tomatoes, melons and cucumbers; also such fruits as apples, pears, plums, cherries and the smaller kinds, these being now (August, 1871) in fruit." General Hazen would have his readers believe that the only agricultural lands to be found in Montana are confined to "the narrow valleys of the streams." Professor Hayden's report to which I refer by advice of General Hazen, states that although there is considerable timber between Deer Lodge and Bitter Root valleys, yet it may be considered an open country, furnishing a large number of extensive grazing fields. And I may remark here that all of Montana from the east flank of the Belt mountains to the Bitter Root range, may be considered as one vast pasture," also "the area lying between the lower part of Blackfoot Valley and Hell Gate is an open and rolling prairie, well covered with grass." The valley of the Hell Gate, from the mouth of the Little Blackfoot to the lower end of the cannon above Missoula, is seventy miles long. The Missoula valley averages fifteen miles wide for a distance of thirty miles. Referring to the considerable numbers of arable

99

areas in the northwestern portion of Montana, the report truthfully states that "in the aggregate they furnish quite an extensive agricultural surface. The detached form surrounded by elevated ridges and mountain ranges, secures to each an ample supply of never failing streams for irrigation. The extensive forests of the west side will also prove a source of wealth whenever a means of distributing the lumber is furnished by railroad communications with less favored sections in this respect."

The climate is also much less rigorous than would be anticipated in "this northern latitude and mountainous region. I must acknowledge that I was generally disappointed in this respect. Mr. Granville Stuart[11] estimated the ratio of farming, grazing and timbered lands in Deer Lodge country as follows: Farming, oneeighth, grazing, five-eighths, timbered, one-fourth. This estimate, with a slight change, will probably apply to the entire section, the proportion of timbered lands being somewhat larger, and that of grazing lands smaller. Following along the route of the railroad in our progress eastward, we read from the report of valleys fifty and eighty miles in length, and a third or fourth that extent in width, well grassed and affording very superior grazing fields. Large herds of cattle, horses and sheep are spoken of as having been brought into this section of the Territory where they graze the winter without protection and without other food than what they can chip from the open pastures. Yet General Hazen's letter states that: "This entire northwestern country is subject to those terrific winter storms which animal life cannot withstand unless thoroughly protected." In the extreme southern portion of Montana and extending to the junction of the three rivers which form the Missouri, the valleys of the streams are generally narrow and already well-settled. It was a knowledge of these facts perhaps which led General Hazen to erroneously believe that the agricultural lands throughout the Territory were confined to these narrow valleys.

---

[11] Granville Stuart was one of Montana's most famous pioneers. He had come to the territory in 1858 and literally grown up with the country. One of the first discoverers of gold, he had later engaged in the cattle business in the Judith Basin. He was later United States Minister to Paraguay and Uruguay.

I now invite the attention of the reader, particularly if they have read the sweeping statements of General Hazen, to the following description of the extreme northern portion of Montana in which is located General Hazen's post of duty, Fort Buford, and from which the deductions contained in his letter are drawn. The description is taken from Professor Hayden's report, which General Hazen may have read and then committed the error of applying it to the entire expanse of the Montana and adjoining territories. It is to be regretted that General Hazen did not read the report more understandingly, as he would then have seen that the engineers of the Northern Pacific Railroad, who first explored the various routes, and rejected that running up the valley of the Upper Missouri and past the very door of General Hazen's post, for the reason, among others, that the adjacent country is comparatively worthless and unproductive, were only confirming the opinions which follow: "The section comprises all that part of the territory lying east of the Rocky Mountains, and north of the *divide which separates the waters of the Missouri from those of the Yellowstone.* It is an extensive region, stretching from east to west some three hundred and fifty or four hundred miles, and varying in width, north and south, from one hundred to one hundred and seventy-five miles."

These limits include the post of Fort Buford, from which General Hazen writes. After deducting thousands of square miles of what is pronounced arable land of good quality, well supplied with water and wood, the report states, "the bordering regions as we approach the Missouri" (which includes the country surrounding General Hazen's post of duty) grow barren "and assume the appearance to which the name 'mauvaises terres' or 'bad lands' has been applied," yet the lands just described are more than one hundred miles north of the Northern Pacific railroad route at the nearest point. And even by the exact words of the report the land is shown to "grow barren" and assume the appearance of "bad lands" only as we approach the Missouri. Lieutenant Mullins,[12]

---

[12] There were two men with similar names. One was Lieutenant John Mullan, who was with Governor Isaac Stevens and who later was in charge of construction of

whose evidence General Hazen wishes to discard, also pronounces the country between Fort Buford and Fort Benton worthless.

With one more reference to Professor Hayden's report upon the value of Montana as a grazing country, and I am done with that portion of it. "Without injustice to any other part of the west, it may truly be said of Montana that it is the best grazing section of the Rocky Mountain region. Not only are the open plains and prairies covered with rich and nutritious grasses but also the smooth hills and naked mountain slopes and the same rich carpet sometimes extends beyond these far up into the timber. Wherever a fire has swept up the mountain side, destroying the pine trees, leaving the blackened stems and stumps to mark the place where the forest stood, there springs up in a remarkably short space of time, a tall green grass covering every spot where it can gain a foothold. Here, as in other parts of the western country, as is well known, the grass cures on the ground, instead of rotting, remaining in this state all winter, furnishing in fact a better food than if cut and cured. "Cows pass the winter season with no other food than what they clip from the grazing field, and although regularly milked, come out in the spring in excellent condition. At one place I saw cows which had thus passed the winter on the range, giving milk the entire season, yet they were in such fine condition that they would have made excellent beef; some of them gave as much as three gallons of milk morning and evening as I can testify from personal observation."

But perhaps it may be said, the most of the testimony extracted from Professor Hayden's report, relates principally to Montana; what are the facts regarding the country farther east—say in Dakota, west of the Missouri River and along the line of the Northern Pacific Railroad. I have given my impressions derived from careful and repeated examination, but of course to the present wild and unsettled condition of the country there have

the Mullan Road. He apparently is the one referred to by General Hazen as the "enthusiast." The other was Lieutenant John Mullins of the Second Dragoons, who commanded a small detachment which marched overland from Fort Benton to Fort Union as a part of the Raynolds survey of 1859. His opinion of the country traversed was distinctly unfavorable.

been no experiments made in testing the agricultural resources of the soil and climate west of this point. But I will offer facts based upon actual knowledge and experience at this point which will go far to answer the question.

General Hazen endeavors to fortify his assertions by alluding to a portion of his life having been passed as a farmer. Judging by the results obtained by his two years put in that little ten feet by forty patch, I would infer that the long years which have elapsed since he was numbered among the "sons of honest toil" must have somewhat dimmed his ideas of practical agriculture. This impression is strengthened since I have met parties connected with the service who have been stationed at Fort Buford and who state that they were quite successful in the production and culture of flowers. Be this as it may, I too, like General Hazen can boast, as I do with pride, of having passed several years of my later boyhood in practical farming, and up to the period of my entering the military service, in 1857, I was practically familiar with the arts of agriculture, as practiced in Eastern Ohio, and year after year, assisted in preparing the ground, first with the axe, then with the plow, and afterwards in maturing and gathering the products, so that, while I scarcely think that either General Hazen or myself would be considered eligible as "Grangers" of good standing —unless the General can squeeze himself in on his recently avowed hostility to monopolies—yet I claim to base my knowledge and opinions upon matters connected with the soil, more or less, upon the teachings of experience.

This post—Fort Lincoln—has but recently been established and I find that no meteorological record was kept prior to last July, but by comparison of a table of the mean monthly temperatures of this post during the last six months of 1873, prepared by the Post Surgeon, John LaBaree, A. A. Surgeon, U. S. A., with a corresponding table prepared from the records of Fort Buford, as published by General Hazen, I find that the prevailing temperature at Fort Lincoln on the line of the Northern Pacific Railroad, is not only far more regular and unvarying than that at Fort Buford, but the climate at this post is milder by several degrees

103

both summer and winter. The same comparison holds good also between the temperatures at Fort Lincoln and those of Fort Rice, twenty-five miles distant from the line of the Northern Pacific road. The correctness of the table from Fort Rice being certified to by Colonel J. G. Tilford, U. S. A., commanding that post. General Hazen's letter shows that on the 5th of last December the thermometer at Fort Buford stood at 27° below zero whereas I find by reference to the official record kept here shows that the lowest point marked by the thermometer on that day, which was the coldest of the month, was 16° below zero, a difference of 11° in favor of this station. An examination of the subjoined table of temperatures at the three posts will show that the difference extends generally throughout the year.

For example: in August the thermometer fell to 36° at Fort Buford, while at Fort Lincoln it only reached 50°, a difference of 14°. In September this difference is shown to have been 12°, and yet General Hazen's letter informs the public that when it was being posted he had before him "the meteorological reports from the other military posts in this region" and that they did "not differ widely" from that at Fort Buford.

Fort Lincoln, Dakota, from which point I now write, is on the west bank of the Missouri River, directly opposite the present western terminus of the completed portion of the Northern Pacific Railroad. The surveyed route on this side of the Missouri passes through this military reservation. I was absent with the Yellowstone expedition during the growing season last year but I addressed a note of inquiry to the officer who was here in command and his reply follows. The officer referred to is Brevet Major General William P. Carlin, U. S. Army, whose services during the war, added to his present high standing in and out of the army will be accepted as a sufficient guarantee of not only the strict accuracy, but the impartial and non-prejudiced character of his statements.

Fort Abraham Lincoln, D. T.

March 7th, 1874

Dear General:—I received your note yesterday. I regret that I am

Station	1873 July			1873 August			1873 September			1873 October			1873 November			1873 December		
Buford	100	48	68.77	102	35	62.92	81	16	45.82	80	5	36.83	60	-2	28.30	43	-27	5.27
Lincoln	96	53	70.06	96	50	72.74	93	28	55.07	92	9	42.16	65	4	30.65	50	-16	25.03
Rice	104	58	71.33	96	57	68.33	94	28	56.00	88	12	41.00	70	-3	33.00	42	-22	12.00

unable to find the record of the results of the Post Garden of last year. I directed Dr. Boughter to keep such a record, and I suppose he did keep it; but he has gone away and may have taken it with him.

We broke up eight acres for our garden in May, 1873, it was the first breaking. It was harrowed for the purpose of tearing the sod, and planted partly in May and partly in June. Last spring was considered a very late one—from two weeks to a month later than usual.

We planted potatoes, turnips, carrots, beets, cabbages, squashes, cucumbers, water melons, muskmelons, radishes, lettuce, onions, beans, peas, tomatoes, egg plant and Minnesota early corn. The corn matured and was consumed long before frost. Some of the watermelons ripened before frost though not of an early kind. The troops had all of the vegetables they could use until about the 21st of September when the garden was taken by the troops and teamsters of the Yellowstone Expedition. I never saw a more luxuriant growth of vegetables than we had in the garden last year. If it had been broken the year before and planted early and some care had been taken to protect the melon and tomato vines with boxes, the top of which[13] should have had an abundance of melons and tomatoes. No irrigation was required here last year. Rains were frequent and copious. As you are aware the garden was on the bench about thirty feet above the river. The old post where the infantry are now stationed is about two hundred and ninety feet above the river. On this high point I sowed a strip of oats about two feet wide, two hundred feet in length. The oats grew to about thirty inches in height, though thickly sown and matured early. Better oats could not be found. Samples of them were taken away by several visitors for exhibition in the east.

Last spring I transplanted one hundred and sixty-five cottonwood trees from the low bottoms near the river to the parade ground of this post. Three or four of these trees were unsound when transplanted and they died. All the others grew most luxuriantly. When transplanting, all the branches and tops were cut off, leaving bare poles eight feet high. When the leaves fell from these trees in October, the branches on many of them were over three feet in length which was the growth of one short season.[14]

So far as the land about this point has been tested, the results have been all that could be desired or expected in this latitude. Of course

---

[13] Some words were omitted here. He undoubtedly meant to say that the plants should have been protected by boxes with the tops knocked out.

[14] Later most of these trees died. Contrast Colonel Carlin's experience with that of Mrs. Elizabeth Custer as recorded in *Boots and Saddles* (Norman, University of Oklahoma Press, 1961), 137–40.

the growing season is shorter than in Illinois or Kansas; but it proved to be long enough to produce all that is necessary to support a good population. I consider the land in this vicinity very good, especially the bottoms along Heart River, Apple Creek[15] and the Missouri. I think that land that produces grass in such abundance as this, must be worth something. I am not familiar with the names of the wild flowers that grow here, but I know that there are very many beautiful wild flowers that grow all over the country. They are so plentiful that beautiful bouquets can be gathered in a few minutes in a short walk from our quarters. I have never seen so many beautiful wild flowers in any part of the United States, as we have here.

I am, General, very truly yours.

W. P. CARLIN.

The facts set forth in the foregoing letter of General Carlin are known to hundreds if not thousands of persons, while the opinions of that officer as expressed above find concurrence in the minds of all people in this section who have given the subject their consideration.

In regard to the question of hay, alluded to in General Hazen's letter, I have made careful inquiry of parties here familiar with the resources of this country in that respect, and am convinced that hay sufficient in quantity to satisfy all probable demands, and of most excellent quality can be contracted for in the stack at a price not exceeding four dollars per ton. In this country also, the grass cures on the ground, furnishing, as in Montana, as good if not better food than if cut and cured. I have seen within the past few days stock, consisting of horses, mules and cattle, which have wintered on the open pasture within five miles of this post, receiving neither hay, grain nor shelter, and their condition was as good as that of animals usually seen at this period of the year on well conducted farms in Ohio.

Equally erroneous with the statements offered by General Hazen, regarding the general character and value of the country through which the Northern Pacific passes, are those contained in his letter bearing upon the climate and its influences. Upon this

15 The Heart River, from the west, and Apple Creek, from the east, flow into the Missouri River, almost opposite one another and a few miles below Bismarck.

point he starts out with the announcement that "the theoretical isothermals of Captain Maury and Mr. Blodgett, which have given rise to so much speculation and are used so extravagantly by those who have use for them, although true along the Pacific coast, are not found to be true by actual experience and observation in this middle region."

Examine this question and it is found that Blodgett's standard charts represent the isothermal of $70°$, mean summer temperature as running just south of the mouth of the Yellowstone, within sight of which Fort Buford stands, and General Hazen's own statistics declare that for eight years past the mean summer heat at Fort Buford has been $60°$. What better, or more positive, confirmation could be offered, of the absolute correctness of Blodgett's chart?

No person familiar with the subject but will acknowledge that in this section of country, as in all our Northern and Northwestern States and Territories, there are occasional brief periods of severe cold weather, and that during those periods which rarely continue longer than from three to four days, a careless and imprudent exposure of life may result seriously. The same is true of all northern latitudes. General Hazen's statement in regard to loss of life and limbs by persons belonging to his garrison is doubtless true, but had he given the details of such losses it is more than probable that the loss was due to a lack of proper precautions, in fact I have even within the past few days seen an official communication, addressed to General Hazen by one of his subordinates, referring to an officer and some men belonging to General Hazen's command who were severely frost-bitten the present winter, but the communication charges it to the imprudence and lack of precaution on the part of the officer referred to.

Several persons have frozen to death in this vicinity during the present winter: two of them were soldiers belonging to my command, but in every single instance brought to my notice it was the result of intoxication, the men having become drunk on the other side of the river and in endeavoring to make their way home in this condition during the night they were overcome by the influence of the liquor, laid down on the ice or near the river and were found frozen in the morning, although our guards remained at their posts in the open air during the same period and did not suffer. An idea of the climate can better be obtained from reference to the routine of our life as practiced here.

For instance, during the past winter the trains of the Northern Pacific Railroad, between here and Fargo, were taken off last November. From here to Fargo is two hundred miles, consequently our mails have to be carried by soldiers from this place to Fargo. The mail is carried from this point to Fort Seward, midway between here and Fargo by non-commissioned officers belonging to this post, and at Fort Seward another mail party of one or two soldiers takes the mail and conveys it to Fargo. Our mail leaves us every Tuesday morning—we keep two parties on the road—one going east while the other is coming west. Our mails from the east arrive on Wednesday, and so regularly and uninterruptedly have these round trips of four hundred miles been made, every mile of which extends along the Northern Pacific Railroad, during the entire winter that we can calculate almost to the exact hour when to look for our newspaper from the east. These mail parties travel in sleds yet so little snow has fallen in this section that during the winter it has been necessary to use a wagon for the first eight or nine miles east of this point. No complaint has ever been made by the mail-carriers as to the cold, on the contrary non-commissioned officers have sought to be placed upon this duty.

From the middle of November up to the present date, scarcely a week has elapsed that I have not been out at least one entire day, hunting. I usually go from three to eight miles from the post and remain until near night. I have never had occasion to wear an overcoat, rarely wear gloves, or if so very light ones, and have never felt the unpleasant effects of cold weather. Often during these hunting expeditions and while waiting the movements of the dogs and the other hunters, I have lain down in the open air and slept comfortably, this too in the months of January and December. Nor has mine been an exceptional instance. My companions

109

in the hunt who, like myself, discarded overcoats, have rarely if ever suffered from cold. I have, in addition to these hunting trips, had occasion to go into the open air every day during the present winter, and up to the present time I have not worn an overcoat nor desired one. The usual guard mounting common to all military posts, has been conducted at this post every morning in the open air, without a single exception. We have had dress parades both in December and January, when officers and men appeared without overcoats, while the ladies of the garrison, without requiring extra wrappings, witnessed the ceremony from the front porches of the officers' quarters.

I have passed winters in Michigan, Ohio, Virginia, New York, Kentucky, Kansas and Texas, yet I have never experienced a winter in either of those States, which possessed all the advantages, and so few of the disadvantages, as have been attainable here during the present season. There has not been a single day during the entire winter when trains might not have been run regularly over the Northern Pacific Railroad to this point, so far as any obstacle from the climate may have determined the matter. General Hazen unsuspectingly asserts that he has seen an area of country 20 miles across strewn with the carcasses of buffalo that must have perished in one of these storms. I fear that someone has been imposing upon the General's credulity, or upon his well-known sympathetic disposition. He, no doubt, may have seen the carcasses of the buffalo. But as well might I assert that on our return march in September last, we saw an area of the country over one hundred miles across strewn thickly with the carcasses of antelope (which was the fact) and then lead General Hazen and others to infer these same antelope "must have perished in one of these storms." But this we know to be untrue as the carcasses were those of animals which had died within the few weeks previous, and were not there when we passed through the country going west. An epidemic of some malignant form had no doubt produced the death of thousands of these beautiful animals along our line of march, and I have no doubt a similar explanation would be correct if applied to account for the buffalo carcasses seen by General Hazen in some part of the country, which unfortunately he omits to state.

The healthful properties of this climate can scarcely be overestimated; no diseases of a malarial, or pulmonary character are known. I can do no better perhaps than to here offer the following statement of the medical officer of this Post:

Fort Abraham Lincoln
March 9th, 1874

To Brevet Major General G. A. Custer, Com. Fort Abraham Lincoln, D. T.

Sir:—Referring to the climate surrounding this post, I would respectfully state it to be my professional opinion, that it is remarkably healthful. Not liable to any of the low type of fevers, that so annoy our friends in Michigan, Indiana, Illinois, Tennessee and many of the other western and southwestern States. The atmosphere being clear, bracing and buoyant, a greater part of the time, renders the climate peculiarly adapted to the treatment of those worn-out by business anxieties, or whose mental and nervous powers are developed (*sic*) by other causes.

I have the honor to be, very respectfully, your obedient servant.

John La Baree
Acting Surgeon, U. S. A.
Post Surgeon

A few observations of a general nature and I will conclude this letter which has only been permitted to attain this length by the great public interest centering in the subjects of which it treats.

General Hazen has attempted to convey the impression to the uninformed reader that he writes from and of a point on the Northern Pacific Railroad and within its land grant when in fact he was at least 120 miles north of the located line and 200 miles west of the westernmost acre owned by the railroad company. He implies and endeavors to make his readers understand that the Northern Pacific Railroad Company is endeavoring to build a railroad through the region adjacent to Fort Buford, and that the company is trying to convince the public that said region is unfit for agriculture, when the facts are that *the Company thoroughly examined this Buford region, rejected it as unfit for its purpose, and has never, directly or indirectly, pretended, or wished to convey the impression, that this region is desirable for agriculture, or anything else.* He writes of a section of the country which he has never seen, and of which he has no personal knowledge; and in so doing his course recalls the fable of the toad who formed its opinion of the appearance of the world from the view it obtained from looking up from the bottom of the well. I ask the impartial reader to compare the statements of General Hazen with those contained in this letter, and then judge whether his universal denunciation of a large and valuable portion of the public domain, and of those who are endeavoring, honestly as I believe, to develop its untold resources, is either just or merited.

I feel assured, from inquiry and from conversation with officers of the army and others who have spent years in the extended region to the west and southwest of this post, and from official reports of reliable parties sent out under government auspices, and who have gathered specimens of the precious metals, that an immense surface covering rich mines of gold, silver, lead, copper, iron and coal, are only awaiting the coming of that most enterprizing and persevering member of our western population—the miner—to uncover its hidden treasure, and add to the individual and collective wealth of our people. Of the intermediate region, the greater part of that, not arable, is excellent grazing land.

It is to utter my protest against a sweeping and unfounded denunciation of this great northwest that I write these lines. So far as the Northern Pacific Railroad is to be regarded as a mighty instrument to be used in the development of this country, so far am I anxious that it should succeed. At the same time I am aware that it has become popular recently to denounce this enterprise. Whether it succeeds at present or not in the gigantic undertaking with which its projectors have manfully grappled, and which extraneous conditions have magnified and embarrassed, it is sure ultimately and at no distant period to realize all that the friends and promoters have hoped or claimed for it. The beneficial influence which the Northern Pacific Railroad, if completed, would exercise in the final and peaceable solution of the Indian question, and which in this very region assumes its most serious aspect, might well warrant the general government in considering this enterprise one of national importance, and in giving to it at least its hearty encouragement.

(Signed) G. A. CUSTER

9. The Black Hills

Under the heading of "A New Gold Country," the New York *Tribune*, on August 10, 1874, had published two dispatches from the special correspondent of the *Tribune* with Custer's expedition to the Black Hills. A special credit line said that the messages had been forwarded to Fort Laramie by a special scout. This was the well-known frontiersman "Lonesome Charley" Reynolds, who alone made the trip from the camp near Harney Peak to Fort Laramie with reports, letters, and dispatches. Riding an unshod Indian pony so that there would be no "soldier sign" to arouse the suspicions of any Indians who might happen to cross his trail, traveling by night and hiding by day, Reynolds made his way through the Sioux-infested region, arriving safely at Fort Laramie, where the news of the discovery created wild excitement. Here the dispatches, as well as Custer's report, were put on the wires, giving the nation its first real news of something that had been long suspected, that there was gold in the Black Hills.

The correspondent of the *Tribune* who had accompanied the Yellowstone Expedition of 1873, had not been as favorably impressed by the region over which they passed as had the General. The discrepancy had been explained by General Rosser as being due to the fact that Custer had accompanied the engineering party, the correspondent had been with the main body of the expedition and thus they had not seen the same country. Also the correspondent, on the return trip, had taken a steamer at Glendive Creek and returned to Bismarck by way of the river, while Custer with his cavalry had marched overland. The report of the correspondent with the Black Hills expedition of 1874 was even more enthusiastic than that of General Custer. Naturally it was seized upon by Custer's partisans as substantiating their point of view. The column in the *Tribune* read as follows:

DISCOVERIES OF THE BLACK HILLS EXPEDITION

Indications of Gold Everywhere in the Black Hills Region—The Surface Soil Well Repays Washing— A Country of Great Beauty and Productiveness—Nature's Efforts for the Husbandman—A Diversified Flora—The Highest Point in the Black Hills Scaled.

Headquarters Black Hills Expedition, Eight and a Half Miles South-East of Harney's Peak, Dakota Territory, August 2.—The country which the expedition has traversed has proved to be one of the most fertile and beautiful sections in the United States. Indications of gold were discovered about a week ago, and within two days its presence in sufficient quantities abundantly to repay working has been established beyond a doubt. How large an area the gold section covers cannot be determined without further exploration, but the geological characteristics of the country, the researches of our prospectors, and all the indications point to valuable fields. So far we have obtained surface gold alone. Our miners hope yet to find a good quartz lead. The expiration of the Sioux treaty will open to settlement a beautiful and highly productive area of country, hitherto entirely unknown. Grass, water and timber of several varieties are found in abundance, and all of excellent quality; small fruits abound; game is plentiful. The valleys are well adapted for cattle raising or for agricultural purposes, while the scenery is lovely beyond description. The flora is the most varied and exuberant of any section this side of California. In this respect it is a new Florida: it may prove to be a new Eldorado. The command is in good health and explorations are being rapidly conducted.

Black Hills Expedition, Within Two Miles of South Fork Chey-

115

enne River, August 3.—We have reached this camp by a march of 45 miles today. I send by Charley Reynolds, a special messenger, the following summary of General Custer's official report, as made to date, covering the history of the expedition from July 15, starting from Prospect Valley, Dakota. Leaving this point, the expedition moved in a south-west direction until it reached the valley of the Little Missouri, up which we moved 24 miles. The valley was almost destitute of grass, and we left it in search of a better camping ground, making a march of over 30 miles and a dry camp. In order to secure camp during our passage up the Little Missouri we entered the Territory of Montana for a short time. From the Little Missouri to the valley of the Belle Fourché the country was generally barren and uninviting. The Belle Fourché was reached on the 18th of July, and good grass, water, and wood were abundant. From this point just west of the line separating Dakota from Wyoming we began a skirmish through the outlying ranges of hills. The country was a very superior one, covered with excellent grass, and having an abundance of timber, principally pine, oak and poplar. On the 22nd we halted and encamped within four miles of a prominent peak in Wyoming, called Inyan Kara, 6,600 feet high, which peak we ascended, lying over here one day. The expedition then turned due east, and attempted the passage of the Black Hills. After a short march we came into a most beautiful valley. "Its equal," said General Custer, "I have never seen." Such, too, was the testimony of all those who beheld the panorama spread out before us. Every step of our march that day was amid flowers of the most exquisite color and perfume: some belonging to new or unclassified species. The total flora of the valley embraces 440 species. The water in the streams stood at 44°. This beautiful vale was named Floral Valley. We followed this valley to the top of the western ridge of the Black Hills, winding our way through a little park of great natural beauty.

During our march through the valley, we came to a recent camping ground of a small party of Indians, and soon after discovered five lodges four miles beyond. To avoid a collision a party of Indian scouts were sent ahead to counsel with them, preceded by a guide bearing a flag of truce. General Custer followed with an escort and, entering the village, assured them of his friendship and promised them presents if they would come to his camp. The village contained five men, seven squaws and fifteen children. The Indians promised to camp near us for a few days and assist us in our explorations. That afternoon three of them came to camp and secured the presents and promised to move their camp near us in the morning, to protect their camp from the Rees. General Custer ordered a guard of soldiers to accompany them to their camp, but the Indians, who had not been acting in good faith, suddenly departed, and two scouts were sent after them with directions to request them to return, but to use no violence. The Indians refused and one of them tried to wrest a gun from one of the scouts. The scout disengaged himself and fired his gun, wounding both the Indian and his pony, though probably not seriously. The Indian who was hit escaped, One Stab, the Chief, being brought back to camp. The Indian village, during the visit of the chief to camp, had packed up and departed. One Stab has recently returned from the hostile camp on Powder River, and says that the Indians lost 10 killed in the fight with the Bozeman Exploring Party. He remains with us three days longer, when he will take his departure and rejoin his band.

On the 30th we camped within four miles of the western base of Harney's Peak, which the next day General Custer ascended with the engineers and a small escort. The peak was found to be the highest point in the Black Hills. Yesterday we moved to our present camp. This morning two companies under Colonel Hart were dispatched to extend our explorations in a southerly direction to the South Fork of the Cheyenne. Tomorrow General Custer with five companies of cavalry will endeavor to reach the same stream in a south-westerly direction from Harney's Peak, the wagon train remaining at or near the present camp.

In no portion of the United States, not excepting the famous Blue Grass region of Kentucky, have I ever found grazing superior to that which grows wild in these hitherto unknown regions. I know of no portion of our country where nature has done so much to prepare homes for husbandmen and left so little for them to do as here. Everything indicates an abundance of moisture within the space occupied by the Black Hills. Gold has been found in several places, and it is the opinion of those who are giving attention to the subject that it will be discovered in paying quantities. I have upon my table 40 or 50 small particles of pure gold, in size about that of a small pin-head. Most of it was obtained to-day from a single pan of earth, but as we have not remained longer at any camp than one day, it will be readily understood that there is no opportunity to make a satisfactory examination in regard to deposits of valuable minerals. Until further investigation is had regarding the richness of the deposits of gold, no opinion should be formed. Veins of what the geologists call "bearing quartz" crop out on almost every hillside. All existing geological or geographical maps of the region have been found incorrect.

The northward march begins in a few days from this date, and General Custer expects to reach Fort Lincoln by the 31st of August.

The persons who cited these dispatches as evidence that General Hazen was misinformed about the agricultural possibilities of the region west of the Missouri River, conveniently failed to notice another article by the same correspondent. This account, which was published in the New York *Weekly Tribune* for September 16, 1874, was dated September 1, from Fort Lincoln, Dakota Territory, and read:

On the 22nd of August, resuming our march, we struck General Stanley's trail of 1872, and the next day came upon his trail of last year. From this point we were sure of a good road to Fort Lincoln, and knew every camp we should make. Finding this trail was like striking an old familiar turnpike, although devoid of tollgates and keepers. Concerning this trail and the men who made it, your readers were informed in the Yellowstone correspondence of last year. Returning over this trail a second time for nearly 150 miles, I found that impressions of the country received last year were again renewed. Of the country traversed by that expedition, the tracts along the Yellowstone were altogether the best. But even this offers few inducements for the settler, while the region west of the Little Missouri and east of the Yellowstone is hardly worth giving away. The admirable letter of Gen. Hazen to the *Tribune* last winter, giving a full accurate description of the country in the vicinity of Fort Buford well characterizes the region of which I speak. It is part and parcel of the same lot. Northern Pacific Railroad speculators are still making strenuous efforts to persuade emigrants of the fertility of this section of the North American desert. But while there are thousands of acres of good farming land still unoccupied, no one who has a modicum of practical wisdom will select his homestead here. It is useless to deny that the country is a desert. The sad necessity of redeeming it has not yet arrived.

10. Haas Report

In the controversy over the value of the lands west of the Missouri River, frequent reference was made to the Haas Report. Although it gives little attention to the subject matter of the dispute between Generals Hazen and Custer, it is reproduced here, because of those references.[1]

NORTHERN PACIFIC
The Suppressed Reports of the Berlin and Vienna Experts
An Unfavorable Opinion—the Road Cannot Pay Interest on Its
Bonds—The Investment Not a Safe One

Two years ago the Northern Pacific Railroad Company attempted to negotiate the sale of large quantities of its bonds into Europe. Application was made to the Union Bank of Vienna, and also to certain capitalists in Berlin, and the result was the appointment of two commissions which came over to America and made a personal examination of the road and a part of the region through which it was to pass. Two reports were made—one to the Berlin capitalists by Herr Haas, a Government director of the Prussian railways, the other to the Union Bank of Vienna by Herr Foltz. Both are able and well-considered documents, and both present in a pretty strong light the advantages of the Northern Pacific route and the extent of the traffic which the road must ultimately

---

[1] I did not succeed in locating this article in the New York *Tribune* but rather in a collection of newspaper clippings in the William Robertson Coe Collection in the Beinecke Library at Yale University.

obtain. Both however concurred in the opinion that for some years after its completion the company would be unable to pay interest on its bonds, and agreed in advising European capitalists not to invest in it. The advice of the experts was adopted, and the negotiations in Berlin and Vienna fell through.

Copies of these unfavorable reports are known to have been in New York for some time, but they have hitherto been suppressed, and even in Europe it has been impossible to get at them. The *Tribune* has secured translations, however, and presents below the report of Herr Haas in full:

The Report of Herr Haas

1. Commissioned as an expert to inquire into the prospects of the Northern Pacific Railway enterprise, I have visited America and endeavored to collect on the spot—as well as by traveling over the extent of the line already in working order, and the adjoining districts which that road is to traverse, as by gathering the most exact information which is possible to obtain concerning the state of traffic and commercial intercourse—the material necessary for the formation of a competent judgment on the enterprise of the Northern Pacific Railway. In expressing this judgment in the following reports, I premise that I consider it expedient to waive all specialties which may not necessarily have a real bearing upon that enterprise, and that I regard it my duty to confine my statement to describing in brief outlines the enterprise itself, and connecting with it a test of the question whether it will be in a position to discharge all these obligations, which according to the promises made by the projectors, it is in duty bound to fulfill.

2. According to the charter granted to the Northern Pacific Railway Company by the Congress of the United States, with the consent of the Executive government, the Company is authorized to build and work an uninterrupted line of railway, commencing at Lake Superior, in Minnesota or Wisconsin, and proceeding westward, within the territory of the United States, to a point on Puget Sound, along the valley of the Columbia River, with a

branch line from a suitable point on the main line over the Cascade Range to Puget Sound.

3. In support of this enterprise the charter grants the Company 20 alternating sections, or 12,800 acres of public land for every mile of completed rails, in the States through which the line runs, and 40 alternating sections, or 25,000 acres, for every mile in those districts not situated in States, but in Territories. These land grants apply to the branch line as well as to the main line. The charter further grants the right of way, as well as the privilege of taking from the public lands, cost free, all the materials necessary for the construction of the line.

4. The conveyance of the land to the Railway Company takes place whenever 25 miles of uninterrupted line have been soundly and solidly completed, and simultaneously the Government enters into a covenant not to dispose of any public land, at any sale in the alternating sections along the line, for less than $2.50 an acre.

5. By virtue of these privileges, the Northern Pacific Railway Company has commenced building operations, intending in the first place to construct a length of line from Duluth, Lake Superior, crossing the Mississippi, Red River, Dakota River,[2] and the Missouri, along the Yellowstone River as far as Bozeman's Pass of the Rocky Mountains; thence along Clarkes Fork as far as Lake Pend d'Oreille; thence over the Columbia Plains as far as Lewis River,[3] and along this and Columbia River as far as Cowlitz River;[4] and lastly, along the Valley of the Cowlitz to the southern end of Puget Sound, a length of about 2,000 miles, for which 50,000,000 acres of public land will have to be conveyed to the Company.

6. The branch line commencing at any suitable point on the main line and leading over the Cascade Range to Puget Sound,

---

[2] The present James River.

[3] The Snake River. The Northern Pacific reached this stream at its confluence with the Columbia.

[4] The Cowlitz River enters the Columbia from the north slightly below Portland, Oregon. Since the source of the stream is just south of the head of Puget Sound, it offered an easy, water-level route between Portland and Tacoma, the original terminus of the railroad.

which has likewise been provided for by the charter—a line about 400 or 600 miles long, which would reduce the distance between Lake Superior and Puget Sound to 1,775 miles—is not to be taken up at present, but to be reserved for a future period. Accordingly, the estimates prepared for building the Northern Pacific Railway are limited to the present project, the cost of the branch line not being included.

7. These estimates calculate the cost of construction of the main line as follows:

1. Grading, masonry, bridges, rails, and entire surface
   works of the line $60,320,000
2. Sidings   4,200,000
3. Sundry expenses inclusive of engineering   5,000,000
4. Telegraph lines   600,000
5. Buildings   2,312,000
6. Working capital   3,615,000
7. Small branch line   1,200,000
8. Extra expenses   800,000
9. Interest on capital during construction, minus the
   income derived from the working of already finished lengths during that time   7,230,000

                                      Total $85,277,000

8. To raise this sum the Northern Pacific Railway Company intends issuing bonds to the amount of $100,000,000, and pledges itself to pay interest at the rate of 7.30 per cent per annum in gold out of the surplus revenue from the traffic of the line, and to redeem the bonds within 30 years.

9. As security for the payment of interest and the redemption of the bonds the whole of the property of the Northern Pacific Railway Company, the line and buildings, as well as the land grants have been made over to the trustees, as representing the bondholders, by a general mortgage deed, registered July 1, 1870, in the office of the Secretary of the Interior of the United States.

By these data the extent and aims of the Northern Pacific Railway enterprise and the means by which it is to be accomplished, are clearly set forth. Adding to this the fact that up to August,

1871, a length of line of 140 miles extending from Duluth, Lake Superior, to 20 miles beyond the Mississippi, was already completed and in working order; that 120 miles additional as far as the border of the State of Dakota are, save little interruptions, almost complete, and that lastly, in the Western division of the road, in the vicinity of Portland, Oregon, 25 miles of the line, through Washington Territory, in the direction of Puget Sound, are so far advanced that they can be opened for traffic by the end of this year, we have all that can be stated about the present condition of the Northern Pacific Railway, and we can turn to the consideration of the future.

10. The consideration of the future, in order to keep within bounds, should be limited to answering the following three questions: First: Are the means provided for the construction of the Northern Pacific Railway adequate to complete the line ready for traffic? Second: Does the finished line offer the necessary guarantee that the net profit of its income will yield the sums required for the half yearly payment of the stipulated rate of interest on the bonds? Third: Will the sums realized from the sale of lands suffice to redeem the bonds within 30 years?

11. Respecting the first of these questions, whether the building capital is adequate to the completion of the line, we must revert to the detailed estimates. The first item of these estimates, which provides $60,320,000 for the construction of the line, or $30,000 a mile, leaves no cause for uneasiness, inasmuch as the contracts already disposed of afford proof that the lengths contracted for can not only be completed for the amount, but that savings are made so considerable that by means of them the more expensive mountainous parts can be undertaken. The chief engineer of the Company is a well-tried man, his honesty, experience, and capacity are beyond question, and he has positively declared that the item in question will not be exceeded.

12. As little can be said about items 2, 3, 4 and 7; but 5, 6 and 9 produce serious misgivings. Item 5 of the estimate, providing $2,312,000 for buildings, includes $850,000 for repair-shops for machinery and cars, 134 stations at $2,000 each, or $268,000;

lastly, 10 principal stations at $25,000 each, or $250,000. These figures are out of all proportion low; for a length of line of 2,000 miles, workshops at the collective amount of $800,000, stations the whole arrangements of which are put down at $2,000 only, and principal stations at $25,000 each, cannot be looked upon as adequate to the requirements. This item, therefore, will have to be increased. The same remark applies to item 6, which provides $3,615,000 as the working capital, and out of this are to be procured 120 locomotives, 100 first-class passenger cars, 30 smoking cars, 30 mail and baggage cars, and 1,500 freight and cattle cars. This working capital is so small, and stands in such glaring contrast with the length of line, that much more will be required than has been provided by the estimates. In North Germany a line of similar length would require more than 25,000,000 thalers; and though it may not be quite fair to measure American expenses by a German standard—a maxim which underlies this report—still the most superficial critic must perceive that here a very considerable augmentation is needed. With regard to item 9, providing $7,250,000 for the payment of interest during construction, a similar claim will have to be put forward. Suppose the time of building to be four years—a supposition based upon exact information obtained—the works would consume a quarter of the building capital in every year during the building period. This interest will have to be paid at the end of the first year upon one quarter; at the end of the second year upon one-half; at the end of the third year upon three-quarters, and at the end of the fourth year upon the whole building capital. Hence the interest during the four years will be 2½ times the annual interest.

13. With an emission of bonds to the amount of $100,000,000, at a rate of interest of 7.30, gold, the interest during the building period will foot up $18,250,000, gold, and though the building fund need not be burdened with that, since the money obtained for bonds and not immediately required for building purposes may be otherwise employed with advantage, and since also the intermediate finished portions of the line will yield a revenue before the whole line is opened, nevertheless, what may be gained in

this way must not be overestimated. The estimate of $3,250,000 is sufficiently high, so therefore, will have to be increased in proportion.

14. If according to these calculations, the estimates require manifold augmentations on the one hand, we must not lose sight of the fact that on the other hand the fixed building capital $100,000,000 is not reached by the sum total of $85,000,000 of the estimates, but exceeds these estimates by $15,000,000. In case, therefore, the bonds are not issued too much below par, the respective items may be augmented by this surplus, and this may be more easily effected, as, according to the communications of Mr. Jay Cooke, in a conversation on the subject, that gentleman is prepared to consider the matter with a view to such augmentation.

15. With regard to this last point, but only in view of the possibility of these anticipations being realized, there is no cause for anxiety about the estimates, and after such augmentation no occasion for an unfavorable judgment.

16. Turning to the second question, whether the Northern Pacific Railway, after its completion, offers the necessary guarantee that the surplus accruing out of the traffic revenues will suffice to pay the half-yearly rates of interest on the bonds, it is to be observed in the first place that the interest at the rate of 7.30 per cent on a capital of $100,000,000 amounts to $7,300,000. To obtain a net profit of a similar amount requires a gross income of $20,000,000 a year. It is proved by official data that the net profits of the American railways are equal to 35 per cent of the gross income, 65 per cent of the total being consumed by the working expenses.

17. Whether the completed Northern Pacific Railway will be able to count on a traffic that will yield an income of $20,000,000 a year can only be ascertained by an inquiry into the state of the population of its industrial and commercial relations, and it will be important to keep the actual state of these relations very carefully in view. The tract of country traversed by the Northern Pacific Railway upon which at the outset the line depends for acquiring and securing a local traffic, is situated in the states of

Minnesota, Dakota, Montana, Idaho, and Oregon, and in Washington Territory. These have, according to the Census of 1870:

	Area in square miles	*Inhabitants*
Minnesota	83,531	435,511
Dakota	147,490	14,181
Montana	143,776	20,594
Idaho	90,932	14,998
Oregon	95,244	90,922
Washington Territory	69,994	23,901

This is an aggregate area of 630,917 square miles and an aggregate population of 598,147 while in the year 1860 they had a population of only 250,000 persons. According to this the population has increased, but this increase belongs for the most part to the State of Minnesota only, since the population of that State has grown from 172,000 to 435,500 during the period in question—an increase of 263,000 persons. There is hardly any room for doubt that 600,000 people, scattered over an area of 30,000 German square miles, even if all are taken as contributing to the success of the Northern Pacific Railway, will not be able to insure a traffic that will produce an annual income of $20,000,000.

18. The enthusiastic adherents of the undertakers of the Northern Pacific Railway will not deny the truth of this assertion, and they are only able to hold out hopes for the future by pointing to a possible rapid increase of population in the adjacent districts consequent upon the completion of the line, and a corresponding increase of the income of the Company. Willing as I am to acknowledge, respecting America, the well approved fact that, contrary to what we see in Germany, where railways are the product of already cultivated and well-populated regions, the railways in America have hitherto drawn culture and population after them into uncultivated regions, and thereby drawn an income to themselves, yet the deductions from these facts must always be made with certain reserve. We must not forget that though a growth of the population in regions newly traversed by railways

is certain, it is not sufficiently rapid to cover thinly inhabited regions within a few years with numerous and densely peopled settlements of a commercially agricultural or industrial character, particularly when it is a question of filling a region of 2,000 miles with such settlements.

We learn, by way of example, from a comparison of the population of the United States in 1870 and 1860, that in that decennial period the population increased from 31,500,000 to 38,500,000, an increase of 7,000,000—very considerable in itself, but not of very great importance compared with the proportional increase of railways, when we bear in mind that the railways in the United States increased during the same period from 31,286 miles to 53,400 miles. Even the most favorable rate of increase of the population during the last ten years, namely, that of Minnesota, or about 150 per cent, would, extended over the whole region of the Northern Pacific Railway, during another ten years, only result in an aggregate population of 1,500,000, or one-third of the present population of the State of New York. That such a population—which, by the way, would not exist at the time of the completion of the line, nor till ten years afterward—will not yield the required income to pay out of the net profits the interest on the capital invested in the enterprise, I think I am, according to my conviction, bound to maintain.

Of course an increase of population beyond the percentage mentioned is possible, in consequence of accelerated exertions and efforts of direct immigration toward the hitherto neglected States of Dakota, Idaho, and Oregon, and Washington Territory; but we must not ignore the fact that such exertions and efforts will always have to contend with great difficulties. The stream of immigration has hitherto flowed notoriously and preferably in the direction of the more Southern States, its diversion northward, particularly in the States of Dakota, Idaho, and Montana, where the Indian tribes are still hostile, will not succeed until after years of struggles and perseverance. Take, for instance, Minnesota, which has only just succeeded in attracting the influx of population already mentioned, though its emigration agents have for years traversed

128

the length and breadth of Europe, and though the State has for considerable time been provided with railways. To rely so confidently and strongly upon the exertions and efforts in favor of an immigration the results of which must be reserved for a future day, and to deduce with certainty that they will necessarily produce a considerable local traffic for the Northern Pacific Railway, from the time of completion of the line, I consider hazardous.

19. If thus, according to my conviction, the prospects for an advantageous local traffic on the Northern Pacific Railway during the first years of its operation do not exist, the through traffic will hardly offer any better chances. The Northern Pacific Railway, one terminus of which is situated at Duluth, on Lake Superior, in Minnesota, and the other at Puget Sound, will hardly be able to reckon on a through traffic in the course of a series of years so far as it relates solely to American products, since the termini do not furnish any basis for such a traffic. Puget Sound, favorably as it may be situated for shipping, has, for the time being, nothing in the shape of industrial establishments except a few embryo colliers, as yet insignificant, and some important saw-mills, which procure their raw material by water, and whose selling markets are not on American soil but abroad, requiring ships to export their product, while Duluth, a town of about 4,000 inhabitants, is still in embryo, so that it is hard to tell what traffic it may afford hereafter.

20. The Asiatic through trade, so far as it affects the existing Pacific lines, and the importance of which must not be too highly estimated since it consists of two articles only, tea and silk, will only be attracted with difficulty to the Northern Pacific road, because on the one hand, until the branch provided for in the charter is completed, which will reduce the distance from Puget Sound to Duluth from 2,000 miles on the main line to 1,775 miles on the branch line, the distance on the existing Pacific lines is about equal to that of the Northern Pacific, which offers no shortening of the journey by land, and because, on the other hand the commercial relations between New York and Chicago and San Francisco are so closely tied that the removal of the agency of the San

129

Francisco houses concerned in this commerce can hardly be thought of.[5]

21. After this exposition, though I readily acknowledge that the Northern Pacific road will come in for something at the opening—for instance, the important consignments to supply the military forts with provisions, the transport of provisions for the Hudson's Bay Company, the products of the mines of Montana, Idaho, and Washington, insignificant at present—I must incline to the opinion that after completion of the line and the simultaneous cessation of paying interest out of the capital, a longer or shorter period of time will intervene during which the working of the road will not produce the required income to pay an interest of 7.30 per cent on the capital invested after deducting the working expenses. As the means provided in the statutory regulations, of which I shall speak further on, by which supplies are to be raised in cases when the regular income does not suffice to pay the interest, will fail to afford a remedy, as I shall endeavor to prove, I have no hesitation in saying that the obligations undertaken by the promoters of the enterprise respecting the payment of interest cannot be fulfilled during the period immediately following the opening of the line.

22. With regard to the third question whether the sale of land will realize the amounts by which the redemption of the entire bonded debt can be effected within the 30 years specified, I must, first of all, contradict an opinion which has been widely circulated, representing the regions traversed by the Northern Pacific Railway as unfavorable to civilization, agriculture, and industry. The experience I have acquired from personal inspection as well as the most trustworthy information from official sources I have everywhere gathered on the spot, has convinced me that the region through which the Northern Pacific Railway passes is one of the most fertile on the American Continent, and is in every respect suitable for colonization. Minnesota and Dakota belong to the grain-growing region, Montana and Idaho are rich in minerals

[5] This statement is of interest especially in view of the contention of President Cass that Herr Haas had made his report without ever seeing Puget Sound.

and pastures, and Oregon and Washington Territory belong to the region of minerals, furs, timber, and agriculture.

The Government land grant to the Northern Pacific Railway Company representing as already mentioned, 50,000,000 acres for the main line, has an appreciable value, the money price of which at the rate at which the Illinois Central sold its land, would amount to $550,000,000; at the rate at which Minnesota disposed of her school land, it would amount to $350,000,000; and at the rate at which the Kansas Pacific realized, it would amount to $165,000,000. Granted that even the last figure is put too high, we may fall back on the minimum price below which the United States Government has bound itself to the Northern Pacific Railway Company not to sell land in the alternating sections adjoining the line. At $2.50 an acre the land grant of the Company is worth $125,000,000—an amount still more than sufficient to redeem the entire $100,000,000 of bonds; even the redemption of 10 per cent above par permitted by the statutory regulations requiring $110,-000,000 to redeem the bonds, would still leave a handsome surplus. However, another question is whether the land can really be disposed of by way of sale within the 30 years fixed for the redemption of the bonds, and whether the demand for these lands will so nearly equal the supply that sales can be made at the given prices and during the specified period of time? The answer to this question is essentially dependent on the same points which have been already considered in connection with the security for the payment of interest on the bonds, namely, whether in this case the population of the respective regions will increase at a rate sufficiently rapid to insure that after the lapse of 30 years the whole land of the Company shall have changed hands and been transferred to private owners. So far as human calculations can at all forecast what may be accomplished in periods of such duration, this question may be answered in the affirmative. The experience of the past in the United States as well as what is seen every day, gives ample proof that, as a rule, after a number of years have passed subsequent to the opening of a line in new and uncultivated regions, and new settlements have been established in conse-

131

quence of the railway, such land can be sold well and easier than any other land. Thus though a period of several years following immediately upon the opening of a line may have few sales to show, yet in the long run all will be right and the period of redemption is low enough to warrant a confidence, based upon experience, that within the period of redemption the area of the Northern Pacific Railway Company will have changed hands for the benefit of the Company. However, that during the first few years after the opening of the line the sales will assume but small dimensions, can hardly be doubted, since, as has been already observed, the immigration turning toward the newly-opened region of the Northern Pacific Railway will not be of sufficient magnitude to create an active demand, and as furthermore a great many immigrants who may turn in that direction to look out for new settlements will prefer to avail themselves of the facilities offered by the Homestead law, according to which every man on American soil, above 21 years of age, and declaring that he will remain, may secure on easy terms the possession of 80 acres of public land by simply paying a fee. Now, as in the regions crossed by the Northern Pacific Railway the public land lies adjacent in alternating sections, and is consequently without any difference of quality, the immigrants will, at the outset, prefer the public land, and the railway company will only be able to effect exceptional sales.

23. To what extent public land is disposed of under the Homestead law may be gathered from the fact that during the year 1869 the Government of the United States sold for cash 2,900,000 acres and allotted under the Homestead law 2,737,000 acres; during the year 1870 it sold for cash 2,150,000 acres and allotted under the Homestead law 3,700,000 acres. If thus the land sales of the railway company should be of little account for several years, one of the means already alluded to of supplementing the fund out of which interest on the bonds is to be paid in years of deficiency, will simultaneously fail. The statutory regulations stipulate that the bonds shall be successively bought up with the proceeds of the land sales and cancelled. At the same time, however, it is permitted in case of the treasury of the Company being exhausted,

and consequently without the necessary means for paying the interest on the bonds, to make up the deficiency out of the proceeds of the land sales. Of course the Company is bound to make restitution to the land fund of the amount taken out, by handing over the first net profits of the line. But if the land sales are only of a limited extent at first, and the proceeds correspondingly small, it will not be possible to make any substantial advances toward paying the interest, and simultaneously, as I have previously asserted, the line will not produce the requisite amount for the payment of the interest on the bonds and thus, in my opinion, it is certain that a longer or shorter period will ensue, immediately upon the opening of the line, during which the bondholders will have to forego interest.

24. In continuation of the foregoing, I have yet to mention in what manner the rights of the bondholders are to be guarded under such critical circumstances. The Mortgage of July 1, 1870, executed by the railway company to the trustees as representatives of the bondholders on the other side—to which, the bondholders have to submit—stipulates that in case the Company should not be able to fulfill their obligations respecting the payment of interest on the bonds and (1) the delay in the payment has lasted three months, the trustees shall have the power to sell so much land out of the area of the Company as will be necessary to realize the amount required to pay the interest; (2) when the delay in the payment has lasted six months the trustees shall be empowered to take charge of the line and work it themselves, and to make all the necessary arrangements for that purpose; (3) when the delay in the payment has lasted three years the trustees shall be empowered to sell the line and all the possessions pertaining to it for the benefit of the bondholders. These stipulations, however if acted upon, would do the bondholders little good. With reference to the powers conferred upon the trustees by Article 1, it is difficult to see what advantage would be gained for the bondholders by making use of them. If the land were salable the Company could and would sell to pay the interest on the bonds, and it will only be on account of the land not being salable, shortly after the opening

133

of the line, that no proceeds of the land sale will be available to supplement the interest-paying fund, and that the circumstances will arise for which the sale of land is to furnish a remedy. How the trustees can realize money by the sale of unsalable land is not very clear. The same objection applies to the measures provided for in Article 2, empowering the trustees to take charge of the line and work it themselves. What benefits are the bondholders likely to derive from that? The trustees will hardly be able to convert a non-paying line into a paying line, and it might even be hazardous to take the management out of the hands of people acquainted with local and other conditions simply because a crisis had ensued which by no exertions could by any human possibility have been averted. Finally, the powers conferred upon the trustees by Article 3, ought to have been given in my opinion, by Article 1. If the interest on the bonds should not be paid, the bondholders—the mortgagees of the Northern Pacific Railway—must, according to my view of the matter, have the power to bring the object mortgaged, in the case before us the property of the Northern Pacific Railway Company, under the hammer of the auctioneer, in order to realize out of the proceeds a pro rata dividend upon their claims, as in any other case of insolvency; but this power must not be withheld for a space of three years, and only conceded when other and questionable measures have proved fruitless.

I find in the mortgage of July 1, 1870, which determines the rights of the bondholders, less a security for the exercise of those rights than a troublesome obstacle to the execution of rights guaranteed to the bondholders by the general laws of the United States of America.

25. To sum up, I cannot deem it advisable that European capitalists should be encouraged to participate in the enterprise of the Northern Pacific Railway, as in my opinion, after the completion of the line a period will ensue during which the Company will not be able to fulfill the obligation it is under respecting the payment of interest on the bonds. It is certainly possible that this period will not ensue immediately upon the completion of the

main line, inasmuch as the branch line equally provided by the charter, will issue new mortgage bonds out of which the interest may be paid for a while, but this will postpone, not avert the crisis.

That the Northern Pacific Railway may be a good and profitable enterprise after the years of its childhood and troubles have been survived will not be enough to commend it to the European money market; it will be able during the early years of the enterprise to fulfill all the engagements entered into. In the full consciousness of the responsibility incumbent on me as a member of the European Commission of Experts, I cannot consider that this proof is forthcoming.

HAAS

Berlin, Nov. 30, 1871

THE REPLY OF THE COMPANY
The President Denies That the Reports Were Ever Suppressed, and Asserts That the Officers of the Road Never Saw Them— the Report of Haas Claimed to Be a Favorable One

The report of Haas was shown to Mr. Cass, the President of the Northern Pacific Railroad Company, on Saturday morning last by a *Tribune* representative, and his views in defense of the character of the road were requested. While reading the report carefully over, Mr. Cass frequently made ejaculations of disgust at the Commissioner's unfamiliarity with American land values, and his lack of appreciation of the country's rapid growth and increasing prosperity. Mr. Samuel Wilkeson, who was also shown the report, declared that Haas didn't know anything about the subject. Why, said he, the man did not go over all the road as he was sent to do, but quarreled with his fellow commissioners in regard to the management of the expedition, and finally left them altogether and made his own report without ever having seen Puget Sound, unless through glasses of lager-beer which he was continually swilling down.

Did you see his report, and that of his fellow-Commissioner, Foltz?

135

Never, Sir! nor did we ever try in any shape to suppress them. They were offered to us for from $35,000 all the way down to $500, but we would never have anything to do with them, but only replied, "Publish them as much as you like. We don't care." They were published in the German papers, although I believe never translated into English.

Who paid the expenses of the visit of these German gentlemen?

We paid them finally. Jay Cooke and Co., our fiscal agents, paid the bills immediately. It was through the rose-colored representations of their agent in Vienna, George P. Sargeant,[6] who duped them, that they were induced to attempt the negotiation of this loan there.

At the conclusion of the interview with Mr. Wilkeson, a consultation between him and the President resulted in the preparation of the following statement, to which Mr. Cass appended his signature:

To the Editor of the Tribune.

Sir:—I acknowledge myself indebted to you for a copy of the report of Commissioner Haas of Berlin to his principals in Europe relative to the Northern Pacific Railroad. I never saw the report until you were so good as to allow me to read it, nor has it been seen by any officer or member of this Company's Board of Directors. The report was made by Mr. Haas to his principals after his return to Europe; and although, as I understand, a copy was asked for by some of the officers of this company, it was refused to them, notwithstanding the entire expenses of Mr. Haas in obtaining the material for his report in this country were ultimately paid by this company. I had heard that the report was quite unfavorable. I am glad to find on reading it that it is much more favorable than could have been expected from a European, especially one from the Continent, who had never been in the United States, and who was not familiar with its rapid development in railroad enterprises and the rapid settlement along the railway lines throughout the Western country. He was not unaware of the fact that railroads

---

[6] This may, or may not, be the person described on page 227. If it is, it would account for the anonymity of the pamphlet.

had been built in the United States through regions where the voice of civilization had hardly been heard and where the sound of the last stroke of the hammer in driving the last spike in the last rail had scarcely ceased to reverberate, before a large business was established upon the roads. This fact I, as well as every other person familiar with our Western States and Territories, have knowledge of.

I have heard it said that this report was suppressed by the officers of this company, or through its agency, in some way, and I now repeat that the report was never seen by any officer of the Northern Pacific until that day; nor were its contents known to us. Therefore it was impossible that any anxiety should have arisen among our directors for its suppression. But the fact is, it never was suppressed, nor attempted to be suppressed, by any officer or director of the Northern Pacific Railroad Company, nor any one in their interest, so far as is known.

But to the report itself. Any one who will read it carefully will find that it is on the whole a most favorable report for this great enterprise; and if it establishes anything, it establishes:

1. That the estimated cost of the construction of the road is entirely reasonable, and that the Chief Engineer of the Company is a well-tried man of a reputation for honesty, experience, and capacity beyond question.

2. That the lands are sufficient to redeem the entire issue of bonds at 10 per cent premium, and leave a handsome surplus of these at a minimum price, at which Mr. Haas estimates them, and that, as compared with existing land grant roads, the amount of the sales may exceed by three or four times, the issue of bonds. That is the second point which he admits.

3. That the region of country through which the Northern Pacific Railroad is building is one of the most fertile on the American Continent, and is in every respect suitable for colonization.

These three admissions establish, in the opinion of Mr. Haas, the Berlin Commissioner, the value of the Northern Pacific Railroad beyond a controversy. His objections to the enterprise may

137

be stated thus: That owing to the sparseness of the population and the slowness of emigration along the line of the road for a period of years not definitely stated, the earnings of the road would not be sufficient to protect the interest on the bonds. These objections have been advanced to every land-grant road that has been built in this country, not only by foreigners, but by our own people, who might be supposed to know better. And yet, in the fact of these fears and apprehensions, the business of all these roads is rapidly developing, the property greatly enhanced in value, and their interest on their bonds protected in every case. There is no good reason to suppose that the Northern Pacific is going to be an exception to similar land grant roads. On the contrary, the Northern Pacific Railroad has far greater elements of undeveloped wealth and resources than the Illinois Central road had in the earlier stages of its existence.

I presume that Mr. Foltz and Mr. Dexter, Associate Commissioners with Mr. Haas, have also prepared reports which may receive publication at this juncture. I have not seen either of these reports, nor do I know, even by rumor, their character; but I have no belief that they contain statements against the practicability of the Northern Pacific Railroad enterprise, and reasonable promise of abundant success for the undertaking when completed, which cannot be refuted with testimony that all unprejudiced men shall feel to be sufficient.

G. W. CASS
President of the Northern Pacific Railroad Company
Office of the Northern Pacific Railway Company
Sept. 27, 1873

11. Our Barren Lands

The region of country, about which this paper is written, lies between the 100th meridian on the east, the Sierra Nevada Mountains on the west, with British America for its northern border, and Mexico on the south. It is a vast section of country, thousands of miles in extent. These wide plains, mountains, and valleys, for many years, have been the subject, sometimes of romantic interest, always of more or less of mystery, and later of various speculations.

The early maps condemned it, for the most part, as an arid desert, and the adventurous traveller who wandered beyond the line of civilization, was warned, that even should he not encounter the savage Indians, hunger and thirst and death accompanied his every step.

Until the discovery of gold on the Pacific coast, very few civilized men were so hardy as to venture across this land, known only as desolate.[1] And when expeditions were undertaken—like those of Lewis and Clarke, [sic] in the beginning of the century, and later, of Fremont and others—the explorers who escaped those dangers and told of their discoveries, gained world-wide celebrity. When that illusive struggle for wealth, the search for gold,

[1] Gold was discovered in California in 1848, but well before that time there had been a considerable movement of population to the Pacific Coast and the Oregon Trail had become an American institution. The migration of 1843 to Oregon Territory was so large that it became known as the "Great Migration."

139

began, thousands of men attempted that perilous passage across the plains. In the following years, a ghastly spectacle of bleaching bones of men and animals marked a roadway from the settlements to the mountains. The burning sun cracked and parched the earth; the merciless snow-storms, the arctic cold, did a work of death whose story has never yet been told.[2]

With the continued discoveries of gold and silver in the Rocky Mountains, and the immense migration to the Pacific coast, came the demand for more expeditions and more frequent means of communication. Railroads were exploited in many directions across the border. Some of these were justified by commerce—more were cheating schemes for the purpose of getting subsidies of land from the United States. Once in possession of this land, every effort, honest and dishonest, was made to induce persons to purchase it and settle upon it. And so, suddenly, by means of that magic power, the Press, those "bad lands," "sandy plains," "wasted deserts," "el llano estacado," "basins of salt," "black hills," and so on, became fruitful as the Vale of Cashmere. Here were "homes" for the "homeless" and "lands" for the "landless." These and other catchwords were used to ensnare the unwary.

The efforts which were and are made to sell lands thus acquired, are familiar to the public. The fruitless, exhaustive struggle of the settler to produce something from barren soil, his misery and destitution, only those can know whose duties station them within the confines of those worthless lands, and where they have the opportunities for personal observation.

Letter to the New York Tribune

In the New York *Tribune* of February 27, 1874, there was published a letter, which I had prepared, pronouncing a large proportion of the lands of the Northern Pacific Railroad Company, worthless, both for agriculture and as a security for money. The last part of this statement is already verified, as the completed road is now in possession of its maximum quantity of land, excepting perhaps some formal drawbacks, and more good land to

2 Here, General Hazen's rhetoric is running away with his judgment.

140

the mile than it can ever again have, should the construction of the road be resumed.

By the term "worthless for agriculture," I mean in a strictly commercial sense; for there is no kind of agriculture in those distant countries, except in a very limited way, that can return to the farmer the money he invests, and a very large proportion of this land will not raise crops at all. It is barren through want of summer rains. There is much of it, however, composed of alkali, where it would be impossible to raise crops were there an abundance of rain. But even with plenteous rain-falls and no alkali, past experience shows that the dreadful scourge of insects would destroy all vegetable life, many of the seasons.

In the *Tribune* letter, it was emphatically stated that what is proclaimed by the Northern Pacific as the "Northern Tropical Belt," is a myth; that notwithstanding we have a very high temperature in summer—sometimes 104 degrees Fahrenheit, in the shade—and delightful autumns, we have a corresponding degree of cold in the winter, sometimes 45 degrees below zero, and accompanied with storms destructive of life; that we have comparatively no spring, summer immediately succeeding winter, while our average of temperature is but 42 degrees, or ten degrees above the freezing point. As evidence of the correctness of this statement, see Professor Blodgett's standard charts, and the meteorological reports in the office of the Surgeon-General of the army.

The *Tribune* letter has called out, as was expected, much criticism and contradiction. I have been accused of hostility to a great interest, ignorance of the subject, and bribery. These charges have often been couched in insolent language. A few of these criticisms will be referred to in this paper.

Why the Middle Region Is not Arable

My main proposition, that there can be no general agriculture along the line of this road, is equally true of all that immense country lying between the 100 degree meridian west longitude, the Sierra Nevada Mountains, the British Possessions, and Mexico. The comparative worthlessness of this great tract of land is owing

141

to the insufficient fall of rain. From this general statement is to be expected the very limited valleys that can be irrigated, and the beneficial effects of an occasional wet season.

These facts have been incontrovertibly proven. They are recorded in the archives of the government, with positive statistical evidence, and this information, so well known to the intelligent people resident in the middle region, has been gained by long experience.

Meteorological Reports

For fifty years the government has been engaged in a system of accurate instrumental measurements of the rainfall and temperature, at all its military posts, and at many other places. These observations are made with the best instruments, under the direction of officers of the army, and I do not know that any intelligent person has ever questioned their perfect accuracy. The snow-fall of winter is melted and measured, or carefully computed, as water.

By examining closely these tables, which extend to the readings of millions of observations, and which are available in most libraries of the country, we find that single, simultaneous observations at different points, as well as separate observations at the same points at different times, either of temperature or of rains, give widely different results. By taking the averages of a great number of these consecutive observations at the same point through a great number of years, we get a general average that is constant. That is, while for consecutive years we get variations in rain-fall sometimes of twenty inches, by taking the average of eight or ten consecutive years at the same point, anywhere in the tables for the last fifty years, we get practically similar results. The yearly averages so obtained will not vary more than two or three inches from each other. In other words, for periods of eight or ten years the amount of rain-fall in any given locality is practically constant. Another point shown is, that these quantities do not change abruptly in changing latitude or longitude, but are regularly and gradually graded into each other. This has proven, beyond all controversy, that the laws controlling this phenomenon are constant through such periods of time as we have need to deal with, and, although we can not portend what the rain-fall of any one year may be, yet by taking several years long enough to embrace the full average, say eight or ten, we can tell what the sum of them will be. This has enabled the construction of maps so shaded as to accurately represent the different quantities of rain falling on the various parts of the country. Line of equal temperature have also been marked out with great accuracy. These are not fanciful displays of color upon paper, but are results of faithful labor intelligently bestowed upon data that has taken fifty years to gather.

There has not been so long a time devoted continuously upon the observations along the Missouri river, but for a very long time the different posts of the Hudson Bay and Northwest Fur Companies have kept these records, from which, with other trusty information, the government has constructed these charts. By these calculations there has been given this region fifteen inches of rain annually, and lines of equal heat running near this point, that very nearly correspond with the observations for years past made at Fort Buford. Our reports at this post, which for eight years have been continuously and accurately kept, show an average of but 12.50 inches of rainfall, two and a half inches less than shown on the rainchart. The following is taken from the public records at the post, the upper line of figures showing the annual rain-fall, and the lower line the rain-fall for the four growing months of May, June, July, and August for the same years:

REPORT OF RAIN-FALL

1867,	6.58;	1868, 11.50;	1869, 9.74;	1870, 9.19;	1871, 9.42;
	5.17	9.31	5.23	6.25	3.98

1872, 19.90;	1873, 21.11;	1874, 4.09	to August 11.
6.77	10.73	3.34,	

The above is an exact copy taken from the records of the post. The actual rain for the last twelve months, ending November 1, 1874, is $6\frac{47}{100}$ inches, less than a third of that of last year.

(Signed) J. F. MUNSON
1st Lieut. and Adjt., 6th Infantry
Post Adj't

143

Rainy Seasons of 1872 and 1873

I desire to call especial attention to the amount of rain that fell in the years of 1872 and 1873, as upon these facts will rest much of this discussion. It will be noticed that, while in all the other six years only 57.06 inches fell altogether, a little more than one year's rain in the productive States, or an annual fall of 9.50 inches, an average of more than double that amount, or 20.55 inches, fell each year for 1872 and 1873.

It will be remembered that it was during these two years of very unusual growth that the Northern Pacific Railroad to Bismarck was built. This work was done by men who had no other experiences of the seasons in Dakota, and it is no more than natural that they should honestly believe that they had seen a fair example of the seasons of the country. All they said of it corresponded with what they had always known of other countries.

General Custer's Letter

The experiences which deceived the builders of the road must have been those of General George A. Custer (but in a more decided way), who wrote a nine column article in reply to my letter, the plain intent being to throw discredit upon my statements. The Custer plea was written after he had seen one season only, and that the last of the two most exceptionally rainy seasons on record. He accurately described the only example of a season he had ever seen in this country, and that appeared like those he had been accustomed to see in productive countries. He so published it to the world, not reminding the reader that he was substituting an example, and the only one he had knowledge of, for a general result. Had he served in this interior country, or had he given the statistics, which he calls hospital reports, the attention due them, he might then have had a knowledge that would' give his writings weight.

All I had written upon this subject I believed to be true, and had evidence for all my statements. It should be said in the outset of this brochure, that the frequent and prominent presence of General Custer in this discussion is unavoidable. It is the result of his interference and question of my statements and motives. The personalities involved in such a discussion are extremely unpleasant to the public, even more than to the individuals concerned; yet justice can not be done, either to the parties involved, to the public, or to the truth, which in this case, is of transcendant importance, without bringing forward General Custer. And if he becomes the chief witness against himself, he may thank the "cacoethes scribendi" which has sometimes brought disaster upon other and more prudent men.

The difficulty of understanding the character of a dry country like this, so entirely different from the countries we have been familiar with all our lives, where there are continuous rains, may well be understood.

General Custer states, in general terms, that this Western Dakota, along the line of the Northern Pacific Railroad route, is a valuable agricultural country, attractive to the emigrant, with an abundant rainfall, and that it will produce in profusion the cereals and fruits common to the Eastern States. He also declares that I wrote without seeing or knowing the country, or from impure and wicked motives, and from a point far from the line of the road. He admits that the land is really worthless at this particular post. He strives to make the reader believe that I knew the land along the railroad was good, and that in my statement I was guilty of unfair motives. General Custer says that I attempted to depreciate a valuable property in the hands of poor people, while, had I desired to do them a kindness, as I pretended, I ought to have pronounced the country valuable, and that I had founded my declarations upon rumor and ignorance. In all this he avers I was committing a great moral offense, and that he proposed to satisfactorily prove that my statements regarding the unfitness of this interior country for general agriculture "were not only untrue, but were actually the reverse, and written in ignorance thereof."

General Custer further says: "What would be thought of a person who should attempt to form and publish an opinion of the rich, fertile soil composing the sugar and cotton lands of the Southern

145

States, when such opinion was only based upon an examination of the swamp lands of Florida, Louisiana and Mississippi; yet a similar course has been pursued by General Hazen."

Each of these grave personal charges of my brother officer will be considered in its proper place. The General asserts his philanthropical intent by saying: It is to utter my protest against a sweeping and unfounded denunciation of this great Northwest that I write these lines." And then closes with the sage and unselfish advice to our national legislators, that this railroad scheme "might well warrant the general government in considering this enterprise one of national importance, and in giving to it at least its hearty encouragement."

What Some of the Newspapers Said

General Custer's nine column reply to my letter of a column and a half, appeared in the Minneapolis *Tribune*, the principal western organ of the Northern Pacific Railroad, in April, just before the bill for the relief of the road was introduced in Congress. The following is a portion of the editor's rather extraordinary heading:

"General George A. Custer in reply to General Hazen. Personal observations and experience vs. prejudice and unfounded rumors. General Custer describes what he and hundreds of others saw last summer. And refutes General Hazen's sweeping condemnations. Wheat, corn, oats, potatoes, vegetables of all kinds, and many varieties of fruits grow luxuriantly, are excellent in quality, and yield enormously."

This newspaper further says:

"General Hazen's condemnation of the Northern Pacific lands, and of the Northwest generally, was made up of prejudices and rumors of an exceptional character, while General Custer speaks from personal observation and experience, and brings abundant corroborations for any assertion he makes. His letter is an able vindication of the country, and we trust his statements will be given as wide publicity as the *false* and groundless *misstatements* of General Hazen. (Italics in original.)

146

Custer versus *Hazen*

Minneapolis *Tribune*, April 21st: "The *Tribune* of the 18th instant contains an article from General Custer, in reply to General Hazen, in relation to the country through which the Northern Pacific passes. The General has examined the matter thoroughly, and knowing whereof he speaks, refutes every statement made by Hazen, intended to injure the country, adducing facts and figures which can not be controverted."

The following is from the Bismarck *Tribune*:

"Some time ago, the editor of this paper, in replying to the wild assertions of General Hazen, relating to the Northern Pacific, took the liberty to use the name of General Custer, quoting him favorable to the country. The General has justified our reference by defending the country in an eight-column letter in the Minneapolis *Tribune* of Saturday last."

From the same paper:

"Among the latest articles in reply to General Hazen is one from General G. A. Custer, who has taken up the statements of Hazen in detail, proving their falsity."

These sayings I have thought best to notice and see how far the letter referred to accomplishes what is claimed for it.

I have endeavored to describe the country truly, that others may not be injured by what I conceive to be misrepresentations about it. I sought to incite such discussion as might tend to the same end, thus averting injury both to private individuals and to the country.

I will now introduce a letter about this region from the veteran soldier, General Sully,[3] and then other letters and statements bearing upon the same subject. I will first state, however, that from three years' observations along the Missouri river, I find that portion of the land about this post, Fort Buford, and the mouth of the Yellowstone, fully equal in quality to that about Bismarck and Fort A. Lincoln, and greatly superior to nine-tenths of the country for a thousand miles below it.

[3] General Sully at this time was the colonel of the Twenty-first Infantry, stationed at Fort Vancouver, Washington Territory.

General Sully's Letter

FORT VANCOUVER, WASHINGTON, T.

June 18, 1874

DEAR GENERAL:—Your letter of the 3d of June reached me at this post yesterday. I have not seen your letter about the N. P. R. R. published in the New York *Tribune* but saw in the *Army and Navy Journal* an article in regard to it. In answer to your question about my opinion as to the climate, character of the soil, etc., of the section of the country through which the N. P. R. R. passes, I would state as follows: My experience of that section of country dates back as far as 1854, when I was stationed in what was then the Territory of Minnesota, near what is now the western frontier of the State, from that time till 1859, when I marched across the country to the Platte river. I was on duty in different sections of the country between the Missouri river and Minnesota, and on the Upper Missouri. From the fall of 1863 to 1866 I was in command of troops operating against the Sioux nation, who were then in a state of war, both in the east and west of the Missouri river, as far west as the Yellowstone river and north to the British Possessions. In 1867, I was again sent into that country to visit the different lands of the Sioux, and went up the Missouri river as far as the mouth of the Yellowstone. In 1869 and 1870, I was stationed in Montana; visited the Yellowstone valley and the head waters of the Columbia river, on the west side of the Rocky Mountains, and now I am located in Washington Territory. I have thus had some opportunity of judging of the nature of the country through which the N. P. R. R. is to pass. The country west of Minnesota, till you come to the Missouri, is decidedly bad—a high, dry, rolling prairie, unfit for cultivation, except in a very few detached places. Alongside the very few springs in that country, there are several ponds or small lakes, but very few of them contain water that you can drink, and many of them dry up in summer; there is very little, in fact you may say no timber in the country, and as a general rule very little rain falls during the summer. The country might do for grazing, but cattle would be obliged to roam over large sections of it, and in winter would perish for want of timber, or other means of protection against the climate, which is very severe. There are heavy snows and heavy winds, and it is very cold. The country west of the Missouri to the Yellowstone is much better in every respect, more arable land, more timber, more drinkable water, and I found on my trip across the country many large deposits of coal or lignite. Still I would not recommend it as a good country to settle in, and large portions of it can never be inhabited, not even by Indians.

As regards to the climate, it is about the same as in the country east of the Missouri. I saw by General Stanley's report of his expedition with the railroad company through that section, that he had considerable difficulty with high water in the streams. I found no such difficulty when I crossed through that country. The season, however, was very dry and the rivers so low that I forded both the Yellowstone and the Missouri, just above the mouth of the Yellowstone, with my command, some 2,000 cavalry. . . .

> Yours, with respect,
> (Signed) ALF. SULLY
> *Colonel 21st Infantry*

To Gen. W. B. Hazen, U.S. Army

General Sully also speaks highly of the valleys of Montana and of the Pacific coast country, and especially of the timber. The climate, he says, "is far better than east of the mountains." The drought he encountered was that of ordinary seasons here, differing widely from the anomalous seasons of 1872 and 1873, which have done so much to mislead the hopeful people all along the border, and to encourage settlements that must be and are now being abandoned all along the line.

Of serious importance is the subjoined description of the character of the country along the northern international line by an officer who was of the escort to the boundary commission. Especial attention should be given to this letter, because the route described crosses a large portion of that country, marked out on the large advertising map of the Northern Pacific as the "International Wheat Garden." Across the entire breadth of the "Garden" there was not found one drop of running water. As the boundary crosses the country following an ideal line, it gives us a true picture of the land, while parties following the beds of rivers and other routes practicable for roads, gain no really accurate knowledge of the whole. General Sully's statement embraced the country from Minnesota to this point. The following letter continues the description on to the Rocky Mountains:

149

Lieutenant Crowell's Statement

FORT BUFORD, D.T., September 7, 1874.

GENERAL:—That portion of the Northern Boundary Survey[4] to which I was attached, marched up the Quaking Ash creek,[5] which rises near the line and runs due south, emptying into the Missouri river about sixty miles west of this post. At a point ten or fifteen miles from its mouth, the timber disappears altogether, and not a stick or bush is found on it from that point on to its source, a distance of at least seventy miles.

The bottom land on the Quaking Ash is, for the most part, covered with cactus, with occasional patches of sage-brush. Our line of march was from 105° of west longitude, along the 49th parallel, with occasional debouches to the south, from eight to twenty miles, to avoid bad lands through which it was impracticable to take a wagon-train. From the initial point on our line to the Sweet Grass hills, a distance of from four hundred and fifty to five hundred miles, we crossed but two running streams, namely "Frenchman's creek and Rock creek," the latter a small stream that later in the season becomes dry.

I do not believe it was possible to have gathered a ton of hay on a strip of territory extending two and a half miles each side of the line and running west five hundred miles. We crossed the Milk River eight miles south of the line—bed of river at crossing perfectly dry; water was found near by, however, in standing pools. All of the country I saw, with the exceptions hereafter noted, is, in my opinion, wholly worthless—its only productions being the cactus, prairie dog, and rattlesnake. There is not an acre of arable land, and can not be made so for the want of moisture, between 105° and 112° of west longitude, that I saw, excepting perhaps a hundred miles of the valley of Milk river. At a point on the Milk river some seventy miles south of the line, running water is abundant. As we approach the Missouri from this point, the valley widens out, vegetation becomes more luxuriant, timber increases in size and quantity, and in some localities the growth of grass was quite heavy, and, altogether, the country improves, resembling somewhat the valley of the Yellowstone. On our return march, we crossed no reliable running streams, except

---

[4] The survey of the northern boundary from the Lake of the Woods to the Rocky Mountains is well described in John E. Parsons, *West on the 49th Parallel* (New York, William Morrow and Company, 1963). The military escort to the surveyors was commanded by Major Marcus A. Reno, Seventh United States Cavalry.

[5] Poplar River.

Milk river and Frenchman's creek, and I am not sure that the latter could be depended on the year round.

Very respectfully,
Your ob't servant,
(Signed) W. H. H. CROWELL
1st Lieut. 6th Infantry[6]

What Others of the International Boundary Survey Say

The other officers of the expedition confirm every word of the above, and state explicitly that their route, until they arrived near the Rocky Mountains, meridian 112, was over a worthless country.

Major Bryant, in command of the infantry escort, says of the country: "It is a blank to the Rocky Mountains, eight degrees of longitude."

Major Twining, the astronomer of the U.S. Commission, says: "The country can not be settled, except near the Rocky Mountains."

Other officers, of perfect reliability, have informed me that there is not a drop of running water along the international boundary, from the vicinity of Devil's Lake, longitude 99, to the Rocky mountains, fifteen degrees.

Testimony of Correspondents with the Black Hills Expedition

The New York *Tribune* correspondent, in his letter from the Black Hills, of June 17th, published August 20th, gives a description of the country, which is accurate. It is an exact verification of my account. The report of General Custer is exactly the reverse of that of the correspondent and of mine. He says:

"Dakota, the year round, is a very dry country." And, after alluding to the untrustworthiness of the Northern Pacific's advertising circulars, says:

"The northwestern part of Dakota, on a line from Fort Lincoln to the Black Hills, I am obliged to say, is a better region of country than on the line due west of Lincoln or, rather, the route of the Northern Pacific Railroad. In each section there are tolerably large areas of good grazing land, and the country would be good

[6] Lieutenant Crowell was a member of Hazen's command.

151

for stock-raising if water and timber were abundant. At the same time, there are much larger areas of cactus and alkali, utterly unfit for the habitation of man or beast. Even the grass-growing districts, valuable for grass-growing purposes, offer little inducement for agriculture, the insufficient rain-fall being an insurmountable objection. The native grasses furnish no argument for the success of grains, since they are thoroughly acclimated."

This is the first thoroughly comprehensive and accurate statement upon this subject I have ever seen in print, and it will be found true, with limited exceptions, to the line of Mexico southward, and the Sierra Nevadas westward. The portion of the Northern Pacific route here alluded to is that portion described by General Custer last summer. He quotes from his diary, that on his return, the volunteer crop of oats was found grown, where they were scattered going out. He also describes limitless meadows. As the correspondent had not, at the time this was written, seen that country since last summer, when he was in company with General Custer, his impressions of it must have been formed at that time. On reaching the Cheyenne river, the St. Paul correspondent takes up the description thus:

"The last twenty miles is through a poor and hilly country; the soil, naturally thin, is rendered almost barren by drouth. The timber gradually runs out. On the river only a few cottonwoods grow, and to the southward, the treeless arid plains extend indefinitely."

The following was written by the New York *Tribune* correspondent, Mr. Barrow, after returning from the expedition. It is introduced here to show, that in writing from Fort Buford, I was correct in making my description of the country apply to that along the proposed line of the North Pacific:

"Returning over this trail a second time for nearly a hundred and fifty miles, I found that impressions of the country received last year were again renewed. Of the country traversed by that expedition, the section between the Big and Little Missouri rivers, excepting occasional tracks along the Yellowstone river and the valley of the Missouri river, was altogether the best. But even this offers few inducements for the settler, while the region west of the Little Missouri and west of the Yellowstone is hardly worth giving away. The admirable letter of General Hazen to the *Tribune* last winter, giving a full and accurate description of the country in the vicinity of Fort Buford, well characterizes the region of which I speak. It is part and parcel of the same lot. Northern Pacific Railroad speculators are still making strenuous efforts to persuade emigrants of the fertility of this section of the North American desert. But while there are thousands of acres of good farming land still unoccupied, no one who has a modicum of practical wisdom will select his homestead here. It is useless to deny that the country is a desert. The sad necessity of redeeming it has not yet arrived."

From Lewis and Clarke's [sic] Report

On page 326, Lewis and Clarke's Expedition, we find the following:

"From the Cobalt Bluffs to the Yellowstone (where Fort Buford is now situated) a distance of about one thousand miles, the hills follow the banks of the river, with scarcely any variation. From the James river,[7] the lower grounds are confined within a narrow space by the hills on both sides, which now continue near each other up to the mountains. This space is from one to three miles, as high up as the Muscleshell river (*sic*), beyond which the hills approach so near as to leave scarcely any low ground on the Missouri; and, as you approach the falls, they reach the water's edge."

This accurately describes the valley of the Upper Missouri. As to its soil, he says:

"The soil is still rich, yet the almost total absence of timber, and particularly the want of good water, there being but a small supply in the creeks and even that brackish, oppose powerful obstacles to its settlement."

At the town of Bismarck, water is hauled from the Missouri river, and peddled by the gallon; and at the military posts along the river it is obtained from the same source.

[7] This stream, one of the longest non-navigable rivers in the world, enters the Missouri a few miles from Yankton, South Dakota.

The following is a letter from the hay contractor of this post for this year:

Statement of Hay Contractor

FORT BUFORD, D.T., September 6, 1874.

GENERAL W. B. HAZEN:

In reply to your communication of August 31st, I would most respectfully state that, with regard to the supply of hay for Fort Buford, this year, I was able to find about 275 tons of hay between eight and nine miles from this post, but, owing to the thinness and shortness of the grass, I was compelled to keep three machines running, in order to cut from twelve to fifteen tons of grass per day. After that, I was compelled to haul the remaining 125 tons twenty-five miles, and to keep the three machines running, in order to cut grass enough to keep ten two-horse teams employed, *the teams making one trip in three days.* I then had to move a distance of thirty miles above the post—having previously cut below it—in order to get hay for my own use. I found about 100 tons at this point, but it was short, the same as at the other two places. The grass I had to haul twenty-five miles cost me $21.75 per ton and that does not include anything for the labor of the teams, nor the repairs on wagons, machines, etc.

I have been talking with Mr. Joseph Sparks, who has been employed by the contractors at this post and at Fort Stevenson[8] for the past six years, and he says that, in an average season at Stevenson, they would generally get about 300 tons, and any amount above this they had to haul not less than twenty-five miles.

Respectfully,
JAMES LEIGHTON,
Contractor.

This is a fair exhibit of the ordinary trouble and cost of securing hay in this country.

What the Bismarck Farmers Say

The following was published by the Bismarck *Tribune* last spring:

"Farming in Bismarck.—It has been stated that this is not a farming country, and in a review of General Hazen's letter, the

[8] Fort Stevenson was located eighty-nine miles above Bismarck on the north bank of the Missouri River.

editor of this paper stated that he knew better. There are others who know better also—practical men—some of whom raised good crops here last season, and who are willing to risk their time and money again.

"The following named gentlemen, for instance, will plant the number of acres set opposite their respective names, viz:

"Oscar Ward and son, 28; H. N. Holloway, 15; R. M. Douglass, 40; J. M. Ayres, 15; Colonel Donnelly, 15; Colonel Lounsbury, 20; Charles McCarty, 15; Henry Waller, 10; Mr. McNeill, 4; W. E. Cahill, 20; Messrs. Bonner and Demarsh, 30; Fred. Girard, 40.

"Many others, whose names we have not learned, will also put in from two to ten acres; and they will succeed, because every farming experiment tried here has succeeded."

At the close of the season, when the crops are harvested, it will be conclusive evidence to give the reports of the degree of success of these individuals from their own lips.

CAMP HANCOCK, D.T., September 14, 1874.

MY DEAR GENERAL HAZEN:

. . . R. M. Douglas planted ten acres of potatoes, oats and garden-truck. Said he would get nothing but a few potatoes.

W. E. Cahill planted fifteen acres. Grasshoppers destroyed all but one-half acre of potatoes.

Colonel Donnelly has about two acres of potatoes.

Mr. Ayres told me he had planted ten acres, and would get nothing.

Mr. Ward planted thirteen acres. Said he would get about sixty bushels potatoes, besides a few squash and melons.

Colonel Lounsberry, editor of the Bismarck *Tribune*, expects to have 300 bushels of potatoes. [After gathering them, he informed the writer he had twenty bushels only.]

Henry Waller planted twenty-five bushels of potatoes on three acres, and gathered five bushels.

[The foregoing is all directly from the the mouths of the parties mentioned. The other four have been heard from indirectly, but just as accurately, and their lack of success is similar.]

The season has been very warm, and dry. Grasshoppers destroyed nearly everything that survived the drouth. . . .

Farming here this year has been nearly, if not quite, a failure.

Some of the men are disgusted, and say they will not try it again; others are bound to try it one more year. . . .

Very respectfully,
Your obedient servant,
(Signed) H. R. PORTER

With all these facts, the government, at the instance of the Northern Pacific, has surveyed the railroad strip for one hundred miles before reaching the Missouri River, and has even been induced to open a land-office in the country for the sale of this arid land. And now, to complete the farce, the railroad company, who, by the terms of their land-grant, are to pay the cost of surveying their lands, are petitioning Congress to be released from this part of their engagement.

Statement of a Gentleman at Fort Berthold[9]

The following interesting letter, giving the general results of agriculture in this region, this season, is from a most worthy gentleman, who asks me to omit his name for reasons that seem perfectly good, but adds:

"If any person should impugn this statement as an invention of your own, you may use my name as authority, without hesitation."

BISMARCK, D.T., September 6, 1874.

GENERAL:—I have recently made a trip extending from Fort Buford to this place, and carefully examined, personally, the agricultural operations at various points along this route. At Fort Berthold, the wheat and oats have been entirely destroyed by grasshoppers, and, owing to the long continued and severe drouth, the other crops of corn, potatoes, squash, pumpkins, etc., will not amount to half a crop. At Fort Stevenson, the post garden and patches cultivated by the post-trader and others will produce almost nothing. . . . At Bismarck, it is the same story. Grasshoppers and drouth, with the additional accompaniment of bugs, have destroyed the hopes of the farmer, and given another year's experience to prove that farming in Dakota is a total impossibility.

It is a monstrous fraud and a great wrong for interested parties to induce immigration to this territory, under the plea that it is a good farming country, whereas every truthful man must know directly to

9 Fort Berthold was nineteen miles above Fort Stevenson.

the contrary. A residence of nearly nine years in Montana and Dakota has afforded me some knowledge of the agricultural resources of these territories; and I fearlessly assert that, without irrigation, successful farming is an impossibility. . . .

Nor can irrigation be successfully employed, except in a few places in Montana, and not at all in Dakota. That farming is a complete failure in that part of Dakota alluded to in the beginning of this communication, can be, I think, proved conclusively, by the fact that, where it has been tried under the most favorable auspices as at Fort Berthold, my home, where there is fine land, as fertile as any in the territory, and where the government has yearly lavished large sums of money, the agency farm, in general terms, from first to last, has been a dead failure. It has swallowed up the chief part of the appropriation to the Ree Indians, in fruitless and disheartening experiments. Then, at Bismarck, and in this vicinity, in spite of all the puffs and poetry of sanguine writers, the hard, naked fact remains, that it can not raise anything like a supply even of vegetables—which, for the daily market, are being brought from the Red River, two hundred miles—not to mention cereals, for its wants. Every one knows this, and why it is persistently stated that this is a good farming country, passes comprehension.

The want of moisture exists in all the country lying between the 100th meridian and the Rocky Mountains, and from the British line on the north to the Mexican border on the south, no successful farming is known, except by irrigation.

I will quote here the opinion given by Mr. Meeker,[10] the founder of the Greeley colony in Colorado, who states that "agriculture, without irrigation, in the countries lying between the 100th meridian and the Rocky Mountains is an *impossibility*."

In Dakota, stock must be kept up during the winter, and very frequently the hay is of so inferior a quality (a good deal being cut on the bottom lands, where it is mixed with rose-bush and weeds), that stock fed on it alone can hardly live throughout the long severe winters, even when well-housed and sheltered. Indeed, if I mistake not, cattle at Forts Lincoln and Berthold have perished during the winter, owing to the inferior quality of the hay and its want of nutritive qualities, rendering it insufficient to support life during the long, terribly cold, and inclement Dakota winter.

---

[10] This was Nathan Meeker, a friend of Horace Greeley and agricultural editor of New York *Tribune,* for which he wrote a series of articles on the farming possibilities of Colorado. He was killed by the Utes in the Meeker Massacre of 1879.

157

In this connection, I may state that I know something of the country contiguous to the Yellowstone and Muscleshell rivers. . . . I have walked over a great deal of it, and a more dreary, desolate, and forbidding region, it would indeed be difficult to find.

I do not forget that a few years ago some parties represented that the Muscleshell country was a paradise, and they had a map published of Muscleshell City, laid out with beautiful wide streets, adorned by magnificent buildings, etc. The effect of this was to induce a number of credulous people to sell off their homesteads, and seek their fortune in this new El Dorado. Extending up the Muscleshell River are to be found the decaying houses and rotten stakes of claims, long since abandoned by the deluded victims.

I confess, when I think of the enormous lies promulgated by paid advocates of the Northern Pacific Railroad Company, who describe the land as "a scene of never-ending beauty," etc., I am constrained in charity to ascribe this, not to a deliberate desire to falsify, but to the poetic tendency of the times. . . .

Let me give, for the benefit of farmers thinking of immigrating here, another hard fact—the official record of the rain-fall at Fort A. Lincoln for the following months of this year: May, 0.45 inches; June, 0.97 inches; July, 0.14 inches; August, 1.28 inches. Total, 2.79 inches.

The following gives you an idea of the hay difficulty: . . .

At Fort A. Lincoln, where the government contracted for about 3,000 tons, at an average price of $9.75 per ton, the contractor has been able to furnish but 106 tons, and has abandoned his contract, and the government is purchasing from private individuals, in open market, in such quantities as can be picked up, at about $14, and it is thought that the quality required can not be had at a less price than $15 per ton. The chief part of the hay has been brought by steamer, a distance of about fifty-five miles by water and thirty-five by land. There has been perhaps about 2,000 tons of hay cut within a distance of fifteen miles from Fort Lincoln, in small lots, at points widely separated. It was cut by a great number of parties, who gleaned it out of ravines, cooleys, etc., and it will probably be all required to supply the wants of Bismarck. . . .

At Heart river and Apple creek, there was considerable hay cut; but a large part of the hay gathered at the former place has been condemned, on account of its being so mixed with weeds and sage as to be unfit for use, and at the latter, the hay obtained will share the fate of the Heart River hay, unless the necessities of the government compel its acceptance.

At Fort Stevenson, the government contracted for about 400 tons of hay, at an average price of about $8 per ton, which is not as yet supplied, and the hay which is now being furnished is badly injured by frost, and would not, I presume, be accepted, if good hay could be obtained anywhere in the vicinity. A great part of the hay cut for that post, was cut by hand, in small lots, gleaned out of ravines. The contract will probably be filled.

At Fort Berthold, the contractor, after "hard scratching," managed to complete his contract for 150 tons; but it had to be gathered principally about twenty-five miles from the agency, and had to be cut in small patches at increased cost, by the employment of extra labor and additional time. The price paid by the government was $15 per ton.

Owing to the extreme dryness of this climate and the scanty rainfall, the hay crop, like all other crops in the country, will be always precarious and uncertain.

Yours respectfully,

——— ———

General Custer—His Power of Observation and Description

In order that the reader of General Custer's descriptions of this country may understand them, it is well to compare his statements by the side of other writers who were with him at the time.

I will quote the following description given by him of a portion of the country toward the Black Hills. It is written of a place twelve miles before reaching the line of Montana:

"After the second day from Lincoln, we marched over a beautiful country; the grazing was excellent and abundant for our wants, and water in great plenty every ten miles. When we struck the tributaries of Grand River, we entered a less desirable country, the streams being alkaline, but we found a plentiful supply of grass, wood and water. Upon leaving the head waters of Grand River, we ascended a plateau separating the water of the two Missouris, and found a country of surpassing beauty and richness of soil; timber abundant, and water both good and plentiful."

This is a fair example of all the Black Hills compositions of

General Custer, and gives to the uninformed reader the impression of at least a fair country.

Eight miles farther along on the journey, the correspondent of the St. Paul *Pioneer* writes to his paper, of the same part of the route and country, as follows:

"The country is sterile and drying up. We circled around knobs, marched and countermarched along ravines, halting in the burning sun, until glad at last to find shelter in our tents. . . . Sometimes, while delayed at crossing a treacherous alkaline flat, and while the sun smote us with its powerful heat, we have found a resting place 'in the shadow of a rock in a weary land.' Such a rest and such a shadow! Oh, how grateful and thankfully enjoyed!"

No one can properly appreciate the full meaning of these last sentences who has not had a similar experience on the furnace-like plains of Texas and New Mexico.

"When the wind blows hard, the fine dust and alkali is lifted and mingled with the air; is painfully irritating to the eyes, and chapping to the skin. All the next day, we travelled over the poor cactusy alkaline flats, crossing a number of dry channels, finding no water except in stagnant pools. Hills, from 150 to 200 feet high, are standing here and there, and their bald, weather-beaten sides only add to the dreariness of the scene. Travelling through such a country as this, with the thermometer at a hundred in the shade, takes the enthusiasm out of a neophyte. . . .

"The next day brought us across the territorial line into Montana. The first nine miles, the country grew no better, but rather worse—the same barren flats and naked hills. Just before reaching our present station, we climbed a long hill, out of the bad land bottoms, and reached a beautiful plain. Except for the lack of timber, it can hardly be excelled anywhere."

From this point on to the Black Hills, the New York *Tribune* correspondent says:

"The expedition moved in a southwest direction, until it reached the valley of the Little Missouri. . . . This valley was almost destitute of grass, and we left it in search of a better camping ground, marching over thirty miles, and found a dry camp. From the Little

Missouri to the Belle Fourche, the country was generally barren and uninviting."

Here they met the rains of August, so copious in all the West at that time, and found good grass and water, and it was here they commenced entering the Black Hills, where were found beautiful valleys, some good timber, flowing streams, and the enchanting scenery which forms such a striking feature of all that interior region vaguely known as the Rocky Mountains. With these most marked exceptions, which may be found in all the Territories, the description given by these two correspondents, here and previously in this paper, will apply very accurately to this great interior region three seasons out of four, as the writer can affirm from personal experience. Arid and fruitless as it is, it does not approach the extreme barrenness of much of the country between the Rocky and Sierra Nevada Mountains. As we ascend to the higher altitudes of these mountains, the rains increase proportionately. It is not uncommon, in these lower regions, to see aerial showers of rain, when not a drop reaches the earth, it all being absorbed in the more dense atmosphere near the earth's surface. These correspondents also state that for 155 miles before reaching the Black Hills, there was no running water.

There is no discrepancy in these accounts, although conveying widely different impressions. Let us not do this enterprising officer injustice. General Custer is full of enthusiasm. At every ten miles he finds wood, water and grass in abundance. But abundance to him is abundance for his military command two or three times a day. Everything is beautiful to him so long as his command is well and prospering in the journey for which he is responsible, and which absorbs his thoughts. He knows that thousands of people in every part of the land are watching with a kind and hearty interest the success of his expedition, and he has succeeded in carrying into his reports his own wishes and feelings. On the whole, the newspaper correspondent describes things as he sees them. The correspondents on this expedition evidently had already lost whatever enthusiasm they may have set forth with. Having no personal interest but to report correctly for their papers, they write with unbiased minds and report those more general characteristics of the country which first impress the civilian. They found a parched country, without running water, wood, or grass, excepting in very small quantities, with cactus, alkali, and stagnant pools all the way to the Black Hills and back. At the Black Hills they found the usual interesting features of all mountainous regions.

Where General Custer saw plenty of water, the correspondents noticed it was stagnant, and for 155 miles they saw not a drop of it running. Where the General saw grass in abundance for his stock, the citizens noticed the country was all dried up, and the good grass only in occasional patches; and where the commander saw wood for fuel, the others noticed that it grew scraggily and sparsely, and only near the water.

I have noticed this with no unkind intent to General Custer, whom I genuinely admire, but merely to show how necessary it is to know men and understand their peculiar tendencies and their standpoint of observation in order to properly interpret their writings. Enthusiasm is a most admirable trait when properly directed, but it often deals with colors so bright that facts are transformed into fiction.

To better illustrate the truth of this remark, on the return of the Black Hills expedition, General Custer made a statement to a reporter about the gold discoveries. He said:

"The reports are not exaggerated in the least, but prospects are even better than represented. . . . The product of one pan of earth was laid on my table which was worth not less than two dollars. . . . The scientific gentlemen are satisfied that far richer discoveries will be made."

And of the agricultural characteristics:

"Too much can not be said in favor of the agricultural worth of the Black Hills."

To all this, Professor Winchell, the chief *savant* of the expedition has already spoken, alleging that his conscience will not permit him to keep silent. He says that the country is not fruitful, and there is no evidence of rich mines. Colonel Grant also says:

"All the good land in the Black Hills will not make more than twelve good farms."

No one believes that these gentlemen have uttered what they believed untrue.

The expedition was understood and always mentioned out here as the "Custer gold-hunting expedition." The search for gold was believed by many persons to be its sole purpose. The belief that gold existed in the Black Hills was pretty general before the expedition started, so that the report of discoveries was fully anticipated before it was made, and, so far as I know, no one's opinion was influenced by that report. The miners of the expedition were shopkeepers of Bismarck, who expected to mine their gold, not in the Black Hills, but in their shops when miners came that way. It is evident from the diversity of opinion which has been quoted about the Black Hills affair, that there was no positive data which could justify the belief that these lands were arable, or concealed the mines of Golconda.

Some Other Letter-Writers

According to the report of his interviewer, General Rosser states that I am discussing a subject I have not taken the pains to inform myself upon. He sharply attempts to refute my statements with regard to lack of rains. He says within a range of five miles of Lincoln 2,500 tons of hay were cut and cured at $4 a ton. Let the reader refer to the history of the hay-gathering at Lincoln this season, given in another place in this paper. He also refers to an interviewer who was at Minneapolis, and points to the fine farms along the line of the road, as a refutation of what I had said of the country. General Rosser could hardly help knowing when he uttered this, as does every person in this part of the country, that there was not then, as there is not now, a farm along the N. P. R. R. between the Red River valley and the Rocky Mountains, nor is there a farm at any place in this entire section of the country,[11] the few Indian fields at Berthold being the nearest approach to it.

[11] General Hazen failed to mention that the Sioux Indians were responsible for much of this lack of settlement.

Some farming was attempted at Bismarck this season, but it has failed, as may be seen by evidence given elsewhere in this paper.

The letter of Major McGinnis, delegate from Montana, written in answer to my *Tribune* letter, does not appear to require notice.

The very gentlemanly letter of my esteemed friend, J. Milner (*sic*) Roberts, has certainly impressed me kindly. I think, however, he should carefully review his estimates, if he expects to support a Pacific railroad upon the business of a sparsely settled pastoral community, the lignite of Montana, or the timber of Washington.[12] His estimates of the value of Dakota as an agricultural country, that "not more than one-tenth or one-twelfth is unsuitable for farming," is entirely erroneous. In this connection, I respectfully refer to the letter of General Sully, whose opportunities for judging are very much superior to any Mr. Roberts could have had.

Opportunities for Knowing the Country

Mr. Roberts also claims that I am not familiar with this subject, and have never seen the country. I will state that I have served six years at different times, commencing in 1855, along and near the line of this road, in every State and Territory it touches. For eight years longer I have been on duty in other portions of this interior country having similar characteristics.

In addition to this, I have observed it closely, its atmospheric changes, and have experimented with its soils. I have seen every imaginable effort made to raise crops in its barren earth. I have availed myself of whatever statistics there are bearing upon this subject that the facilities of the country afford, and they are very numerous; and I claim that my knowledge of its value and general characteristics is to be relied upon, even though my feet have not trod upon every acre of its wide extent.

Since Mr. Roberts mentions the death of General Stevens as having taken place on the line of the N. P. road, giving the impression that he was a martyr to its interests, I will simply make this correction. The gallant and lamented Major-General Isaac I.

12 The success of the Northern Pacific is the best refutation of this argument.

Stevens, the pioneer explorer was killed in the war while leading his command at Fort Wagner, Charleston Harbor. [See page 73.]

The Very Limited Volume of Running Water

It is well established by tradition that ever since this country has been known, it has been dry and unfruitful. Professor Blodgett says of it, page 747, U.S. Meteorological Reports:

"There is known to be great deficiency of rain, and a large portion of that great area inclosed partially by the long curve of the Missouri river is set down as an arid and uncultivable district by explorers. Its amount of drainage is too small to permit the supposition that it is otherwise, as all the tributaries of the Missouri below Powder River are small and comparatively unimportant streams, belonging to that class of shoal rivers of the plains, falling off to a very small volume in summer."

Lewis and Clark, as well as later explorers, make particular mention of these facts.

So remarkably true is this, that in coming from the James River to this post, in the month of August of this year, via Bismarck, a distance of 325 miles, I crossed but three running streams, and each of these could be spanned by a single step dry shod. The Black Hills Expedition at the same time saw no running water on the other side of the river for 155 miles. At least half of that was so alkaline as to render it unfit for irrigation, and if all of the remainder on the route I travelled had been gathered into one ditch and used for irrigation, it would not suffice for the cultivation of a space of ground to exceed one-half mile in breadth.

As has been said, there was comparatively no running water found on the Black Hills expedition, while the officers with the Northern Boundary Commission say there is comparatively no water in that country. The Milk River, the most considerable northern tributary of the Upper Missouri above the State of Iowa, has no water in its bed after ascending fifty miles from its mouth. The officers of the Boundary Commission expedition further report that for fourteen degrees of longitude along the international boundary there was no running water.

165

Here we have distinct accounts of what a thousand miles of this country, in various directions from Bismarck, which report comparatively no water, while it is reported by Professor Blodgett, and is well known from other sources, that, excepting the Yellowstone, the Upper Missouri has no tributaries that yield more than a mere rivulet of water in the summer season. Now, it is a well-recognized fact that, where the summer rains are so inconsiderable as to make no streams, there can be no general agriculture, and of course no water for irrigation. This example of a river without tributaries is only equalled by the Nile which, for 1,500 miles, has no tributary at all. Compare these instances with the thousands of running streams one crosses in passing over the less distance from Boston to Omaha, and one can form a vague idea of the remarkable drouth of this country. The Missouri, unlike the Nile, from the great fluctuations of high and low water and high hillsides, is not available, even for its narrow valley.

Extreme Drouth

This fact of drouth is shown not only by the traditions of the country, but by exact measurements, which, although they extend back but eight years, are associated with other like measurements extending back fifty years, which prove that by taking the mean of eight consecutive years of rain-fall anywhere in these countries, we get a practically true expression of the rain-fall of that section. With all these facts, so potent and perfectly established, we still find many men preferring the evidence of the past two years to that of fifty, because it is what they wish to believe.

Something can not come from nothing. The rains are not created to order in the midst of these plains, but are evaporation from the oceans. The Sierras shut off what would come from the Pacific, as the atmosphere that is rare enough to pass over them is not dense enough to carry much water, while that coming from the Atlantic is well-nigh precipitated before it reaches the 100th meridian. The rain-fall over this interior region has been measured, and it is insufficient for agriculture; and, unless Heaven provides the rains in some other way than by nature's present laws, the American farmer will not take up his residence here for a long time to come.

The readers of the New York *Tribune* can not have failed to notice the very interesting letters of its Greeley (Colorado) correspondent, Mr. Meeker. He describes how they have already reached the limit of water that can be used for irrigation, what a very insignificant portion of the land it irrigates, and how utterly impossible it is to raise trees, gardens, and grains without irrigation. Now, by referring to the rain-charts of this country, prepared by Professor Blodgett, it will be seen that in this portion of Dakota we have five inches less annual rain-fall than in Colorado, agreeing with our recorded reports, while they have the advantage of the proximity of the mountain belts that always furnish limited but unfailing streams.

We have seen by our tables, that in eight years there have been two, and perhaps three seasons, when farming might have been carried on in favorable locations, and five with a rain-fall like the present year, that will not permit of agriculture. And this, judging from the unchangeableness of natural laws, will be true in the future. In Michigan and Wisconsin, where the fire-scourge treats them so harshly, they have a rain-fall of thirty inches per annum, and in Iowa, Illinois, Indiana, Ohio and New York, thirty-five and forty inches; while in the more southern States, fifty inches. (See U.S. Meteorological Report.) Yet in these states it is seldom that there is too much rain. Notice the marked difference between these States and the desert, where, during five years out of the last eight, there has been but nine and one-half inches per annum. To describe the present year, is to describe them all, except the exceptionally wet ones. The diary of a single season, the impressions of a voyager who comes and is gone in a day, or the success of a single kitchen-garden, or the temporary growth of a few shade-trees— these incidents taken by themselves, and not in connection with like experiments in other seasons, can have but little value in weighing this question. It is a problem that can not be demonstrated with mathematical completeness, and can be dealt with only by taking from the greatest number of examples the prevailing characteristics. In this manner we get probabilities amounting almost to certainties.

The prairies of Illinois can not be compared with these of the far distant West, for they are visited with abundant rains, and the trees were kept down by fires. But even the destitution of this neighborhood is made plenteous by comparison, for we have reports come up to us from far off El Paso, the other end of this same barren, rainless region, that they have not had a drop of rain for 365 days.

General Custer's Observations

The "personal observations" of this country by General Custer, at the time he wrote his letter, were confined to a single season, the summer of 1873, which had the greatest rain-fall ever recorded in the country, and about two and a half times as much as the average of 1867–1871 and 1874. Much of the soil being good, only lacking moisture, the rains of 1873 produced the same results as they would anywhere else. General Custer saw this, as did many others, and accurately described it. He could have seen one or, at the most, two other like seasons in Western Dakota in eight years. In Ohio, once in six or seven years, we have a drouth so great that the grasses die, and the meadows have to be newly seeded. To judge by one such example would be as good evidence that Ohio is a worthless country, as the experience of one year is that this is a good one. I will now take extracts from my own journal, for the same period this season, while coming from Fargo to Fort Buford, D.T., a distance of 425 miles—about as great a tract of land as the route observed by General Custer last year:

"*August* 3. Left Fargo today at 8 A.M. travelling over two hundred miles. At Fargo, meridian 96°20′, the vegetation is rank, crops abundant and good, about one-tenth injured by grasshoppers. The whole Red River valley is a dense meadow, with grass waist high. The people claim to have had showers every second day all the season, and vegetation justifies the statement. After coming westward sixty miles the grasses were shorter, and less rains for the summer were apparent. Continuing on to the James

168

River, one hundred miles, about meridian 98½°, we found that stream a mere rivulet, the grass crisp and short, the country dried, and the people complained of no rains. The gardens about the station and military post were badly parched and pronounced failures. Passing on to Crystal Springs, some thirty miles, the country continued parched, the grasses not more than one and a half inches high, and burned brown by the sun. Here was a small patch of about two acres plowed and planted, partly in a little valley, and the remainder on a low bluff. After passing half-way up the bluff, there was no longer any green thing visible. In the valley, the land gave promise to yield very little except potatoes. From this on to Bismarck, meridian 101°, it continues crisp and brown, without any running water, Apple Creek, even, standing in stagnant pools. The patches about this place, where cultivation has been attempted, present a sickly, parched appearance, as if they would produce about a tenth of a crop, the people claiming it to be the work of grasshoppers; but they only preceded the drouth by a week. Looking through the town, I find but one shop where vegetables can be had, and these, poor and sickly, have been brought from the Red River, more than two hundred miles."

Proceeding by land to this post—Fort Buford—225 miles, there was one uninterrupted succession of brown, and sometimes yellow, earthen-colored hills. When approaching Bismarck, and some twelve miles from it, we saw haying-parties in the narrow ravines. But there was no hay that could be cut in the valley of Apple Creek, and I was told that there was none on Hart [*sic*] River. The grass was, in fact, as short in these narrow valleys as on the hills. After leaving the town, there were seen, at intervals of five or six miles, parties gathering hay for many miles up and down ravines so narrow, that often one or two swaths with the scythe would cut it all. There was no more bottom land where hay could be cut for twenty-five miles. At this distance, near the Missouri River, there were a thousand acres. It was in a basin, where the spring rains gather and keep the soil wet a long time. Here a large party were cutting hay. They will gather about four hundred tons, and hold it at starvation prices. There was no more grass that would do for cutting until we arrived within six miles of Fort Stevenson, where, by meandering up the narrow valleys of Snake Creek, from three to twenty yards wide, and some twelve miles long, hay is found. Some three hundred tons only were cut there. No other hay grounds of importance were found for a hundred and thirty miles, until we reached the Buford hay-party, twenty miles from the post. During this entire distance of 325 miles, after crossing the 100° meridian, I only crossed four running streams, and they were so small that a single step would span them. The difference of the two seasons, '73 and '74, was most plainly shown by the growth of the grass. The grass of last season had been burned off, leaving only the stalks, too green to be consumed. These scattering stalks were standing two feet high all over the country, while the present year's growth was but from one to two inches, and both equally dry and crisp. Like this have been five of the last eight years, as may be seen by extracts from meteorological reports.

From the 15th of May to the 1st of August there were no rains in useful quantities in this section of the country. This has prevented the growth of grass for hay, except in a few low places, and has made the raising of all small grains and early vegetables an entire failure. The grasshoppers about Bismarck consumed the early vegetation; but they only destroyed what the drouth would have done a few years later, and what it did do where the grasshoppers did not appear.

General Custer's Statement upon the Hay Supply

My statement, that, in 1872, the small amount of hay required at this post compelled the contractor to search over an area of the country embracing twelve hundred square miles, met with general contradictions. From General Custer came the courteous and confident criticism, that he had "made careful inquiries of parties acquainted with the resources in this respect, and am convinced that hay in sufficient quantities to satisfy all probable demands (about 5000 tons), of excellent quality, can be contracted for in the stack at a price not exceeding four dollars a ton." The reader may judge as to the facts about hay by referring to the statement and letters bearing upon this subject for the present year, already given in these pages.

Let me record the results of the united efforts of men and nature in this vicinity in the way of vegetable growth. The grasses commenced growing about the twenty-fifth of April; but by May 15th, when about two inches high, it had already been checked by the drouth, nor did it grow more until the first of August, during which period there were practically no rains. At this time, and during the whole month of August, rains were ample, and the grass started up anew, giving the whole country the appearance of spring. But the cereals and many of the vegetables had perished. The experiments at farming had failed. Potatoes, however, and turnips, beets, cabbages, tomatoes, carrots—the root crop generally, and native Indian corn, came on finely, until, on the night of September 13th, a severe frost cut everything down. These late vegetables, here mentioned, with a few tomatoes which had commenced to turn, will be about a fourth of a crop. This is the third year we have tried to raise garden-truck, and this is our greatest success. In these notes of garden cultivation it may be said that melons have never ripened, though growing well. Occasionally there is found a hill of potatoes or a head of cabbage of remarkable growth and perfection; and these are the examples it has been the habit to exhibit at agricultural fairs in different parts of the country.

General Custer's Experiences

Among "General Custer's Experiences" is recorded one of a nap in the open air. This incident, common in a tropical climate, is mentioned by this officer to show that this really is a "banana region" as has been claimed. There is nothing at all improbable in that narration. And in the possibility of this nap out of doors, we have the very worst feature of the country—that is, its great and speedy changes of temperature; for the guide and interpreter of Fort Lincoln, who was with the General when he took that ground-nap, says: "If he had tried it next day, he would have told a different story." The thermometer in this section is known to

171

have varied seventy degrees in twelve hours. During the year it varies 150°; and from thirty to fifty days of the winter it is below zero, reaching as low as 45°. General Custer says the troops who were frozen were not properly clad. It might as well be said that all the people who lost their lives in the storm in Minnesota, in the winter of 1872, were carelessly or improperly clad. The troops are better and more warmly clad than citizens generally; but no people in ordinary life are prepared for such serious and sudden changes. For a complete confirmation of all I have said about the extreme cold of winter in this country, read Lewis and Clarke's narrative of the winter of 1804–5, which they passed at Fort Mandan, at a point about fifty miles above Fort Lincoln. The mercury that winter was as low as 45 degrees. The winter of 1873–4 was the mildest known here for many years.

Unfounded Rumors

By "unfounded rumors," it is presumed, is meant my own sources of knowledge of the country. As I have said elsewhere, I have passed six years of military service along this proposed line of road, in every State and Territory it touches. I have drawn my facts largely from the archives of the government, from the official reports of its officers, from its recorded tables of the rain-fall extending over a period of fifty years, from the reports of explorers from Lewis and Clarke down, and last of all, the report already given of the veteran General Sully, and many other well-known officers of the army, and citizens of known reliability. Such testimony is not usually classed as "unfounded rumor."

Every intelligent man in the country knows that there is not a farm between the valley of the Red river and the Rocky Mountains. The little patches about Bismarck, which have failed so signally this season, can not be counted as farms. With the exception of an occasional wet season, like that of 1873, there has never been raised in this country either wheat, American corn, oats, or vegetables, except a few kinds. Some potatoes, other roots, and a little native Indian corn will be raised this year, as they probably can be in favorable spots every year; but no small grains, to any extent, of any kind. The growth of fruit has never been tried.

Views of Other Persons

General Custer, in a vague way, says that the officers who were with him on the Yellowstone expedition, were prepared to substantiate his expressed views of that country. The voluntary statements of very many of them, whom I have met incidentally since that time, fail to confirm his views, but quite to the contrary, oppose them. General Custer can have no doubt of the opposite opinions of the *Tribune* correspondent, who was with him, for that clear-sighted gentleman expressed himself unequivocally.

Captain Charles E. Clarke, of the 17th Infantry,[13] a brother of Grace Greenwood,[14] and a most estimable man, who has been stationed in this country, near Fort Lincoln, several years longer than either General Custer or myself, informs me that although the military posts in this vicinity have tried to make gardens each year in the country, yet they have never succeeded, except in the two years of 1872 and 1873.

Grains, vegetables, and, I have no doubt, fruits grow luxuriantly in the narrow valleys of Montana, west of the mountains. No one has tried them east of the mountains in that Territory.

Military Meaning of Terms

As has been before remarked, the reader should not misunderstand what a military man means by plenty of grass, wood and water. In 1866 I went across the country with my own teams, with a guard of twenty-five men, leaving Omaha in July, and arriving at Sacramento, California, in November, travelling by the way of Wyoming, Montana, Idaho, Utah and Nevada.[15] In all that

[13] The Seventeenth Infantry spent many years in frontier garrison duty in Minnesota and the Dakotas.

[14] Grace Greenwood. This was the pen name of Sara Jane Clarke Lippincott, a popular writer of the day.

[15] It was on this trip that he made his inspection of Fort Phil Kearny and the other posts on the Bozeman Trail.

time I passed but one night without an "abundance of wood, grass, and water"—that is, for my military needs; yet I reported to the government, on my return as follows:

Report Crossing the Country

"For about two hundred miles after leaving Omaha, the soil of the Platte River is highly productive. At about that point, the soil begins to become weak and thin. The atmosphere is dry, and continues so all the way to the divide of the Rocky Mountains, and to the west of them in Montana, Idaho and Utah. Of this entire country, one-half may be considered of no value. Of the other half, it is worth about one-tenth as much for pastoral purposes as good grazing land in the Northern States, and of this last half, one acre in a thousand can be made abundantly productive by irrigation, and in no other way. These last points are to be found near springs under mountains, or on the immediate borders of Sun, Jefferson, Madison, Gallatin, and a few other streams, and at the western foot of the Wasatch mountains, now occupied by the Mormons. Three-fourths of the country passed over is mountain, the sides of a small proportion being covered with pine, and the streams bordered with cottonwood. Whatever mineral wealth the country contains, can only be known when developed. The precious metals, as now produced, are damaging to the country at large, as they divert much more capital and labor than finds profitable employment. The country has little value, and can only be sold by the government at nominal rates, and insufficient to pay the cost of surveying. It will in time be settled by a thinly scattered pastoral population. No amount of railroads, schemes of colonization, or government encouragement, can make more of it.

"As to the troops on the Upper Missouri, I am of the opinion that the posts should all be broken up. They are very remote, and supplied at great expense. They give little protection to the navigation of the river, and can never form nuclei of colonization, because of the utter poverty of the country. Then, if detachments of a few companies were sent up the river with the earliest navigation, to return with the latest, I would consider the river much more advantageously occupied than at present, besides releasing large numbers of troops for more active operations.

"By reason of the great number of small posts, more than half the military force is exhausted in taking care of them." Ex. Doc. No. 45, 39th Congress, 2d Session.

In the journey above referred to, my route was across the country and water-courses, not threading up the course of the stream, thus making my facilties the best possible for becoming familiar with the character of the land.

In crossing the region of country from the Big Horn River to Fort Benton, it carried me over the proposed route of the Northern Pacific R. R., about ten miles below the mouth of Prior's Fork. "I found the right valley of the Yellowstone about two miles broad, the mile farthest from the river being rather high and covered with sage. Then came a strip of good grass, and near the water a fine growth of cottonwood, the best I ever saw. Sometimes the grass and then the wood strip would occupy the greater part of the lower bank near the river. On the left bank we came at once to a clayey side hill with no vegetation of any kind. The different character of the banks, as above given, often shifted from side to side in passing along the river. We reached the Muscleshell, a distance of forty-five miles in a day and a half, finding water in but one place on our route, and that was strongly impregnated with the urine of the buffalo. The country was dried up, and the Muscleshell, as well as the Yellowwater, one of its main branches, were stationary bodies of water, about knee deep. The waters were of a whitish, stagnant appearance, bordered by an extremely meager soil, with quite a breadth of a poor sort of second-growth cottonwood. We had no grain at all for our animals, yet we found grass to take us through to Benton."

I have spent nearly all the eight intervening years in this interior country, and it has all tended to strengthen my opinion then formed, and I believe my report not exaggerated.

Lewis and Clarke's Narrative

Lewis and Clarke, in their narrative, Vol. 1, p. 253, writing from the Falls of the Missouri, say: "The country exhibits its usual appearances, the timber being confined to the river; while back from it, on both sides, as far as the eye can reach, it is entirely destitute of trees and bushes." Excepting some mountainous tracts, this remark can, in general terms, be applied to all this great interior country. And on page 316, it again says, at the head waters of the Jefferson: "From the top of this eminence I could discover but three trees in this whole country." They confirm, as far as their observations gave them the opportunity, all I have said about the cold of winter, the character and narrow dimensions of the Missouri valley, and also of the rain-fall. On pages 171 and 207, it will be seen that they had only one shower of rain from October 15, 1804, until May 28, 1805. Their narrative states particularly the almost total absence of timber, except on the mountains, until they reached the Sierra Nevada or Cascade range.

In passing on from the Missouri to the Sierras, they repeat the same story of alternating heat, cold, mountainous, timberless country, with wild sage, cactus, briars, drouth, alkali and utter barrenness. To this are made a few notable exceptions, the principal being the valley of the Koos-koos-kie.

All persons having an interest in this region should read the record of this remarkable expedition. It was written with no other intent than to convey exact information, fifty years before any other interest was dreamed of, and, with some few inaccuracies, is the most complete and truthful account of the general features and character of this region in print.

Need for Correct Information of This Country

It is of vast importance that the true character of this country be made known. Every wet season, like the last two, brings great numbers of immigrants west of the productive line, who finally have to return with great loss and discouragement, as has been seen in Kansas during the present season. It is not strange that the steadily moving wave of immigration, which has gone westward uninterruptedly for a hundred years, should have gathered an impetus that is now carrying it beyond the line of productiveness; but it has reached its outposts, and should be warned to halt, and not encouraged to go farther.

Bad Lands

During this discussion I have made no reference to what is technically called "bad lands," which comprise a large extent of the Upper Missouri country. This region is deeply cut by the rains, forming a continuation of clayey hills and ravines. It is merely a sloping cross section of the drift of this region, worn by the winds and rains into barren mounds of all shapes, along these cuts made by the water. By going up the ravines a mile or two, you invariably gain the table-lands. By substituting rocks for clay, we find large stretches of this kind of country in every Territory of the West. It has nothing whatever to do with the rain-fall, however, which controls this question of agriculture.

Isothermal Lines

The isothermal lines upon the maps of Professor Blodgett and Captain Maury are correctly placed. I was led to pronounce them wrong, by supposing the Northern Pacific had used them. But a closer examination of the large map, compiled by the N. P. R. R. in 1871, reveals the fact that they have placed their lines of the same temperature three degrees farther north than Blodgett. By suppressing the annual winter, spring, and autumn, using only the isothermal of the three summer months, they show a summer isothermal of 70° at the intersection of the 104° meridian west longitude, with the 51° north latitude while Blodgett puts the same line at 104° and 48°. By using only the summer isothermals, they show at this point a reading of only 70° Fahrenheit while the annual isothermal of this point is 35° only. Upon scanning this map, unless one is especially familiar with these lines, he at once takes them for annual lines, such being the lines expected to be found, but called summer from their summer temperature. Whether so intended, they are well calculated to mislead.

On their large map, very conspicuously placed, will also be

177

noticed the latitude of Paris, London, Hamburg, and Stockholm, as if to say, "See in what latitudes these great and wealthy people live." By examining the isothermals of Baron Von Humboldt and Professor Dove, it will be seen that the annual isothermals of Northern Europe, from 14° to 50° Fahrenheit, are all of them, in their range across North America, deflected southward from 13° to 18° of latitude. This is true, notwithstanding the line of excessive summer heat extending north and south, between 95° and 115° of west longitude, in our western country, caused by atmospheric condensation.

For the past three years, and on some days in every month of each year except those of June, July, and August, the number of days the thermometer has fallen below 32° has been respectively 208, 208, 206.

Wintering American Stock

The statement that American stock does well in winter without other food than what nature provides, unaided by the care of man, so prominently noticed by General Custer as one of the valuable features of the country, is a deception, as has always been such a report. I have sought for this locality so often told about, during these nineteen years, and although I have been at all the places mentioned, at none of them can stock be safely wintered out of doors. American stock will live under favorable circumstances, and in exceptionally mild winters, in this and in nearly all the Territories; but what wintering! Every few years a storm will come that kills the greater part of the stock, while its quality constantly deteriorates, as seen in Texas, which may be considered partially exceptional to this statement.

Tree Culture

General Custer has given an account of his success in tree culture during the past season, at Lincoln. Six hundred and twenty-seven cottonwood trees have been transplanted there, away from the river. Of these, it is true only eighty have died; but except in the very rainy summer of 1873, water has been constantly hauled from the Missouri River to irrigate them, and so long as this is done, the example is of no value, while the fact that this is necessary fully contradicts the theory that trees will grow on these plains. Across the Missouri at Bismarck, nine-tenths of the transplanted trees are dead. In the yard of Mr. Jno. Mason, who kindly invited me to inspect for myself, were forty-eight cottonwood trees. But one had green leaves, although he claimed vitality in five. Of twenty evergreens, all were dead. Of a dozen apple-trees, nearly all had green leaves, but showed no signs of growth; and of a promiscuous lot of other native trees, all were dead.

The fact has been published that the St. Paul and Pacific Railroad Company have succeeded well in tree culture along their road. This entire road, however, is several hundred miles to the east of the hundredth meridian, where the rain-fall is ample.

Publication of General Custer's Letter, and Reference to Its Statements

The time and place of publication of General Custer's letter led many to believe it was written in the immediate interests of the Northern Pacific Railroad. In order that the whole question should be clearly understood, let me recapitulate. General Custer indulges in a vein of personality, not called for by my letter, nor by ingenuous argument. Its statements, based upon the agricultural growth of last year, although true of that year, are none of them, except with late garden vegetables, true of this year, and were not true of but two of the last eight years. It gave the world the example of the most anomalously wet season we have any accurate record of, as an average season by which the country could be judged.

It told what hay could be bought for at Lincoln—the fallacy of its intended argument being shown by their experience at that post the present year. It gave examples of gardens last year, where they have failed this year. It gave the success in tree-raising at Lincoln last year, when they were kept alive this year only by constantly hauling water to them. He says "the best lands of the

Northern Pacific are east of the Missouri River." General Sully answers his statement with regard to these lands.

He speaks of my ingenuousness in writing from a point away from the line of the railroad. He means it to be understood by the reader that I was pretending to write from some point on the road itself. Had he looked upon the rain-charts he would have seen that the rain-fall of the two places is identical, and would also have seen that the isothermal lines passing near Buford, pass southeastwardly from here, crossing the Northern Pacific near Lincoln, and turning eastward, keep to the south of that road, until they pass beyond its eastern terminus; and practically what is true here, is also true of all the section of country lying along the line of the road in Dakota. (See New York *Tribune* correspondent's letter.)

He has drawn from Professor Hayden's Reports of Montana, but fails to find in it anything contradictory to my own statement. The pasture-lands here described are not agricultural lands, and Professor Hayden always associates irrigation with agriculture.

In all this it is difficult to see where General Custer's opportunities for knowing this country, as claimed by a portion of the Western press, were better than my own, or wherein he has refuted what so many others besides myself have asserted. He has said much in contradiction, and nothing in disproof.

Conclusion

No country is known to be valuable, agriculturally, until it has proven itself to be so. This region in dispute has not given such evidence, for there is not, nor has there been, a farm, in the proper sense of the word, between the Red River valley and the Rocky Mountains.

This country has only one-third of the rain-fall that, on an average, falls upon the productive portions of the United States.

Five out of the eight last years, the gardens, and the small agriculture at the Indian agencies and military posts in this country, have failed. Farming this year, the only one that has ever been tried has failed.

The last year, the one upon which General Custer's arguments are founded, was the most productive year in this section of which we have any accurate knowledge. This season, while in the growing months of May, June, July and August, there fell in the Red River valley, meridian 96° and 97°, twelve inches of rain, there fell in Fort Lincoln, near the meridian 101°, but two and ninety-seven hundredths ($2^{97}/_{100}$) inches.

Professor Blodgett says, as does all tradition, that this Upper Missouri country is too dry for agriculture. Experience, in the majority of cases, still confirms it; meteorological measurements confirm it; the correspondents with the Black Hills expedition confirm it; and the boundary commission confirms it.

Excepting the Yellowstone, which rises in the great central snow mountains, as do the Missouri, Columbia, Colorado and Platte rivers, the Missouri has no feeders from the mouth of the Niobrara to the junction of the Gallatin, Jefferson and Madison, a distance of more than two thousand miles. In the drouth of summer it becomes standing pools or the merest rivulets. This of itself establishes the impossibility of general agriculture, for in this parched land there can be no irrigation.

The stories of the "Tropical Belt," the "Continental Wheat Garden," the "Attractive Country," and a "climate and soil that will produce in abundance *all* the cereals and fruits of the Atlantic States," are puerile inventions of the late witness, literary stockholder, and literary agent of the Northern Pacific, aided by other writers of the country, employed and volunteer. If this scheme is knocked as high as he found his literary venture would be, a great good will have been accomplished. These writings have been repeated as lectures, and, by the extravagant use of money, have been published as advertisements, as editorial matter, as pamphlets, charts, maps and books. They have been distributed by the car-load to every portion of the country. The sympathy and good-will of persons in high places have been sought and won in favor of this scheme.

A key to all is given in this quotation, which most readers will remember:

I come to you with a letter just mailed to Jay Cooke, advising him to secure your services as a platform speaker, to turn New England, Old England, or the great West upside down about our Northern Pacific.

(Signed) SAMUEL WILKINSON.

All this has been contrived and animated through the instrumentality of that great moral power, the *"Independent,"* for which services that leading Christian newspaper of the world was given previously unheard-of compensation.

The wonder is that, in the presence of so great a failure, that there should still be found those to give further aid to this scheme. Its originators made a most melancholy mistake in their estimate of this country. In the presence of all the facts, their scheme has been wicked beyond the power of words to express, for it successfully appealed to the poor, the lowly, the widow and the orphan, to loan their little hard-earned savings. This fraud was enacted with impressible artfulness, with high sounding promises, supported by the name of the national government. It was proclaimed with the pious pretenses of greater gains and surer pay than could be obtained from any other source.

Not the least of all these offenses was that of shameful waste, for of the vast sum of money which was spent, that part which went to build a railroad across an arid desert was as if thrown into the sea.

The Northern Pacific Railroad has taken up considerable space in these pages, because its partisans have continued to assert the value of these barren lands. But the truth, which can no longer be denied, is of far greater importance than the profit or loss from many railroads, serious as these interests may be.

There is a long line of territory, extending from the tropical heat of the Gulf of Mexico, in the south, to the regions of eternal ice in the north, where the tide of emigration must halt, or, passing over the barren lands, find homes on the shores of the Pacific.

Within the limits of that vast area of barren lands nature refuses to assist man in the cultivation of the ground. Year after year, with wonderful patience, industry, and endurance, the emi-

182

grant has struggled; and as one winter has followed another, cries of distress have gone forth to their brethren of the East and the West: "Give us bread, give us clothing, or we shall die."

In this region there are many years of famine, and none of plenty, so that provision for the future can never be made. Among the evils which visit it, is that of the plague of insects. Even to-day, as these words are written, there are many thousands of men, women, and children suffering from drouth and the devouring locusts. In their great poverty they ask the people of the productive states to send them help.

Their petition will not be made in vain; but it is time that one and all clearly understand the truth, that animal and vegetable life can not be sustained on these barren lands.

Hereafter, let emigration to these places known not to be arable, be emphatically discouraged. Happily, there is no need to go so far to find so little. All over the United States, from the Atlantic ocean to the one hundredth meridian, and on the shores of the Pacific, there is arable land sufficient to supply all the wants of our people for a long while to come.

W. B. Hazen

12. Arable Land in the Middle Region

The *North American Review* for January, 1875, carried an article by General Hazen entitled "The Great Middle Region of the United States, and Its Limited Space of Arable Land," which has received little attention especially when compared to the same author's pamphlet dealing with *Our Barren Lands*. But this article bears evidence that it was several years in the course of composition—in fact, internal evidence seems to indicate that it had been begun while he was still at Fort Hays—indicating that General Hazen had devoted considerable study to the subject of the territories west of the Missouri River, and that his letter to the New York *Tribune* was not written entirely on the spur of the moment. In February, 1874, William Tecumseh Sherman, General of the Army, had given Congress a detailed statement of the location of the various regiments of the army together with some information as to the nature of the country occupied by each, and since this was published in the *Army and Navy Journal*, General Hazen undoubtedly saw it and appears to have incorporated some of the material in his article, which would seem to have represented his mature and considered judgment on the subject.

The article must have been close to completion when Hazen's attention was directed to the article by Captain Maury (as he calls him) in *Harper's*. In a moment of excitement (and perhaps exasperation) General Hazen, drawing on his familiarity with the subject, wrote his letter to the New York *Tribune*. The reaction to this, especially Custer's letter, led to the pamphlet which was largely an answer to Custer, and which, despite its greater publicity, is not as well written nor as well thought out as the article. That the two publications were completed about the same time is indicated not only by the dates of publication but by the similarity of the argument in the latter part of the *North American Review* article to that in the pamphlet. General Hazen had a well-reasoned argument in the article, and it is regrettable that he did not develop it fully, allowing himself instead to be diverted into another controversy with George Armstrong Custer.

The Great Middle Region of the United States, and Its Limited Space of Arable Land

Of the value and capabilities of the great middle country between the Mississippi Valley and California much is said and little is known. If we are guided by our early school-atlases, we have an arid desert over the whole area. If we take as authority the published statements of corporations and individuals now possessing large interests in that section, we have one uninterrupted field of fruitfulness, capable of producing States like Pennsylvania, Illinois and Missouri. In either case we should be far from right, but the truth is somewhere between these extremes.

It would not be strange if, upon investigation, it were found that the popular estimate of this region is somewhat too high; for there is not an interest of any kind, nor the wish of one individual, that so immense a country, as large as thirty-seven States, should be a valueless waste. On the contrary forty millions of people hope and expect it will give homes to as many families, and add proportionately to our riches and greatness. At the same time the interest of railroad companies that it should be considered valuable land, are measured exactly by the number of millions of dollars for which it can be hypothecated. These interests have perceptibly acted upon the mind of the nation, and the fact has not yet dawned upon the people that the western limit of our agricultural land has already been reached by settlements along the frontier, from the Rio Grande to the 49th parallel of latitude.

There can be no fairer way to get at the general character of all this interior country than by accurate statistical data, and by traversing the entire distance to the Pacific Ocean at intervals of a few degrees. Then, if the traveller judges intelligently what he sees, and describes truthfully, his conclusion should be entitled to some consideration; above all, if his motives are to arrive at truth. Suppose a start is made from the general line along the eastern boundary of Texas, the Indian Territory, Kansas, Nebraska, and Dakota, commencing with the southernmost line,—say nearly along the 32d parallel of north latitude,—passing through Texas, New Mexico, and Arizona. This parallel nearly bisects the State of Texas, but the western portion of our southern boundary deflects so much northward as to make it necessary for our route to deflect also. In going westward through Texas, whether we start from the Sabine, from Galveston, or from Powder Horn, we find, until we reach the meridian of San Antonio, or about the 98th degree west from Greenwich, a region of plains and timber, well watered, a moist atmosphere, and sufficient rainfall, making a valuable agricultural country. For a hundred miles farther, or, in fact, until we come to the 100th meridian, all these features rapidly change, the soil becomes thin, the rainfall less; the streams dry up in summer, timber is more meagre, the grass shorter, and changes into *mesquite*, or buffalo-grass, and the surface becomes broken. The climate varies most singularly in different years. Two or three successive seasons of drought will be followed by as many of abundant rains. Nothing can surpass the fruitfulness and beauty of this section in seasons of plenty,—which has given rise to much beautiful but partial description,—nor its desolation in drought. In the third successive dry season the grass actually disappears altogether, and the earth cracks open in immense fissures. Great difficulty is then found in subsisting stock, and much actually perishes. The annular layers of the timber show this change of seasons to be the regular order there. In going beyond the 100th meridian, we pass at once into a dry, broken, and barren country, with very little timber, except thorny bushes, and, from lack of moisture, unfit for agriculture, excepting along the narrow mar-

186

gins of streams that can be irrigated. Continuing westward through the southern portion of the State, till we reach the Rio Grande at El Paso, we find a few springs, and but one stream, the Pecas [*sic*], that is not liable to go dry in summer; and even the Pecos is not available for irrigation, its waters being alkaline. The surface of Western Texas is covered scatteringly with bunch-grass, and some other varieties of grass, cactus, and some thorny shrubs. In the more northern portion of the State, on leaving the 100th meridian, we at once strike the foothills of the Staked Plains, which are high table-lands, altogether sterile, extending to the river Pecos in New Mexico. Out of these foothills spring numerous small streams, the sources of the Red, Brazos, and Colorado Rivers; nearly all these branches having narrow strips of good land which become broader and better timbered as the streams flow east. Blodgett says of this section: "On the upper plains of Texas, and over all the plains west of the 100th degree of longitude, irrigation is generally necessary to support cultivation which requires the summer for its growth" (page 745 of Report). All Western Texas, except the Staked Plains, is broken up with chains and spurs of rugged, barren hills and mountains, often terminating in high table-lands covered with scant grass, but neither timber nor water, except in holes where the rains have collected. The sides of some of the high mountains are fringed with pine timber. This same general character of country extends across New Mexico, except that the mountains are more regular, and there are a few fertile valleys of very limited extent. In Arizona it becomes still more mountainous, barren, and arid, but, in the extreme southern portion, adjoining Sonora, there is a strip, some fifty miles in breadth, of considerable fertility, in which Fort Buchanan[1] is situated, and where the rainfall is sufficient for limited agriculture without irrigation. This territory of two or three hundred miles in the western part is less mountainous, and has broader plains, but is without permanent water, except in a very few places, and is generally so

---

[1] Fort Buchanan, established in 1856, was twenty-five miles east of Tubac and on the route between Yuma and El Paso.

187

sterile that the travelled routes meander with the larger streams like the Gila, which, with a large number of smaller streams that rise in the great central chain of mountains and empty into the Colorado, has a narrow valley of varying breadth from a few yards to two miles, which can be irrigated, and all the remaining agricultural lands of Arizona are of this character. All these streams are gradually absorbed in the sands as soon as they leave the mountains, and most of them add but little water to the Colorado. Going westward, we cross this stream (which we find has a narrow valley, liable to be overflowed by the swift and changing current), and find ourselves in California, where for a hundred miles, or until we cross the range of mountains about twenty miles from the sea, there is a worthless, sterile plain, like that east of the Colorado. The last twenty miles of this route are moderately good, but very uncertain as agricultural country.

Again, taking a course along the general direction of the 35th parallel, which nearly bisects the Indian Territory, New Mexico, and Arizona, and crosses the southern portion of California, we find the eastern half of the Indian Territory, or that portion east of the meridian running through Fort Arbuckle,[2] to be well watered, with a reasonable amount of timber, a rich and productive soil, a varying surface, and many ranges of hills; about one half of the land is suitable for agriculture, and many of the river bottoms are of great richness. Farther west there are strips of scanty soil, less rainfall, and, after travelling seventy miles, the land susceptible of cultivation is confined to the valleys of the small streams. Going still farther, there is less and less good soil, until it disappears altogether on reaching the vicinity of the 100th meridian. In the northern portion of the Territory this aridity is sooner reached than in the southern part, where there are some very rich valleys, similar to those of Northern Texas before reaching the Staked Plains. The western half of the Indian Territory is too dry and barren to till, and continues so, with some few exceptions, until we reach the Rio Grande in New Mexico. On the river Pecos, at

[2] Near present Davis, Oklahoma, and a short distance north of the Texas line. It was built by Captain Randolph Marcy and was completed in 1851.

Fort Sumner, where the Navajo Indians were carried and kept for several years, the water of that stream was tried for irrigating purposes; but although the Indians are very industrious, and are irrigating farms at home, they failed here, on account of the strongly alkaline water of this stream. Farther south, round about Fort Stanton, there is a good deal of very fine and picturesque country. The Rio Grande runs through this Territory from north to south, a turbulent, rushing torrent. It has, for its whole length, a valley varying in width from a few yards to three miles, and where these broad valleys are found there is some farming by irrigation, and here and there are situated Mexican towns. The western part of the Territory comprises the land occupied by the Navajo and Zuna [*sic*] Indians; it is mountainous, with a few deep gorges, where the semi-primitive people carry on a simple farming and sheep-growing quite successfully.

The lands of any value whatever in this entire Territory are very limited, the estimate of the Surveyor-General (see his Reports of 1867, 1868, and 1869) being that not more than one million acres, or about one acre in seventy, in the whole Territory, are capable of even this style of agriculture. Going west, we cross a high, very broken, and mountainous country, covered with a growth of gramma and bunch-grass, but with very little land that can be tilled; and in Arizona, instead of any improvement, the mountains become higher, with higher table-lands, between more and more broken ravines, of great depth, and much country covered with volcanic deposits, and of entire sterility. Yet there are many large areas in Arizona covered with forests of various trees, sometimes widening into handsome parks. The mountains in these sections are covered with pine, the plateaus with juniper, the borders of the streams with cottonwood, and the valleys with grease-bush and sage. But so very desolate is a large portion of this Territory, that it is destitute of game. The mountains are less rugged as we go south, and afford many grassy spurs suitable for grazing.

Prescott, an American settlement near the centre of the Territory, is situated in a region where, from its position in the moun-

189

tains, the natural rainfall permits some agriculture, but dependence is placed upon irrigation. The Gila, the Colorado near Fort Mahone,[3] and some smaller streams, have valleys that can be irrigated, and are cultivated in some few spots, there being as many as ten thousand acres in a body devoted to the raising of corn and barley; but by the most liberal calculations of the Surveyor-General and others there is not more than one acre in sixty or one hundred that can by any possibility be cultivated. Westward, through California, to the Pacific, the mountains become more rugged, precipitous, and barren. Lieutenant Wheeler,[4] of the Engineer Corps of the Army, says in his Report: "The greater portion of the area examined in Southern California was of the most barren and desolate nature; the bare and brown rocks seldom being relieved by any sort of vegetation." There is, however, along the entire coast some land that can be cultivated.

The third route, nearly on the 39th parallel, follows the Kansas Pacific Railroad, so far as it goes, and this portion is pretty well known. This parallel nearly bisects Kansas, Colorado, Utah, Nevada and California. The eastern half of Kansas, or rather until we reach the neighborhood of the 98th meridian, about Fort Harker,[5] has an excellent soil and, although occasionally subject to drought, has generally a sufficient rainfall, a fair amount of timber, and abundant crops. But at this meridian a very perceptible change takes place. The altitude grows greater, steadily, as we go west, the soil becomes more and more arid, the native grasses shorter, the streams less frequent, and, after passing Fort Hays, we get beyond the country suitable for agriculture. This section, extending west nearly to Denver, is that known as "The Plains." It is a succession of gentle undulations, without timber,

---

[3] This was Fort Mohave. It was constructed in 1858 near Beal's crossing of the Colorado River.

[4] The Wheeler Survey of those parts of the United States territory lying south of the Central Pacific Railroad line is well covered in Richard A. Bartlett, *Great Surveys of the American West* (Norman, University of Oklahoma Press, 1962).

[5] Fort Harker was located near the present town of Ellsworth, Kansas, and was about ninety miles west of Fort Riley.

and covered with buffalo-grass, which is a short native grass, seldom growing more than two inches high. It is very nutritious, almost the exclusive food of the buffalo; maturing in June, it is dry and brown the remainder of the year.

Sometimes in the period of a single day, when the wind sweeps eastward from the great western altitudes and constantly grows more dense, it becomes so hot as to be a perfect sirocco, and the green slopes of the morning are by evening withered and burned to a dull brown. When the grass is green these plains present the most beautiful appearance, and impress one with their great likeness to an unlimited pasture of great fertility; and, to fully appreciate the transformation, one must see the rapid change from green to brown. For the years 1861 and 1862 the Kansas Pacific Railroad Company employed a farmer to experiment on their lands; but the moisture of the spring season has heretofore been of too short duration for him to accomplish much, and there is comparatively little water for purposes of irrigation. I have his Official Report before me. His grains failed, except on "some stalks of moderate length." Some grasses failed, with successes for other varieties. Many kinds of trees failed, others succeeded. Those reported a success were varieties of little value, like the catalpa, box-elder, and honey-locust. But to my directions to cor-respondents on the line of the road within the last few weeks, "Count and report the number of trees alive, planted more than two years," the answer is, "None living." His general results are what can be attained anywhere on the plains by careful experi-ments, in tolerable seasons. They will not answer for the farmer.

At military posts gardens have, only by irrigation, been made possible. The Arkansas runs through the State, and the Solomon, Republican, and Saline Rivers rise in the northern part of it, in numerous small branches, giving some narrow strips for irriga-tion; but as a rule the soil is unsusceptible of agriculture and unfit for settlement. Denver City is situated near the eastern foot-hills of the Rocky Mountains, in which rise the rivers Platte, Arkansas, Red, Rio Grande and one branch of the Colorado, and the prosperity of that city is purely the outgrowth of the mining interests of that region, which support a small agricultural industry by irrigation.

The western half of the Territory of Colorado is broken and mountainous. The snows of winter, when they melt, form a great number of small streams, which all afford limited facilities for irrigation. There are many thousands acres of the finest land so situated on the streams which form the Arkansas, and there are many small areas in the valleys of the mountains, where the rainfall is sufficient to obviate the necessity of irrigation. The grazing is excellent in many parts of this Territory, the mountains afford a great amount of timber, and there are besides several fine parks within its borders. In its southwest corner, and in the contiguous angles of New Mexico, Arizona, and Utah, there is a large area which is nearly a *terra incognita*; there being no definite and accurate account of it. According to the estimate of the Surveyor-General, there are in Colorado, including the strip cut off for Wyoming, from two to four million acres of arable land (but he says he thinks the smaller number nearest the fact) ; that is, from one-fifteenth to one-thirtieth of the whole area. My own observations are confirmatory of this calculation; and yet so vague are the opinions of the mass of the people on this point, that I have been told within the past few days by a high official of this Territory, in reply to the question, what was the proportion of available land in Colorado, "that one half could be cultivated."

The following is taken from the records of the Commissioner of the General Land Office at Washington: "I (the Surveyor-General of the Territories of New Mexico, Arizona and Colorado) estimate the arable lands of New Mexico at one million acres, and of Arizona at about the same." "The term 'arable' is synonymous with 'irrigable.' " He says further: "Those Territories may be divided into mountains, table-lands, and valleys. The valleys can be irrigated, but they form but the small portion above given. The table-lands are too high to admit the water to be carried on to them, but are covered with grass, and form about three fourths of the country. The remainder is mountains."

Again going west, we pass over a high, broken, and mountainous country, covered mainly with wild sage, till we cross the Wahsatch Mountains in Utah, where, at the western foot, there is a thin line of Mormon settlements, using the water coming down from the mountains for irrigation. The remainder of this Territory and Nevada, until we reach the eastern foot of the Sierra Nevadas, is composed of parallel ranges of mountains from fifteen to twenty miles apart, all running north and south, and having sandy, desert valleys between. The Wahsatch range is fringed with pine; the ranges west are covered with short cedar and piñon, a sort of scrub pine, and the ranges farthest west are destitute of timber. All of the mountain slopes and some of the valleys bear grass thinly, and sage-brush and grease-bush. After leaving the Mormon settlements, with the exception of a few oases, a narrow strip at the eastern foot of the Humboldt Mountain, on Deep Creek, and a few other mere patches, none of this country can be cultivated. The whole amount of available land in Utah is so very small as to scarcely admit of comparison. So little is there, that the Mormon authorities are already compelled to seek land in the adjoining Territories for their new arrivals of emigrants. The eastern foot of the Sierra affords fine timber and excellent land, but in limited quantities. As we proceed into the mountains and cross them, there is abundant and excellent timber, but only the merest patches of available land, until we reach the Sacramento Valley in California, which is from ten to thirty miles in width. From there to the sea it is a mountainous country, with many fine, but very narrow valleys. The same is true of this coast section, both north and south. About one third of the western half of the State is available, while not more than a twentieth of the eastern part can be used by any of the processes of farming which will be used in America for a hundred years to come.

Passing rapidly, now, over the route of the 41st parallel, beginning at Omaha, we find for the first two hundred miles, or to Fort Kearney, one of the most beautiful portions of the continent. The Platte and Elkhorn valleys cannot be surpassed in richness by any soil in the world, and greatly resemble the Rhine Valley. A great

193

number of small streams water this region excellently. There is a small quantity of timber, a good rainfall; there has never been a failure of small grains, and spring wheat is almost a certain crop in the twelve years I have known this country. The winters are severe, but easily provided against. Westward from this point we see precisely the same condition of the soil, dryness of the atmosphere, insufficient rainfall, and general aridity noticed on the same meridian in Kansas, Indian Territory, and Texas. The Platte has a narrow valley, which can be irrigated at considerable cost, and good grazing is always found near the streams. In Wyoming there is some fine grazing along Lodge-pole[6] and other creeks, and some meagre strips that can be cultivated, and nearly the whole surface of the country affords some little grass. During all this progress from Omaha we have steadily ascended, and some sixty miles west of Cheyenne we reach Sherman, the summit of the Rocky Mountains. From here we have a broken, barren, mountainous country until we get into Northern Utah. The quantity of agricultural lands in Wyoming is too inconsiderable and too little known to admit of any reliable computation, but it is proportionately less than in Colorado, while Nebraska corresponds with Kansas in this, that while the eastern half is very valuable, the western half is worthless.

Going over the Wahsatch Mountains, we find that the range differs but slightly from what it was where we crossed it in the more southerly part of the Territory. The same strip of Mormon settlements at the western foot, and the same desolate country, save that, until we reach the Sierra, the ranges of mountains in the west are less broken; and from there on to the sea the only difference from California, farther south, is that we do not find the broad valley of the Sacramento, but the entire breadth of the State is taken up with irregular mountains running east and west, as well as north and south. While there are no broad valleys, there are several well-watered narrow ones, and the mountains are well timbered. Many of these valleys have been graded by water as

---

[6] Lodgepole Creek, a northern tributary of the Platte River, had a narrow valley with a limited amount of bottom land.

well as if done by an engineer, and are of wonderful richness and beauty, always jutting against the adjoining hills, which afford scant pasturage, but abundant timber. There is a plentiful rainfall here, and nothing could be more picturesque than the northern portion of California. It is in the States and Territories along the western portion of this line that we find the great lava flow, extending over two hundred thousand square miles. Much of this is not yet covered with mould or vegetation. Sometimes it is in vast masses of rocks, and sometimes in broken fragments.

We will now notice briefly the northernmost route along the 45th and 46th parallels, or, generally, the parallel of St. Paul, bisecting Dakota and Montana, passing through the southern portion of Idaho, Northern Oregon, and Southern Washington Territory. Starting westward from Duluth, for the first hundred miles there is no prairie, but some meadows of wild rice and high grass, a large preponderance of flat tamarack marsh, and lakes, with very little good timber. The remainder of the distance to the Mississippi, about sixty miles, is a barren lake district, but with good timber. Crossing the Mississippi, we find pretty good land well timbered with pine, till we reach the valley of the Red River of the North, and pass into Dakota. The whole valley or drainings of this river, a hundred miles across, and reaching near the branches of the Cheyenne River (meridian of 98°) is an excellent wheat and vegetable country, scantily timbered, but by some thought to be too level for drainage. Going west from this to James River, there is some fair land, but much that is waste, and thence to the Missouri, between the 100th and 101st meridians, little or no available land, except the narrow valleys of the small streams.

The Missouri itself, after passing a few miles above Yankton, may be said to have no available bottom-land; for although there are places where the old river beds spread out and form fine "intervals," or bottom-lands, for one or two miles back from the stream and several in length, yet for the greater part of its course from Fort Benton the river cuts sharply against abrupt, barren bluffs on one or both sides. Whenever this is not the case, the banks are fringed with cottonwood of inferior quality which

195

sometimes thickens into groves of moderate size. As we go west from the Missouri, we pass through what is known as the "Bad Lands," or "Mauvaises Terres."[7] This is a broad section of country, either side the river, extending far to the west, with a superposing layer of drift, orginally several hundred feet thick, but now broken up into bluffs or small hillocks by the action of the elements, and with but little vegetation. The sides and sometimes the tops of the bluffs are entirely bare of vegetation, and every rain or wind storm carries down vast quantities of mud or dust to the lower levels, much of which finally finds its way into the Missouri. It is a visible example of the levelling process of nature, but it has nothing to do with the rainfall of the country, and the district is superior as a grazing country to one half of that lying between the 100th meridian and the Sierra Nevadas. This continues to be the character of the soil until we get through Dakota and well into Montana. The eastern boundary of Dakota is some two degrees farther west than that of the Indian Territory and Kansas, and we find a correspondingly narrower strip of good land. After going one hundred miles into the interior, we cross the 98th meridian, and already see a large amount of waste land, which increases until finally, in the vicinity of the 100th meridian, only a few valleys are available. All through the western portion of this Territory are small strips, like the narrow valleys of Apple Creek and Hart River,[8] which can be cultivated, and a few points, like Fort Berthold, with quite extensive flats, where, by planting early and in favorable seasons, cultivation is exceedingly successful without irrigation, yet irrigation is often needed here. But with these exceptions, and the narrow fertile strip in the east, the proportion of cultivable land does not exceed one acre in a hundred. Good gardens at the various military posts in this section are made without irrigation, in the exceptionally rainy seasons (maturing, however, only the early vegetables), unless eaten up

---

[7] These "bad lands" were not so designated on account of the poorness of their soil, but rather on account of their shape. They were broken and waterworn, thus making them difficult to cross, hence the original name, *mauvaises terres pour traverser.*

[8] The Heart River.

by insects and grasshoppers, which occurs about every other good season. There is limited grazing all over the Territory, and in the southwest corner are situated the Black Hills. Elsewhere, with the exception of strips of cottonwood along the streams, there is virtually no timber.

We now go into Montana, and soon reach the Yellowstone, the valley of which, as generally understood, is a myth. It has a rapid current of clear water, which comes down from the snows of the Big Horn and other mountains. It impinges against bluff banks on one side, while it usually has a valley from a half-mile to a couple of miles on the other, and in one or two places, I am told, even to ten or fifteen miles. The portion near the river is covered with excellent grass and the best of cottonwood timber, while that near the bluffs bears an abundant crop of wild sage. The very numerous branches of this stream, commencing with Powder River, which comes down from the Big Horn Mountains, have valleys of varying breadth and availability, and those farther west, beginning with the Big Horn, are clear mountain streams of great beauty. The last-named stream has a beautiful well-grassed valley all the way from the mountains to its mouth, about sixty miles; and those streams west of it, although smaller and with narrower valleys, are, in other respects, similar to it. There is also a rich grassy strip all along the north foot of the Big Horn Mountains. Crossing the Yellowstone going west we soon reach the Mussel Shell [*sic*], a muddy, whitish-looking stream, with a broken sterile country on both sides. We shortly after reach the many small, clear, and pebbly mountain streams that go to make up the Judith. The country here is well covered with grass, which in rainy seasons grows rank and high like a continuous meadow, is picturesque beyond description, and the mountains bear scattering pine-trees. From here to the Missouri, where it runs north, is a most broken, mountainous country, tormented with broad and almost bottomless ravines and gorges, with immense, high, and sometimes almost isolated, peaks of barren rocks, marshy flats, white with incrustations of various salts, and great ranges of mountains. All the way through Montana we find great sloping

197

hillsides and table-lands, covered with thin grass; high ranges of mountains, always fringed with timber; many streams with beautiful valleys, water-washed and as level as a billiard-table; innumerable brooks; and a few mountain valleys of some value for agriculture. The minor streams with rich valleys are the Gallatin, Jefferson, Madison, and Sun Rivers, and several more which run west into the Columbia. They have valleys from half a mile to three miles in width, are very rich, level as a floor, easily irrigated, and have been settled for several years. There cannot be far from a million acres of this fine land in Montana, giving, according to the usual rate of our farming States thus far, a population of fifty thousand. In the western part of Montana and Northern Idaho there is a good deal of timber, and a sufficient rainfall to produce crops without irrigation.

Rapidly crossing into Oregon and Washington along the Columbia, we look in vain for the "broad, rich valley" of that river, discovered by the early explorers; unless they mean the half-barren Spokane Plains in the north part of Washington Territory. This stream washes the foot of a mountain, or runs through a gorge that sometimes widens into a valley; and whenever its banks can be traversed by wagons, the wheels cut into a loose arid sand, with here and there a sagebrush so large as to have grown into a shrub with a stalk several inches in diameter, and extending its branches over several yards of ground. We find these general features of a broken mountainous country till we cross the Sierra,[9] and then we have a most humid atmosphere, abundant rainfall, immense growth of pine timber, and rich valleys on to the sea. In the northwest portion of Washington is situated a network of straits, commonly known as Olympia Bay and Puget Sound, whose outlet is the Straits of Fuca. This unrivalled body of water, which may be considered entire, embraces not less than a thousand islands of various sizes covered with evergreens and other beautiful foliage. The surrounding country has great richness of soil, is thickly wooded, and is favored by a spring season at least

[9] The northern Sierra, north of Feather River, is now known as the Cascade Range. Mt. Lassen is its southernmost peak.

six weeks earlier than that of New York, a temperature modified by the currents of the sea, and a mild summer. In plain sight are snow-capped ranges of mountains, an active volcano, Mount Baker,[10] and the great white peaks of Hood, Adams and Rainier, which combine to make it one of the most beautiful and attractive regions in the world, and the cause of continual rhapsodies on the part of travellers.

We have now passed hurriedly across the section of country in question, virtually upon the five routes talked of as national lines of communication. The portion east of the Rocky Mountains, and a large part of that west, has been described from personal observation extending through fourteen years of military service on the Plains. It is all supplemented by observations and reports of others extending over a period of forty-eight years, including official reconnaissances and the results of vast numbers of accurate instrumental measurements. For its general accuracy I refer, without permission, however, to General A. A. Humphreys, Chief of the Engineer Corps of the Army, to General G. K. Warren and General William F. Reynolds,[11] also of the Engineer Corps, United States Army, who for many years made reconnaissances of the Upper Missouri country, and have given us our only reliable maps of it; to Lieutenant Wheeler, also of the Engineer Corps, now investigating that country; to Clarence King, Mr. Gardner, Professor Hayden, Brigham Young, or to any officer of the army, or other disinterested persons, whose opportunity for observation, and whose practical knowledge in such matters will give their opinions value. There are, of course, in so summary an account, many fine sections of limited extent which could not be noticed in a sketch which undertakes to give only general characteristics.

It remains to give, in as few words as possible, the rainfall of this section as determined by accurate daily observations of the area, and extending through a period of more than twenty years. It can be seen by any one in the office of the Surgeon-General of

---

[10] Although many of these peaks are volcanic, it is doubtful if Mt. Baker was active at this time.

[11] This was Captain W. F. Raynolds.

the army. As a standard of comparison, the usual average rainfall in the productive States, east of the general line from which I have proceeded, is assumed as about forty-five inches. It rises to sixty in South Florida, the mouth of the Mississippi, and the west coast of North California, Oregon, and Washington; at Sitka it reaches ninety inches; while in Wisconsin and Michigan, where we have such devastating fires, it is but thirty inches; but the general useful and necessary rainfall is from thirty-five to fifty inches, except at some points on the sea-coast, where it is only from twenty to thirty inches, the necessary moisture there being made up by the excessive humidity of the atmosphere, which imperceptibly precipitates moisture.

Along the 98th meridian the rainfall is from twenty-five to thirty inches, and on the 100th meridian it is from twenty to twenty-five inches; as we near the mountains, from ten to fifteen inches, and even higher on the more elevated tablelands. Westward, along the extreme southern route, after leaving the 100th meridian, there is a rainfall ranging from twenty inches, in Middle Texas, to three inches at Fort Yuma, while its average is ten inches. The generally similar rainfall along the middle portion of this route arises from the Rocky Mountain range breaking down to an almost uniform level with the adjoining country in Southern New Mexico, and on no other route does this occur. The zones of uniform rains range from north to south, varying, for the main part, in the mountainous regions, with the altitude. The great altitude of the Rocky Mountain range increases the rainfall largely; much of it falls as snow, which, melting in the spring, produces what is known as the "June rises" in the streams which flow from those mountains. The range is from twenty to thirty inches, with an average of about twenty-five inches. The great basin between the Rocky and Sierra Mountains is the most arid portion of our domain, the range being from three to ten inches, averaging but six inches. Blodgett says of this basin: "This great arid region may be said to embrace ten degrees of longitude and seventeen of latitude in the United States (the whole length of the country in that region from north to south and high into British

America, and between the Rocky and Sierra Nevada Mountains) drained only by the Great Colorado and Columbia Rivers. So arid is the Great Basin, that fully two hundred thousand square miles has not a sufficient rainfall to require any drainage at all." As we ascend the Sierra the rainfall increases rapidly, reaching sixty inches at the summit in Washington and Oregon; nor does it decrease as we continue toward the sea, but only as we go south, until at San Francisco it is only twenty-two inches, fifteen inches at Los Angeles, ten inches at San Diego, and three at Yuma. The effect of this small amount of rain in the interior is to preclude all possibility of general successful agriculture, although in California, by sowing grains early, so as to get the advantage of the rains, which all fall in the spring, a much less rainfall produces good crops. The stinted vegetation that finds life elsewhere has adapted itself to the conditions there found, and much of the season it is dry and crisp, the "siempre vivre" being a marked example. In digging up the soil, after only a few inches, we find it perfectly dry and dusty, and this too even in the rainiest season. All this applies also to most of the country between the Rocky Mountains and the 100th meridian. Blodgett says in 1855 (in the absence of full data, which have been supplied) of this region along the Upper Missouri: "One striking remark is always made of it: it is uncultivable, on account of the absence of summer rains. . . . The atmosphere is so arid that there can be but slight winter precipitation. The rains that fall, for a like reason, do not afford the advantage they otherwise would, they are so soon evaporated." He also says, page 747: "On the Upper Missouri there is known to be a great deficiency of rain in the summer months at times, and a large part of the great area partially enclosed in its long curve is set down as arid and uncultivable by explorers. Its amount of drainage is too small to permit a supposition that it is otherwise, as all its tributaries, except the Yellowstone, are small and unimportant streams." The latter receives its waters largely from the mountains, but in summer they all discharge very little water. The very popular theory that the rainfall is increasing in that country, and that it is due to the effects of

201

civilization, is not supported by accurate measurements. The natural laws that govern these phenomena are too broad and general to be affected by the slight results of civilization already found there. The wish is father to the thought. All over this vast territory, wherever beds of primitive rocks are found, are natural tanks where the rains collect and the water may remain sweet the whole year. In nearly all this section there are also found springs of water, but in some portions very infrequently. Wherever there are high mountains the rains and snows of winter form a great number of streams of pure water; but in many large sections, more especially in the great basin west of the Rocky Mountains, the water both of springs and streams is frequently salt and unfit for use. Wherever pure water can be found for irrigation, even in the most arid and unpromising soil, the most abundant crops can be raised. The amount of water, however, available for this purpose is exceedingly limited, and the popular belief on this point is erroneous. The level spaces along the margins of streams or at the foot of mountains are very narrow, and nowhere else can the water be used cheaply. It would require very great outlay to utilize the large rivers, on account of the great fluctuations between high and low water. The success of artesian wells is not promising. The government, and private enterprises, have already expended much time and money in these projects, without much success, and at too great cost for farming purposes.

There are several small sections of country where, from special causes, agriculture has been made successful. In New Mexico for the last two hundred years the old Spanish population has carried on in its own un-American way its peculiar style of farming,—ploughing the ground with the fork of a tree, and artifically irrigating their crops as the Egyptians did thousands of years ago. A few Americans also, with the certainty of selling their crops at a high price at the military posts, have successfully embarked in this style of farming. In Colorado these experiments are going on with considerable success, being limited by the amount of water available, and the amount of capital that can be raised to secure it. The garden and tree culture about Denver is very successful, and Greeley, some forty miles north of it, is the best example of combined effort in this direction that has come to my notice, but by too great an outlay of capital to be copied. The success of the Mormons in Utah is remarkable, and has been brought about by special causes,—religious fanaticism, a mild but forcible despotism, the industrious habits brought from Northern Europe, and the spur of a lucrative market, produced first by the emigration of 1849, then by military occupancy, and most of all by the discovery of the precious metals in the adjoining Territories. All these have tended to bring about this remarkable state of things. They have settled along the immediate western foot of the Wahsatch Mountains, beginning in Idaho and extending southward for six hundred miles into Arizona. As yet there has been but little combined effort in constructing water-ditches there, nor has it been necessary, for the mountains furnish a great number of small rivulets made applicable to each farm. Yet with all this stretch of cultivated country, the Hon. Mr. Hooper,[12] who has so long represented the Territory in Congress, told me, that if all the available land in the entire Territory could be placed consecutively in one long strip along the whole distance, it would be but a very few miles in breadth, and that it is even now necessary to soak out the alkali, a very slow process, before the land can be used. My own observations quite confirm this statement, giving therefore slightly over a hundredth of the area as arable. The successful farming about Bozeman and some other parts of Montana make up, with the cases already cited, the principal examples of successful agriculture in this great interior country, and will probably be all-sufficient for the wants of that country. Tree culture has been very successful at Denver and other parts of Colorado, in New Mexico, and at Salt Lake City, in Montana and Nevada too; but not one tree have I known to thrive, unless there was, at its roots, an irrigating ditch with running water. When the water ceases the trees die. All over this interior country trees can be raised successfully when artificially watered, and in no

[12] William Henry Hooper had moved to Utah from Illinois in 1850. He served as representative in Congress from 1859 to 1861, and again from 1865 to 1873.

other way, except on the borders of streams where nature has already placed them.

The grazing facilities of this entire country cannot fail, in the aggregate, to become exceedingly valuable. There is much diversity of opinion as to its extent, but it must be very great. But farms for grazing purposes, as we know them in the States, will never be found here. Wherever there is unfailing water there will be an owner of it, who will control the range about it, either by cession or legal assignment, and the next water may be thirty miles away. Many acres will be required to furnish the grass grown on one acre in Ohio or Illinois. Nor will there be successful stock-raising here, in any of the Territories, till people come with capital to build shelter and to provide all the protection and food for stock, as is done in the Eastern States. The following extract shows what now exists in Nevada, which will and does take place every few winters in all the Territories; and until there is proper provision made for such seasons, stock-raising in the Territories will be a snare and a deception. Experience has shown most conclusively that good stock requires the same care and provision in all these Territories that it does in Ohio and New England; and wherever too great reliance is placed on unassisted nature to furnish this food, we find a compensating decrease in the quality of the animal, as is shown in some portions of the Southern States and in Texas.

Hard Times in Nevada

The Reno (Nevada) *Journal* says that after a long, dreary winter, spring has at last opened, and as the snow recedes from the valleys, the farmers are all busy putting in their crops. The past winter has been one of the hardest ever experienced in the country. Many have lost all the live stock they possessed, and all have lost a large per cent of their stock. Honey Lake Valley has probably suffered most; the hay-crop having been short the past year, nearly every one was obliged to buy, and consequently the few men who had any raised the price, demanding whatever they wished. Hay has been sold in Honey Lake for $60 a ton, and in Susanville it commanded at one time $130 per ton. Yet stock are still dying, and a person riding through Honey Lake Valley can hardly get out of sight of dead and dying cattle. Sheep have fared better than cattle; but at present they, too, are dying very fast from the effects of the alkali which they got into their stomachs while eating the short grass which is just sprouting.

My post of duty, the past season, has been at Fort Buford, on the Missouri, at the mouth of the Yellowstone, a point supposed to be exceptionally good. I have before me a letter from the hay-contractor, Mr. Joseph Anderson of St. Paul, in which he informs me that this season, in order to gather nine hundred tons of hay for my post, he has been compelled to search over a country extending twenty-five miles in all directions on the north side of the Missouri River. There was no grass to make hay for as great a distance beyond, making about twelve hundred square miles. I have not noticed the high temperature of this section; for, although the heat of summer is intense in some portions, yet that of itself would not prevent the country from becoming populous. It is proper to speak of the extreme cold of this northern route, not because it is an insuperable obstacle to the populating of the country, but to expose the fraud practised in representing it as desirable. The many excessive changes in temperature, sometimes seventy degrees in twelve hours, are exceedingly trying to all persons with rheumatic or scrofulous tendencies. This post is situated in the midst of the "northern tropical belt" we have heard so much of,—a belt not clearly defined, but supposed to be synonymous with what has been called on the large maps distributed by the Northern Pacific Railroad Company (now before me) as "The Continental Wheat Garden" extending to the Saskatchewan country on the 53d parallel. It has been claimed by the company as one of the great purposes to open this country. It is, in a direct line, two hundred and fifty miles from Bismarck; but the proposed line of the railroad in passing west, makes so small an angle with the river after crossing it, as to be but one degree south when opposite Fort Buford; and whatever is said of the temperature or rainfall at that post is practically true along the line of the railroad. By examining the isothermal lines of Blodgett, it will be seen that the summer, winter, and annual isothermal lines, passing

205

very near Fort Buford, toward the east, deflect southward, crossing the railroad from ten to forty miles east of Bismarck, and remaining south of the road as they pass eastward until beyond its eastern terminus. The Northern Pacific Railroad Company has published and widely distributed, on a large map, what purports to be the correct averages (isothermal lines) of the summer heat of this region. As compared with Blodgett's Charts, published by the government, they have forced these lines three degrees to the north. Thus the summer line of 70° Fahrenheit, passing through this post, latitude 48° N. by Blodgett, will be found on their maps on this meridian at 51°. They also avoid allusion to the summer extremes, 104° Fah. in the shade, and frosts nearly every month, and entirely suppress the spring, autumn, and winter isothermals. The result is that any one not entirely familiar with these subjects is deceived by these maps, thinking that the lines represent the annual temperature, but called summer, seeing no others, from their warmth, while the real spring, autumn, and winter temperatues, corresponding to a summer temperature of 70° in this region, are 32°, 44°, and 15° respectively, with a mean annual temperature of 45°. (See Blodgett's Charts.) Our own records for the past eight years confirm these figures, while we have forty days with the thermometer below zero, and the coldest days at –37° to –40°. It is believed that these maps have been prepared purposely to deceive.

The storms of winter in this region are truly terrific, and it would seem that they must destroy all animal life not securely protected. The Indians never buffet them, but on the approach of one, if travelling, they at once go into camp in some sheltered place, and remain until the storm is over. This is told me by the oldest and most reliable mountain-men of the country, and is confirmed by the large number of deaths occurring in these storms every winter. All remember the storm in Minnesota in the winter of 1872–73, in which hundreds lost their lives, the storm about Yankton the same spring,[13] and the storm in which so many of

---

[13] This famous blizzard is well described in Elizabeth B. Custer's *Boots and Saddles*.

Colonel Cole's cavalry horses were frozen to death at the picket-line in the Powder River country in 1865.[14] These are examples liable to occur any winter. I am informed that the climate is more mild in Montana, but I have not seen accurate reports from there. As we go toward the Pacific, the climate perceptibly moderates, from the influence of the ocean.

The foregoing imperfect description has been presented with the one purpose of calling the attention of the people of the country to the most important fact that we are rapidly approaching the limit of time when the landless and homeless can acquire both lands and homes by merely settling on them. We have reached the border all along, from Dakota to Texas, where land for nothing is no cheaper than good land at thirty dollars an acre. Not but that there is yet a great deal of good land for pre-emption in all the extreme frontier States; yet in all these States some settlements have reached the border, and from the 100th meridian to the Sierra Nevada Mountains, a distance of twelve hundred miles, there is no more than one acre to the hundred that has any appreciable value for agricultural purposes, or that will for the next hundred years sell for any appreciable sum. Moreover, for one hundred miles before reaching that meridian there is comparatively little good land. The authorities for this statement are believed to be unimpeachable. My personal observations have been of the strictest character, accompanied by careful statistical study. I have served in every State and Territory on both the eastern and western frontier, excepting Arizona and Alaska, and in all of these I have seen the land tried in gardens and fields. There is no fault of soil anywhere. The fault is in the want of water. It is possible that, at some remote period, the good lands of the country may be so densely populated as to cause many to seek a precarious existence by such meagre farming as is possible in this region; but until then, the occasional great stock-grower, the scattered groups of miners, and the fortunate farmer, or groups of them, in the narrow valleys, who can control a little water for

---

[14] On September 8, 1865, a cold storm had caused the death of many horses and mules belonging to Colonel Nelson Cole's column in the Powder River country.

irrigation, will comprise the population. As an example of such populations we have Nevada, where about all its capacity in this direction is utilized. It has been represented in Congress by its two senators, for ten years, and it has a population of about forty thousand, or about one-third as many as a single congressional district in the populous States. And New Mexico, which for twenty years has been in our full occupation, is another example. It costs many million dollars for its administration; yet take away the army, its hangers-on, and the transient miners, and the remaining American population could sit in the shade of a good-sized apple-tree.

There is yet a good deal of unoccupied land in Northern Texas, but it is owned by the State, and is fast passing into the hands of railroad corporations. The lands of the Indian Territory are owned by the Indians themselves, not as a reservation set aside for their use, but as compensation for their having surrendered valuable considerations, in farms and other lands to the United States, and they hold patents for them from the Land Office. If there is any one pledge of the government more sacred than another, it is that these may have a perpetual home there.

The phenomenon of the formation and rapid growth of new, rich, and populous States will no more be seen in our present domain, and we must soon face a condition of facts utterly new in the economy of the country, when, not new, but old States must make room for the increase of population, and thereby receive a fresh impetus. And the old song of "Uncle Sam is rich enough to give us all a farm" will no longer be true, unless we take farms incapable of cultivation. I am aware this will startle very many people. There has been a system of misrepresentation practised about the value of this country, which cannot be estimated without considering the extent of the interest involved in such misrepresentation.

The government has, year after year, at great expense, sent parties of scientific men to traverse these countries; to gather up, describe, and publish all that could be found out relative to beasts, birds, insects, fishes, and every conceivable creeping,

208

crawling, or flying creature; also correct reports of its geology. But I have never known any one charged to learn and report that most important of all items, "whether it is good for agriculture." And the Surveyor-General is today surveying, at great expense, large strips of country in some of the Territories which will never be sold by the acre.

It has been common to make up excursion parties of newspaper-men, members of the government, and citizens of large influence (always in the green months of May and June), to visit these sections. The roads all lie along the valleys of streams, and at that season give the idea of fruitfulness. These persons are never taken on transverse routes, where they would inevitably find sterility, nor are they practical agriculturists. After an excursion of this kind, where every human want is anticipated, the press would be unnatural not to applaud, and the members of the government mean, not to encourage, the enterprise. An obligation has been laid upon them all, and they have only seen the country at its best points and in its holiday dress. Men in high places have been employed, and paid for their services, in writing and speaking for these enterprises, and their writings and speeches used as advertisements in disseminating this deception. Their names are synonyms of honor and truth, but they, too, are deceived, and are made to deceive others innocently. For illustration, we will take the example of the North Pacific Railroad. This road, having no resources but its land grant, must make that appear valuable, to enable it to secure the means necessary to build it. By taking these eminent persons, above mentioned, to the rich wheat-growing lands of Minnesota, to the valley of the Red River of the North, or to Corinne on the Union Pacific Railroad, and thence along that most enchanting of all journeys, at the western foot of the Rocky Mountains, and the rich valleys of Montana, or to the most beautiful of lands, the country of Puget's Sound, they are so impressed with these fruitful points as to honestly believe that it is all fruitful; and in just enthusiasm they write an account of what they have truly seen, as being equally true of the whole. This is the route Herr Haas was taken. Many of the advertisements so lavishly printed in all the press contain more or less positive falsehoods. The most flagrant I have seen is "that this grant, for its entire length (meaning, in general acceptation, all of it), is capable of producing all the cereals and fruits of the Atlantic States." Another, more indirect, is by instancing the success of land-subsidies in good sections of the country, for instance the Illinois Central, as illustrations of what may be expected from the whole route. By issuing a series of misrepresentations of the climate on a part of their route; by causing the press to publish, as editorials or current news, the statements of the company; by producing attractive displays of vegetable products at fairs, grown no one knows where, certainly in none of the country mentioned as bad in this article; by a specious literature, as magazine articles, so artfully written as to hide their intent; by engaging the religious press and church influences of the country,—they have succeeded to a large extent, in deceiving the people. Another powerful advertisement which this road has employed with marked success is by securing from the government costly expeditions as escorts, to be known and written about as acting in the interests of this road. They have been readily furnished, which shows to the world a fostering interest next akin to actual government indorsement.

As a single example of the advertisements used in these interests, take the following from the *Nation* of August 22, 1872:—

PROGRESS OF THE NORTHERN PACIFIC RAILROAD.—The entire aspect of the far Northwest is undergoing a rapid change, in consequence of the construction of the Northern Pacific Railroad. . . . Long trains of emigrants follow the track of the railroad surveyors and builders, so that the country is being thoroughly explored, and is filling up with a rapidity which is destined to increase into the largest population.

This statement is entirely false, after passing west from the valley of Red River, where the surveyors and builders then were, nor is that country susceptible of cultivation. The emigration stopped short at the line of the Red River. "Operations are now centred in Montana, where track-laying progresses at the rate of three miles a day." To refute this statement it is only necessary to say, track-laying has in no place on the Northern Pacific Railroad reached nearer to any point in Montana than two hundred and fifty miles. Another equally untrue statement is, "The trunk road is now in progress of construction along the Yellowstone River in Montana." No construction party ever reached within two hundred and fifty miles from any point on that river.

> The observations, so far, amply confirm all that has been said of the fertility of that country along the line of the railroad. In Dakota the climate is genial, and the soil is admirably adapted to the cultivation of grain. . . . Natural water-springs can be found almost anywhere by excavations ten or twelve feet beneath the surface. . . . Of the soil fully nine tenths is arable land.

It would be difficult to invent so many falsehoods in so few words. The country, with the exceptions hitherto mentioned, is practically worthless. The winter climate is given elsewhere. Natural water-springs are often a day's march apart, and to get water at Fort Buford, wells have to be sunk sixty feet to the level of the Missouri, and rise and fall with that river. Farther back from the river they would have to be sunk much deeper.

> The company is fairly entitled to the merit of amicably settling for the United States government, at once and forever, the Indian question on the most difficult and threatening portion of the frontier.

It is well known that construction on this road has never reached the hostile Sioux country, and that whenever surveying parties have gone there, they have been escorted by several regiments of troops.

The audacity of the last quotation, and the boldness of misstatement in all of them, require no comment. These advertisements, asking and advising the people who have safely invested their savings in government securities to exchange them for the securities of these roads, with the promise of a higher rate of interest, have induced thousands of the poor and needy of the country, who have put by the little earnings of a lifetime in safe securities, and those holding funds in trust, to exchange them for these bonds, having a present security of land at two dollars an acre that has

211

no available value. If these roads ought to be built, can there be any sufficient reason why they should be built upon a basis of deception and fraud? But is there any sufficient reason for building five lines of road across the continent, at a gross cost of five hundred millions of dollars, every cent of which must be borrowed; the final return of which must depend upon the value of these lands. The three great reasons urged for building these roads are: First, military or state considerations. These seem sufficient to warrant the construction of one road, which for many reasons should better have been built along the 32d parallel, as it probably would have been had the South been represented in Congress. And, even now, since the Union Pacific is liable to be closed any winter, and is certain to be closed some winters, as was the case for many weeks in 1871–72, it seems suitable at once to build a southern line. But let it be built on a true basis, and not on one of falsehood. The second reason is, to develop the great interior country into rich and populous States. This I deem fallacious, for the country is incapable of it. Look along the lines of road already built; where there were begun thriving towns, with their plats and choice corner-lots, there is now one shanty left. Many have seen, and nearly all remember, such rattling, noisy towns as Phil Sheridan,[15] on the Kansas Pacific Railroad, not far from the 100th meridian. There is not to-day a stake, brick, or shingle to mark the ground where it stood, and this is true of many others. Were this development possible, the advisability of scattering, across great stretches of new country, poor and destitute colonists (as nearly all are who settle new countries), without the aid and co-operation of established neighborhoods, may well be questioned. Successive settlements furnish these. I saw much of this dreadful suffering and almost starvation along the Republican and Solomon Rivers in 1871–72 in Kansas, where these poor people had been induced to come by the Kansas Pacific Railroad,

[15] The town of Phil Sheridan was a typical "end of the line" town which disappeared as soon as railroad construction had passed beyond it. There were many others which suffered a like fate. A few however, managed to survive and become permanent municipalities. Examples are Cheyenne, Wyoming, and Bismarck, North Dakota.

212

entirely beyond schools, and where it took the earnings of a season to secure the attendance of a doctor. Colonization is not increased by scattering it. The other reason given is the great value of the international carrying trade. When it is remembered that a bushel of wheat can be carried from San Francisco to Liverpool in ships—nature supplying in this case both roadway and motive-power—as cheaply as from Chicago to New York by rail, and that proportion of costs in these cases is as one to thirteen per mile, and when time and insurance are the only other elements to be considered, any one may readily calculate the extent to which a railway three thousand miles long can successfully compete for any considerable amount of this trade.

The foregoing article was written some two years since. In the interval much has been said and published which requires comment or reply. Without entering into the region of controversy, a few further remarks may be thought becoming.

The rainfall of this region, which is its controlling characteristic, varies greatly with different years. For the past eight seasons it has been determined by accurate measurement as follows, namely:—

EXTRACT FROM THE PUBLIC RECORDS

Years	Annual	In summer months May, June, July and August	Remarks
In 1867	6.58 inches	5.17 inches	
" 1868	11.50 "	9.36 "	This includes the
" 1869	9.74 "	5.23 "	melted snow of
" 1870	9.19 "	6.25 "	winter.
" 1871	9.42 "	3.98 "	
" 1872	19.99 "	6.77 "	
" 1873	21.11 "	10.73 "	
" 1874	6.50 "	4.49 "	To Aug. 11.

I hereby certify that the foregoing is a true extract from the public records of the post.   J. F. MUNSON
1st Lieut. and Adjutant, 6th Post Adjutant
Fort Buford

213

The rainfall for the four growing summer months is also given in the foregoing table. It will be seen that for 1872 and 1873 was greatly in excess of the others; particularly the summer rains of the second of these years. The result has been an extraordinary growth of vegetation such as has seldom been seen here. This was especially true in the year 1873.

Writers have been employed to describe the country that year, and have well improved their opportunity, honestly believing, no doubt, that it was but an ordinary season. The two most conspicuous examples are a series of letters written, as is supposed, under the pay of the Northern Pacific Railroad Company, by the best letter-writer of the press, and another, written by General George A. Custer, and published in the company's leading Western organ just before the bill for the relief of the road was presented to Congress. The descriptive portions of these letters are, without doubt, accurate. These writers, however, have committed the error so commonly and innocently committed by thousands who undertake to enlighten mankind. They have substituted an example for a general principle. They both pursued the idea that other seasons had been, and would be, like the one they described. In this was their error, since they wrote of the most exceptionally fruitful year on record. The present season alone offsets all they have both said. There has been very little rain during the three summer months of this season; the country is, in consequence, parched and brown, the grasses having grown but one or two inches, where they grew from one to two feet last year. So little water is there, that in coming from the James River to Fort Buford, *via* Bismarck, along the north bank of the Missouri River, a distance of three hundred and twenty-five miles, I have crossed only four running streams, each of which might be spanned at a single step dry-shod. General Custer wrote of this country after serving in it but one summer; Mr. Townsend, after remaining in it about one week. The following letter from General Sully tells its own story:—

214

FORT VANCOUVER, WASHINGTON TERRITORY

June 18, 1874

DEAR GENERAL: ... In answer to your questions about my opinion as to the climate, character of the soil, etc., of the section of country through which the North Pacific passes, I would state as follows. My experience of the country dates back as far as 1854, when I was stationed in what was then the territory of Minnesota, near what is now the western portion of the State. From that time until 1859, when I marched across the country to the Platte River, I was on duty in different sections of the country between the Missouri River and Minnesota, and on the Upper Missouri. From the fall of 1863 to 1866 I was in command of the troops operating against the Sioux nation, who were then in a state of war both on the east and west of the Missouri River, as far west as the Yellowstone River, and north to the British possessions. In 1867 I was again sent into that country to visit the different bands of Sioux, and went up the Missouri as far as the mouth of the Yellowstone. In 1869 and 1870 I was stationed in Montana, and visited the Yellowstone Valley, and the head-waters of the Columbia, on the west side of the Rocky Mountains, and now I am located in Washington Territory. I have thus had some opportunity of judging of the nature of the country through which the North Pacific Railroad is to pass. The country west of Minnesota, till you reach the Missouri, is decidedly bad: a high, dry, rolling prairie, unfit for cultivation, except in a very few detached places along the very few streams. There are several ponds or small lakes, but very few of them contain water that you can drink, and many of them dry up in the summer. There is very little, in fact, you may say no timber, and as a general rule very little rain falls during the summer. The country might do for grazing, but cattle would be obliged to roam over large sections, and in winter would perish for want of timber, or other means of protection against the climate, which is very severe: heavy snows and heavy winds, and very cold. The country west of the Missouri to the Yellowstone is much better in every respect,—more arable land, more timber, more drinkable water, and I found on my trip across it many large deposits of coal or lignite. Still, I would not recommend it as a good country to settle in, and large portions of it can never be inhabited,—not even by Indians. As regards the climate, it is about the same as in the country east of the Missouri. I saw by General Stanley's report of his expedition with the railroad company through that section, he had considerable difficulty with high water in the streams. I found no such difficulty

215

when I crossed through that country. The season, however, was very dry, and I forded both the Yellowstone and the Missouri just above the mouth of the Yellowstone, with my command,—some two thousand cavalry. This was in September. . . . Yours with respect,

(Signed) ALF SULLY
Colonel, 21st Infantry

To General W. B. Hazen, U.S. Army

General Sully also speaks highly of the valleys of Montana and of the Pacific coast, and especially of the timber. The climate he says is "far better than east of Montana."

The drought he encountered was only that of ordinary seasons here, differing widely from the anomalous seasons of 1872 and 1873, which have done so much to deceive the hopeful people all along the border, and to encourage settlements that must be abandoned. The eight seasons, the rainfall of which I have tabulated, give but three years of like rainy character, in summers 1868, 1872, and 1873. In the other five the rainfall was less than ten inches annually. On the 3d of August I left Fargo, about 97° long. west, on the Red River of the North, by the Northern Pacific Railroad for Fort Buford. The boast there was that they had been favored by rains every few days all summer, and the evidence of the fact was clear enough from the rank condition of vegetation. The grasshopper scourge I had read of was not visible. This condition marked the country in going west for about seventy-five miles, when the grasses appeared shorter and the diminishing rains began to be apparent. This continued until we arrived at James River, near the 99th meridian, where the earth and vegetation showed unmistakeable signs of excessive drought. Going westward forty miles farther to Crystal Springs, we found a garden spot of some four acres ploughed, about one half being in a little valley, the other running up a slight bluff. The valley was devoted to ordinary garden vegetables, while the side-hill and bluff had been planted to corn. The vegetables gave promise of a tenth of a crop, while the corn, although showing itself at the foot of the hill, faded out of sight before the eye got half-way to the top. Going still westward to Bismarck, near meridian 101°, the drought had consumed nearly everything. Apple Creek stood a stagnant pool, the grasses in the valley being no higher than on the prairie. About the town the little planted patches were thinly covered in spots with a sickly vegetation, first eaten off by grass-hoppers that only saved it from a universal drought. From that point to Fort Buford, two hundred and twenty-five miles, was one unchanging stretch of brown and yellow hills and valley consumed with drought. With all this we found wood, water, and grass in abundance for our stock; but attempts at gardens at Fort Stevenson, Fort Berthold, and at Fort Buford have failed, as they have done along the whole line of the Upper Missouri. The trees planted at Forts Stevenson and Abraham Lincoln, the two past seasons, and which were growing so boastfully, were about half dead and dying. A few potatoes and a little native Indian corn is all that will be raised. The hay-contractor at the latter post was expected to forfeit his contract, while it was asserted by intelligent men that the quantity of hay required at the two posts, Lincoln and Rice, five thousand tons, could not be had within fifty miles along the river and twenty-five miles back on both sides. At Fort Buford it has taken all the available grass that could be found within twenty miles in all directions to provide four hundred and fifty tons. Near Bismarck men were cutting hay for ten miles along the windings of ravines so narrow that one and sometimes two swaths would cut the entire breadth of grass. The contracts made by the government call for "upland hay," but not in a single case will there be any upland hay to be had, and it will be cut of necessity from swales and low land. There is not a farm for this entire distance of three hundred and twenty-five miles, although there are a few patches where farms are intended; no wheat appears to have been sown anywhere on this line. This is but an example, but with that of last year we have the two extremes. This is the proper season of the year to visit the country to see it at its worst, to offset false impressions gained of it by the universal custom of visiting it in the early season.

The system of meteorological measurements was commenced in 1819, under the direction of the Secretary of War, the Hon.

John C. Calhoun, and has been kept up and constantly improved ever since, extending over the country acquired from Mexico, and to the constantly increasing military posts. Blodget says of them, in great justice: "These observations are taken under the direction of officers, by strict rules, and are the best calculated to give the best results." These compiled reports comprise seventeen hundred printed pages, and are derived from more than fifty million instrumental observations. They are taken from all portions of the country, and their entire accuracy, as a mass of correct averages, has never been questioned by any one competent to deal with them. Differences of simultaneous observations at remote points prove nothing, nor are the sensations any guide, as they are dependent upon the winds more than the temperature. The experiences gained in a single season are quite as apt to mislead as to instruct. These tables prove nothing so conclusively as the great variableness of consecutive seasons, sometimes the rainfall differing as much as twenty inches; but by taking the averages of any eight seasons in the tables, we get a very close approximation to the true law, as the result does not generally vary more than two inches of rainfall from the entire average. An accurate measurement of the rains at Fort Buford for the past eight years gives an annual fall of twelve and a half inches; while Blodget, in his tables, all made previous to 1867, gives fifteen inches,—so near as to prove their practical accuracy. These tables also prove conclusively that the laws have been constant during the period of the formation of the tables, and that the theory, so popular, that the rainfall increases with the cultivation of the land is erroneous. A few changes have been detected, but due to difference of instruments.

These facts seem to establish beyond question an insufficient rainfall for successful agriculture in those regions west of the 100th meridian, and this agrees accurately with the accepted and well-known views of all practical and intelligent men who have a true knowledge of the country, formed upon long experience, and who have no other interest in it than to truthfully represent it. The reasons given by our public men, who know the facts and will not

218

speak out, are probably sufficient to themselves, but will not always bear the strictest tests.

The greater part of this country has places and spots where great labor, a rainy season, or other favorable circumstances may produce encouraging results; but the farmer, whose margin of profits is small at the best, cannot bear such uncertainty, and whatever influence tends to lead him into these sections faster than he would naturally find his way with his eyes open, from the continuous borders of the settlements, will lead to his disappointment and misery.

The plan of "placing" the lands of the Northern Pacific Railroad "where they would do the most good" was varied by Jay Cooke from the example of his illustrious predecessor in this, that while Oakes Ames undertook to place them directly with congressional representatives, Jay Cooke, more radical and shrewd, endeavored to place his with the people, until enough had been so placed as to assure such interest in the road as would compel Congress to subsidize it. If this scheme is ever to be meritorious, and able to stand upon its boasted land grant, why is it not so now? It can never have more acres of land to the mile of road than it has at present, nor can it ever again—should construction go on— have so many acres of *good* land to the mile as it has now.

It is eight years since, with twenty-five men, I passed over the Yellowstone country, where it is now proposed to build a railroad, and saw the iniquity of the scheme, so recently discussed, to build a road upon the credulity of the people, impressed with the belief that the country was valuable. Until there shall arise some more palpable reason in its favor than has, as yet, been produced, it is an act of simple duty to record a protest against the plan.

W. B. HAZEN

13. The Railroad Rings

In January, 1874, another person entered the field against the Northern Pacific Railroad, who perhaps unintentionally ranged himself on the side of General Hazen. This was Elizur Wright, whose contributions have been too little regarded and who argued from an entirely different point of view. He conceded that much of the land lying between the Missouri River and the Rocky Mountains was largely worthless for purposes of agriculture, but that the land grant given to the Northern Pacific was, as a whole, too valuable to be turned over to a private corporation.

Mr. Wright seems to have been an erratic individualist, one of those advocates of reform too radical even for those who agree with them in principle. Of New England ancestry, he had lived in Ohio as a youth but had graduated from Yale College. He then returned to Ohio, where he became one of the first professors at Western Reserve University. Here he became involved in the abolitionist movement and also took a strong stand against a high protective tariff, but he is probably best known for his campaign against the existing practices of the life insurance companies. Some of the companies were so much impressed with the strength of his arguments that they paid him the supreme compliment of employing him to prepare their actuarial tables, and as a result Mr. Wright probably had more to do with the development of sound standards of life insurance than any other person of his generation.[1] In 1872 he was listed as "Consulting Actuary" by the

---

[1] *Dictionary of American Biography*, XX, 548–49. The article is by Gilbert Barnes.

220

St. Louis Mutual Life Insurance Company which advertised itself as the leading insurance company of the West.[2]

In a series of four articles in the Boston *Daily Advertiser*, beginning on January 9, 1874, he argued his case against the Northern Pacific. (These articles were later brought together in pamphlet form to meet the demand for reprints.) In essence his contention was that the United States in its national capacity owned a great isolated domain in the Pacific Northwest which was "destined to be the greatest quarter of its whole extent," and that Congress, "with reckless improvidence," had subsidized a corporation "that has never paid a dollar on its stock," with enough land to build two railroads from Lake Superior to Pudget Sound.

In his first article he defined a "railroad ring" as "a little circle of men who, without paying out a dollar of their own money, except as bribes, procure an act of incorporation and a grant of public lands. Then, pledging the lands and franchise as security, they borrow from the little hoards of honest, simple, and hardworking people, ready money enough to build their road. Then, if the road pays and the lands sell, they are able to refund their loans and be millionaires—they and their offspring—forever. But if the road fails to pay and the land fails to sell, the thousands of honest people who trusted them suffer about as much as if so many thousands of thieves had been let loose without any policemen to look after them." He then characterized the Northern Pacific Railroad as "the biggest of the ring railroads, and a fair sample of the whole class," and declared that its ring, like that of Saturn, was double, consisting as it did of "The Northern Pacific Railroad Company," which held the franchise and the land grant, and "The Lake Superior and Puget Sound Land Company," consisting of the most energetic and sagacious members of the corporation, whose function was to pre-empt the most valuable town sites, corner lots, etc., along the route.

In a later article he declared that "these rings have for a good many years past, in a financial sense, run the national government. Constituting a great debtor class, they have effectually resisted

[2] *Army and Navy Journal*, March 3, 1872.

specie payment and inflicted on the country an essentially dishonest currency to further their own interests. The more they flourish, the less does the country."

Wright was of the opinion that the crisis in the affairs of the railroad caused by the insolvency of Jay Cooke and Company, gave the general government the opportunity to annul the charter and take back from the company a franchise to which they had no honest title. The title would then revert back to the government of the United States, which should also take back the land grant and build the road itself, and thus secure the whole enormous profit of the enterprise for the taxpayers.

Arguing that it had been decided many years before that the Pacific railroads should be built by the government, he stated his belief that the decision of Congress to build them by subsidy rather than by direct contract had been unwise. But for the action of the government these railroads could not be constructed, since to reach the vast hospitable region of the Pacific coast it was necessary to cross "a scarcely habitable desert." He referred to the Pacific Railroad surveys undertaken under the direction of Jefferson Davis when the latter was secretary of war and quoted the Secretary as reporting "almost utter sterility from the western boundary of Minnesota to the Yakima Pass in the Cascade Mountains, that is, from the 97th to the 121st meridian." Mr. Davis was also quoted as saying that "the sum of the cultivable soil in the Rocky Mountain region does not exceed, if it equals, 1000 square miles." While there was said to be good soil and an attractive climate west of the Cascade mountains, east of them there was not only sterility but also winters that were "severely cold."

Then, addressing himself to the question, "Will the Northern Pacific be Finished?" Mr. Wright wrote:

Since the calamity which befell the Northern Pacific in the failure of Jay Cooke and Company, a good many of the leading newspapers not directly under the patronage of the Administration like the "New York Tribune" and "Sun," for example, have fallen back—perhaps unconsciously to themselves—on this opinion of Mr. Jefferson Davis. They pronounce the road one leading from nothing to nowhere, all Mr. Jay Cooke's geography mythical, and the whole scheme an impracticability which should never have been undertaken. One would think these editors must have been borne since Congress printed the thirteen quarto volumes of Pacific Railroad Reports, and that their geographical education had been neglected ever since their birth.

To make a sufficiently strong case for the practicability and wisdom of the Northern Pacific Railroad,—indeed to prove that its speedy completion somehow is inevitable,—it is not necessary to put any faith whatever in the florid prospectuses of Jay Cooke or the indorsements of Schuyler Colfax. It is not even necessary to swallow whole the speeches of Governor Isaac I. Stevens, which read so much like Walt Whitman's poems.

Let us leave out of account as worthless everything between Minnesota and Fort Benton. Here we come to a mountainous belt, seven hundred miles long and three hundred and sixty broad, naturally tributary to the Northern Pacific road, if it should ever be built, to say nothing of the adjacent British territory on the north. And just here I must say that Jeff. Davis objected to this as a *military* road, because it was run so near the British possessions, *his* military idea having a south side of it. This great mountainous belt, sprinkled with snowy peaks and intersected and watered by innumerable rivers, abuts on the Pacific with at least one of the finest harbors in the known world. It has confessedly some of the finest forests in the world. It is of course as large as New England, New York, New Jersey, Pennsylvania, Delaware, Maryland, Ohio and Indiana put together. Taking out the mountains there cannot be less than 150,000 square miles of valleys and plains and rivers and lakes. It is most likely not a good country for any sort of plough, unless it is the side hill plough. Minnesota is the paradise of ploughs and wheat, but not of cattle in the winter season, or even of sheep. This is true of almost the whole of the great arable country which we used to call the North-West. Its winters are too long and hard for profitable stock-raising. It may continue to furnish our own and its grain, but our beef before the next century has got to come mainly from the sheltered and grassy mountain valleys of the new North-West. So has our wool.

If anybody can find where the wild ox or buffalo winters, he will probably find the country from which our beef will come as soon as its distance is annihilated by a railroad leading to it. Not that we are going to eat roast buffalo. But where the wild ox can survive the winter alone, there by the help of man the tame one will flourish best. We can judge of the multitude of the migratory buffaloes that have hitherto roamed over the cis-Rocky Mountain prairies in summer, by the multitude of buffalo robes that one sees everywhere in the United States and Canada, and even in Europe.[3] We know they never wintered on those plains, nor in the countries south of them, to any considerable extent. If a herd of buffaloes were to be caught by one of those snow-storms that traverse these treeless plains in winter, their carcasses would turn into herbage the next summer. An animal whose male knows enough to perform the military duties of a march, and a female to take her calf on her back in crossing a stream likely to drown it,[4] will not be caught much in this way if there is any safe retreat accessible. And such retreats we know do exist in the valleys of the new North-West, as well as those of the adjacent British possessions, where the buffalo is found up to the sixty-fourth parallel.

Early in January, 1854, Lieutenant Cuvier Grover,[5] by order of Governor Stevens, left Fort Benton with a dog-train to test the snow question in the Rocky Mountains. The Missouri had been closed a little while by ice in December, but was then open. They took pack-mules along because there was no snow for the dog-sledges. After ascending the mountain a few days on the Teton River, they met a little snow and sent the mules back. But the next day the south-west wind blew and the snow melted, making the lieutenant sorry he had sent back the mules. After sledging on

---

[3] And yet the senseless slaughter of the buffalo, which was to bring about the almost complete extermination of that animal, had scarcely begun.

[4] The accuracy of this statement is difficult to determine. I have heard it argued, with considerable heat on both sides, many times.

[5] Later, during the Nez Percé War of 1877, colonel of the First United States Cavalry, with headquarters at Fort Walla Walla, Washington Territory.

bare ground awhile, there was more snow, but never more than a foot. The thermometer at the summit of the pass went as low as it does in Maine.

Under the date of January 8, Lieutenant Grover mentions seeing "plenty of deer and a herd of buffaloes." On the fifteenth, he saw "the track of a wood-buffalo." This was the larger kind found on the Saskatchewan farther north. On the eighteenth, he says "On some of these inclined intervals I observed a good many buffalo tracks leading from the mountain defiles to the water." Again, on the twentieth, he says, "Buffalo tracks continue to be observed, but in less numbers than yesterday." This was on the west slope. On the twenty-first, in Bitter Root Valley, the headwaters of the main or northern branch of the Columbia, he says, "Cattle and horses were grazing contentedly on the wide range." "The cattle though never housed or fed, were, with a few exceptions, in market order; and the young calves, were sporting in the sun." Descending the river northward, without snow, on the fourth of February he saw forty horses grazing. Going through the tall and dense pine woods on Lake Pend 'Oreille [*sic*], the snow lay two or three feet, but on emerging into the prairie it was summer and cattle were feeding "fat and sleek," in green grass up to their eyes.

Dr. George Suckley,[6] who descended the Columbia in a canoe a little earlier in the same season, also mentions seeing a buffalo-bull killed at the mouth of the Pend 'Oreille River. Their bones are plenty in all these valleys, and particularly in that of the Salmon River, a little farther south, where the Indians made great havoc of them for their skins. It is obvious enough that the buffalo would never have resorted to these pent-up valleys, where his foe, the Indian, has so much the advantage of him, unless he found there protection from the rigors of winter and the means

---

[6] Dr. George Suckley had been an assistant surgeon in the United States Army before the Civil War. During that conflict he was a staff surgeon of the United States Volunteers. In 1860, in collaboration with Dr. James G. Cooper, he had published *Report on the Natural History, Climate and Physical Geography of Minnesota, Nebraska, Washington and Oregon Territories* (New York, 1860). *Appleton's Cyclopedia of American Biography* (New York, 1891), V, 738. Efforts to locate a copy of the *Report* have, so far, been unsuccessful.

of subsistence. This one fact, considering how much forage the buffaloes that formerly existed in that region must have consumed, is more decisive than the opinion of Jefferson Davis, or even the ablest newspaper editor. And it does not depend upon interested witnesses.

It is quite impossible that the corner of the country best fitted by nature for the production of flesh, fish and wool, to say nothing of its minerals, should escape for many years longer being connected with the rest of it by rail. The only question is whether it shall be done honestly or corruptly.

14. Sargent

Also appearing in 1874 was another pamphlet, entitled "Major-General Hazen on his Post of Duty in the Great American Desert," written, according to the title page, by a former surveyor general, and generally attributed to John O. Sargent, a lawyer and journalist who wrote prolifically upon a number of subjects. Born in Massachusetts in 1811, he was graduated from Harvard in 1830 and admitted to the bar. In 1838 he entered newspaper work and seems to have divided his time about equally between the two occupations until 1872, when he retired from the practice of law. He had written a good many pamphlets, the greater part of them having political overtones. He had also spent much time in literary pursuits, translating a number of foreign works. He also found time to write pamphlets dealing with controversial subjects before the American public.

Although this pamphlet is generally attributed to Mr. Sargent, I have been unable to establish that he ever held the position of surveyor general. However, his interest in politics was so great and continued over so many years that he may very well have written it. It is difficult to fit in the period of years to which he refers when he states (page 251) that he had lived forty years on the frontier and measured "more acres of the Northwest than Major-General Hazen has ever seen." I am inclined to believe that the pamphlet was, rather, the work of George B. Sargent, who, in addition to working as a practical surveyor, had served as surveyor general from 1851 to 1853 and had lectured on the subject of "the West."

Regardless of authorship, however, this pamphlet is an attack —an extremely sarcastic one—upon the argument that Hazen set forth regarding the value of the western lands; it made no mention of Custer's letter nor of other persons who disagreed with Hazen, although reference is made to Elizur Wright. But it is a part of the controversy over the barren lands, and is in itself a valuable and interesting document. In many ways it is the ablest and best written refutation of the Hazen argument to appear. For that reason it is here printed as the final article.

There are useful and in other regards respectable members of society, who are unhappy unless they can see their names in the newspapers. Never a crowd gets together but the victim of this unhappiness is announced in the public prints as being present— every time. Nor is there an important office vacant but you can bet on some of the names that will be telegraphed as imminently in danger of being sent to the Senate. This class of monomaniacs, when they can manage it in no other way, write letters and prevail on humane but inconsiderate editors to publish them; and thus it is, we apprehend, that Major-General W. B. Hazen has been urged into print under his own signature. On the first day of January, 1874, he put the finishing touches to a long and elaborate letter dated at Fort Buford, D. T., which was apparently intended as a sort of New Year's gift to the American people. It was published in due course in the "New York Tribune" with sympathetic edi- torial comments. We learn from this document that the Major- general is grievously discontented with his position. A spot at the intersection of meridian 104 W. with the 48th parallel N., just where the Yellowstone empties into the Missouri, is no place for a gentleman who may have wealth to enjoy and social aspirations to gratify. It would no doubt be more agreeable to almost any major-general, unless he were of the stock and stuff that Zachary Taylors are made of, to be domiciled in the neighborhood of the meridian where the Hudson falls into the Atlantic, or the Charles

228

into Massachusetts Bay. We can well imagine that a first of January in that inhospitable region may have called up old recollections of the day in a far-off city on the banks of the Potomac, with diplomats in uniform at the White House, and friendly tables laden with terrapin and canvas-back, to say nothing of accompanying egg-nog and apple-toddy. All this may have made our frontier major-general quite miserable, but it should not have made him so splenetic and venomous as his unfortunate letter exhibits him.

Being then at this very frigid "post of duty" and hardly concealing his wishes for a very Unhappy New Year to all persons in more favored regions, Major-general Hazen sends out his compliments of the season to the late Governor Stevens, to General Fremont, Lieutenant Mullen, and the author of the "Poetry and Philosophy of Indian Summer" in "Harper's Magazine" of December in particular—and to all the territory running from the meridian 100 W. sixteen hundred miles toward the Pacific, and from the Rio Grande to the British possessions, in general. And it is a little curious to see the distinction he draws between the author and the epauleted gentlemen, though they have written very much in the same vein. The author's statements are shameless falsehoods, deliberately indulged. The governor and the military men are merely enthusiastic persons, whose descriptions are not fully borne out by a more prolonged and intimate knowledge of the country. He draws it very mild with the soldiers, but the bankers and the financiers he abuses without stint. His letter is in the spirit of a papal bull. For himself he claims infallibility. Any one who shall contradict him he denounces in advance as a liar. Major-general Hazen, standing conspicuously on his "post of duty," proclaims from this commanding standpoint that the lands in this vast territory will not sell for one penny an acre, except through the fraud of the seller or the ignorance of the purchaser. They have absolutely "no value." Representations to the contrary are false and wicked deceptions; so false and so wicked that they have evidently chilled the blood and soured the temper of Major-general Hazen on his very "post of duty." This is his positive

229

averment, on his honor, we suppose, as a gentleman, and his responsibility as an officer.

But fortunately this swift witness gives us the means of weighing the value of his testimony, as far as it depends upon his personal knowledge. It is based, he tells us, on eighteen years of military service as an officer of the army, and on the experience of the residue of his days as a practical farmer. Much of his military experience has been upon the frontier, we learn by way of parenthesis. On which side of the Missouri his frontier service was performed, before he was stationed at Fort Buford, he does not inform us. When he descends to details, he gives us none that bear upon any other region than that immediately about the place of his exile. Apropos to this special location he exhibits a transcript from the hospital records, attested by an assistant surgeon of the United States army and a lieutenant of the 6th Infantry; and this transcript is a table of temperature and rainfall at Fort Buford, D. T., from the 1st of August, 1866, to the 31st of December, 1873. Of this table we may have a word to say by and by— allowing here for the purpose of the argument that it shows a degree of cold and an absence of moisture that might seem more or less uncomfortable to a military lounger on Pennsylvania Avenue, but that certainly ought not to appall a major-general in the regular army, on his "post of duty." But whether cold or dry, let us see what this climate and soil enabled our exiled garrison to enjoy in the way of an "extensive garden" at the intersection of the meridians above stated. They could not have *red* tomatoes. This was a hardship, no doubt. A red coat becomes a tomato, no less than a soldier. But what was worse, pumpkins did not mature; there were some pumpkins at the "post of duty," but on the first of January they were not matured. The same was true of squashes and melons. We must prevail on Mr. Gregory,[1] the seedsman of Marblehead, to send the Major-general some of his early varieties, say the Early Nutmeg and the Summer Crook-neck. But as an

---

[1] James John Howard Gregory of Marblehead, Massachusetts, who, from a small and almost accidental beginning, built a seed business which became one of the largest and best known in the United States. He is generally credited with the introduction of the Hubbard squash.

offset to the want of these esculents—not altogether necessary to keep body and soul together even at Fort Buford,—the garrison with "great care" and by "utilizing all the available season" managed to console themselves with an "abundant" and "mature" crop of potatoes, cabbage, early-sown turnips, early peas, early beans, beets, carrots, salsify, cucumbers, lettuce, radishes, asparagus and American corn, reaching to roasting ears. What a list of luxuries for a major-general to groan over! The garrison could not have done better if every soldier of them, instead of his Scott's "Manual," had made a *Vade Mecum* of Peter Henderson's "Gardening for Profit." But it was not vegetables alone that the garrison raised: by expending three barrels of water daily on a garden plot ten feet by forty, the Major-general was enabled to enjoy in the open air about three weeks of flowers. And this is absolutely all the testimony based on his own experience vouchsafed in proof of the averment that the land of the immense territory in question is not worth a penny an acre. It is supplemented, however, by the testimony of a hay contractor, to the effect that he went twenty-four miles toward each point of the compass before he could get together nine hundred tons of hay; and if he had gone twenty-four miles further he would have found no more grass high enough to cut. Did ever an army contractor, or any other contractor, find hay, corn, or cotton abundant in the region where he was to deliver it? And supposing the hay contractor's story true, we must know more of the locality than we learn from Major-general Hazen to understand its significance. We apprehend that there are points in New England and Pennsylvania of which a hay contractor might make the same report, without proving the territory worthless. But did it ever occur to the Major-general that his story seeing twenty miles of this territory strewn with the carcasses of buffalo was a complete answer to this hay contractor? These buffaloes must have been alive some time, and what business had they in a country where there was no grass?

It is no new thing—this disgust of army officers with their frontier accommodations; nor is this the first time it has found its way into print. Less than fifty years ago there was a military post

231

near the mouth of Chicago River—Fort Dearborn,—and the military gentlemen there were as much exercised with their agricultural experiences as our practical farmer at the mouth of the Yellowstone. Indeed they were much more desolate and oppressed. Instead of the rich assortment of mature vegetables set forth as the product of extensive gardens,—a list that might rejoice the heart of an epicure—they were obliged to import their provisions in a schooner from Mackinaw, and sometimes to bring them three hundred and eighty-six miles up the Illinois and Des Plaines rivers from St. Louis. So barren and worthless was the region about Fort Dearborn that it was "impossible" for a garrison of some seventy to ninety men, "although much of their time was devoted to agricultural pursuits," and "with the most active vigilance on the part of the officers," "to subsist themselves upon the grain raised in the country." The soil was shallow; the soil was humid; the soil was exposed to the cold and damp winds that blew most of the year from the lake with great force. The season was short; the season was cold; the grain was devoured by swarms of insects; the grain was devoured by flocks of destructive birds. Of this last plague it was "impossible to avoid the baneful influence," except by keeping a party of soldiers constantly engaged in shooting at the crows and blackbirds that depredated upon the corn planted by them." But to the military eye this was not all, and perhaps not the worst. The appearance of the country was very much against it. The water view was a dread stretch, unrelieved by sail or an island; and on the shore there was nothing in any direction to break the fatiguing monotony but a few patches of thin and scrubby woods. Even the name of the place was an offense to the military nostril, for in the Potowatomi tongue Chicago meant "skunk," or at best a "wild onion." Notwithstanding its "antiquity" the village consisted of only a few filthy huts, tenanted by a miserable race of half-breeds. To be sure, the number of trails centering there indicated that it had been the sometime seat of a large Indian village; but it offered no inducement to the settler as a place of business, for all the trade on the lake, including the importation of provisions from Mackinaw, did not include the cargo of more than five or six schooners. The best that could be hoped for was that at some distant day, when the low prairies between the Illinois River and Fort Wayne should be settled and cultivated, Chicago might become one of the points in the direct line of communication between the lakes and the Mississippi. It is gratifying to know that in the number of "impossibles" found by our military men hereabouts, this result is pronounced "not impossible." Even this, however, could not be entertained without very formidable doubts. The dangers of the lake navigation, the scarcity of lake harbors, and the shocking sand-banks on the southern and eastern shores, were regarded as the most serious obstacles to the commercial importance of Chicago, and such as rendered it almost certain that the intercourse through the direct communciation above mentioned would be a "limited one." Surely the military view of Fort Dearborn on the New Year's day of 1823 was not eminently cheerful. It can hardly be said to compare favorably with that of Fort Buford fifty years later.

But even at that early day, civilians, non-resident and merely visting Fort Dearborn, saw the country and the village with very different eyes. Instead of a bleak and barren waste, Mr. Schoolcraft thought the country about Chicago the most fertile and beautiful that could be imagined. His accurate estimate of its advantages and capabilities, his prevision so singularly contrasting with the blindness of our military friends, and so eminently justified by the results we have been in the habit of witnessing for a quarter of a century, we must copy in his own words: "As a farming country," Mr. Schoolcraft wrote half a hundred years ago,—"it unites the fertile soil of the finest lowland prairies with an elevation which exempts it from the influence of stagnant waters and a summer climate of delightful serenity . . . . To the ordinary advantages of an agricultural market-town it must hereafter add that of a depot for the inland commerce, between the northern and southern sections of the Union, and a great thoroughfare for strangers, merchants and travellers." And all this, notwithstanding even Mr. Schoolcraft doubted if a safe and permanent harbor could be constructed by any human ingenuity upon the bleak and naked shores of that lake "exposed as they are to the most furious tempests." So it would seem that furious tempests are not specialties of the New Northwest.

But civil as well as military officers sometimes take false views of unexplored regions, by generalizing too rapidly from an insufficient experience. By an act of Congress of May 5, 1812, six million acres of land were ordered to be surveyed in the territories Louisiana, Illinois and Michigan, two millions in each territory, to be set apart for our soldiers in the war with Great Britain. A quarter section fit for cultivation was awarded to each soldier. The lands were duly surveyed and appropriated in Louisiana and Illinois, but no lands fit for cultivation could be found by the surveyors in the state of Michigan. It is curious to see by what minute details the worthlessness of these lands is officially established. Fifty miles in one stretch from the Indiana boundary line on a given direction are set down as wet land, mixed in with very bad marshes, but generally very heavily timbered; thence north and and east the swamps get bigger, and there are more of them, with lakes from twenty chains to two or three miles across. And these lakes have extensive marshes on their margins, sometimes "thickly covered with a species of pine called tamarack"—and other places covered with a coarse, high grass, and "uniformly covered from six inches to three feet (and more at times) with water." These swamps are found through the whole country, and what is not swamps and lakes, is with a few exceptions a poor, barren, sandy land, with no vegetation but very small scrubby oaks. There is little dry land confessed to, if such a name can be given to little, short sand-hills, with deep bottoms of marsh intervening. Narrow rivers very deep and with banks swampy beyond description run through this superfluously irrigated country; and it is only with the "utmost difficulty that a place can be found, over which horses *can be conveyed*." So it would seem that these unfortunate explorers and pioneers were obliged to "convey" their horses instead of having the horses "convey" them.

It is mentioned as a circumstance "peculiar" to this country,

234

that the marshes are covered with a thin sward of grass, "by walk-ing on which evinced the existence of water, or a very thin mud," which had the remarkable property of sinking six to eighteen inches under the pressure of the foot, and at the same time rising before and behind. Even the banks of the lakes and the rivers were "literally afloat." Toward the "straits and Lake" there were not so many swamps but there was the same "extreme sterility and barrenness" of the soil. The summing up we must give in the very words of the official who pens this appalling sketch: "Taking the country altogether, so far as has been explored, and to all appear-ances, together with the information received concerning the balance is so bad there would not be more than one acre out of an hundred, if there would be one out of one thousand, that would in any case admit of cultivation."

It will be noted that this account is abridged from an official letter of the Surveyor-general of Ohio to the Commissioner of the General Land Office, written at Chillicothe some time in 1815. Congress recognized the hardship of compelling the soldiers to select their quarter-sections in Michigan, and repealed so much of the bounty act as related to the forlorn region made up of swamps and sand-hills, with no land fit for cultivation. In place of these sterile and floating acres, fit for the residence of neither man nor beast, they substituted the better lands of Illinois and Missouri. One would suppose that this official and governmental condemna-tion would have settled the question for Michigan. With only one acre out of a thousand admitting to cultivation in any case, it was worse than the Hazen desert at least twenty-fold. But how has the result justified the confident statements of the Surveyor-General? The present area of Michigan is some thirty-five millions of acres. Of this number, by the census of 1870, ten millions of acres were embraced in farms, of the cash value in round numbers of four hundred millions of dollars, and an annual production of upwards of eighty-two millions. Twenty millions of acres pay taxes as individual property, of which it was officially averred and official-ly acted upon that only some twenty thousand acres could under any circumstances be capable of cultivation. And it was the mere question of more or less moisture that seemed conclusive to the Surveyor-general and to the Major-general alike. In Michigan there was "water,—water everywhere:" but in Dakota there is "not a drop to drink."

We have seen that the malediction of our Major-general covers a vast extent of territory,—1,600 miles in one direction, and from the Rio Grande to the British possessions in another. But the object it is avowedly aimed at covers a comparatively narrow strip, no more than a belt forty miles wide on each side of the track of the North Pacific [*sic*] Railroad. For two years he had been the witness of the efforts of this corporation to induce the belief that "this section" was a valuable agricultural one. For two years he had "kept silent" although he knew the "falsity of their representations," and had permitted them to go on unchecked in the disposition of their bonds on the sham security of lands that are of no value. For two years he has restrained his "shame and indignation" till they culminated in the perusal of a florid eulogy on the Indian summer in the December number of Harper's "estimable" periodical; evidently written for the benefit of this swindling corporation, and designed to utilize the poetry and philosophy of this marvelous season in the service of their fraudulent securities. Flesh and blood can stand it no longer on a "post of duty" in a region so hyperborean. The steed was stolen and the Major-general felt bound to shut the stable door. That any man should speak well of the Indian summer without a sinister motive, was more than he was willing to believe; and the only solution he could give to this phenomenon was the identification of this gentle enthusiast with the author of Mr. Jay Cooke's advertisements in the interests of the North Pacific Railroad. Two years of pent-up "shame and indignation" broke their flood-gates, and we can hardly measure by meridians the boundless area they overflowed.

The propositions which Major-General Hazen demonstrates by vehement assertion involve not merely the reputation of the promoters of this great enterprise, but the good faith of numerous officers and agents of the United States Government, civil and military. They may be thus briefly stated. The country intended

236

to be traversed by the road through Dakota, Montana, Idaho, Washington and Oregon is worthless. Knowing it to be worthless the corporation in question through their fiscal agents have represented it as valuable, and have negotiated their bonds on the strength of these representations. These bonds therefore are substantially identical with the paper of a swindler who has checked upon a bank where he has no funds. They will prove a total loss, unless they are converted forthwith into the good lands now held by the Company in the valley of the Red River of the North, and east of that river. You will perceive that on his "post of duty" and nowhere else, Major-general Hazen has taken upon himself the responsibility of maintaining these criminatory averments. Not merely as a practical agriculturist and an officer of the regular army long engaged in service on the frontier, but as a financier and economist proclaiming truths of importance in Wall Street, he informs the world that the thirty millions of the North Pacific bonds are utterly worthless unless they are forthwith foreclosed *on the very security on which they have been issued.* Two points here present themselves which we propose to discuss with Major-general Hazen, the first of which is his attack upon the bonds. There are two distinct propositions, because if the lands between the Red River and the Sierras are as bad as Major-general Hazen represents them, it does not follow that the bonds heretofore issued are of necessity worthless.

I. And first with regard to the land. It will be observed that the question involved in this inquiry is not the value of the land grant of a railroad, but one of infinitely more moment, to wit, the value of an empire. It is the New Northwest that Major-general Hazen has made the subject of his violent tirade, and it embraces a territory of more than imperial dimensions. We propose, therefore, to analyze more particularly than we have yet done the peculiar experience on which this gentleman relies as giving value to his testimony, that we may compare it with the opportunities of judging that have been enjoyed by other witnesses whom we shall call upon to contradict him. The portion of his life passed in the pursuit of agriculture is of no special bearing on the case, except so far as his farming experience may be connected with his personal examination of the region he has denounced, and of his eighteen years of military experience on the frontier, those years only are of importance to the present subject that were passed in the country he presumes to describe. His first service was in 1855, at Fort Reading[2] in California, and Fort Lane[3] in a southwestern county of Oregon. Then for some three years he was scouting and skirmishing with the Indians; sometimes in Oregon, but chiefly in Texas, on the Nueces and on the Yanno [*sic*], where he was severely wounded and remained two years on the sick list. At the outbreak of the Rebellion he recruited and organized a regiment of volunteers at Cleveland for the defense of the Ohio frontier, and was subsequently engaged in operations in Kentucky and Tennessee, and was raised from the rank of colonel of Ohio volunteers to be Brevet Major-general of the United States army in 1865. We find him at Washington, D. C., for a short time in the Department of the Platte, and afterwards organizing a regiment at Jefferson Barracks. Some months of European travel, and the composition of a book which no one could wish his worst enemy to have written, filled the gap between his service at Jefferson Barracks and his service at Fort Buford. From this statement of the gentleman's particular whereabouts during his eighteen years of service, "mostly on the frontier," the reader will perceive what an erroneous impression he unintentionally conveys by his general claim to peculiar opportunities of observation in the territory he describes. But from even this statement the reader will hardly be prepared to believe, what we have good authority for asserting—that Major-general Hazen has never seen an acre of the country traversed by the North Pacific Railroad between the Missouri and the Yellowstone, and that he has no personal knowledge whatever of the lands which he so flippantly describes as worthless.[4]

2 Fort Reading was established in 1852 on Cow Creek, a mile and a half above its junction with the Sacramento River, at the site of the present town of Redding, California.

3 Fort Lane was established in 1853 on the Rogue River, a few miles northwest of present Medford, Oregon.

The best opportunity he has enjoyed of learning from personal experience that the territories of Dakota, Montana, Idaho, Washington and Oregon, are not worth a penny an acre, is from two years uncomfortable residence at Fort Buford. And except by broad phrases of the most vague and general character, insinuating everything but distinctly averring nothing, even his remarkable letter fails to connect his military service, any more than his farming experience, with that special personal knowledge, which alone entitles him to give the lie peremptorily to all who have ever written otherwise than himself upon this region, and to all who may hereafter contradict him. A table of temperatures and rainfalls for seven years at Fort Buford, and the really brilliant farming and gardening experience of the Major-general for one or two years in that location are "statistics" and "personal experience" too inconsequent and inconclusive to lend any weight whatever to his sweeping and monstrous generalization.

In aid of his summary valuation of half a dozen States, Major-general Hazen refers the reader to General G. K. Warren of the engineer corps of the army, or to Professor Hayden, both of whom, he says, have been engaged in scientific explorations of the territory in question. We can find no printed reports of either that sustain the extraordinary assertions of Major-general Hazen. We know that but a very small portion of the North Pacific route was ever traversed by General Warren; and we have good reason for believing that the use of Professor Hayden's name as a voucher for the penny-an-acre valuation of Uncle Sam's farm in the New Northwest is altogether unauthorized. It will be time enough, therefore, to handle the testimony of these witnesses when we know what they say. Names are things sometimes, but the mere names of witnesses are not sufficient to confirm the statements of so judicial an observer as Major-general Hazen. It is a maxim of the civil law that witnesses are to be weighed and not numbered. In disposing of the testimony adduced by Major-general Hazen, we have both numbered and weighed his witnesses, and we find

---

[4] As inspector general of the Department of the Platte, General Hazen would have had the opportunity to see some of these lands.

that they count one, and weigh nothing. And now for the other side.

In presenting the opposite view of the New Northwest, we shall not rely at all upon the witnesses who, with the graceful flourish of the Major-general's right hand, are waved aside as enthusiasts. We are not sure that the term may not be well enough applied to Fremont, who seems to have manifested more or less "entusymusy" as miner, financier, and politician, and we can therefore believe that he may have exhibited the same element as a traveller. But as Fremont's explorations were many hundred miles south of the "disputed territory," his testimony either way could not be of any more value than that of Major-general Hazen himself. Governor Stevens we have seen and observed, and a more practical man, and one less liable to be carried away by his imagination, we have never met with. He was not a mere explorer of the penny-an-acre empire. He lived in it for years, was the Governor of one territory carved out of the worthless domain, and died in it[5] with the conviction that it was at no remote period to be the seat of populous and prosperous commonwealths. Nor was Lieutenant Mullan a mere bird of passage. He was for a long period a resident of the country, in the service of the government; and engaged in the location of military roads he enjoyed the advantage which Major-general Hazen does not seem to appreciate—of seeing something of the country of which he speaks. And with this we dismiss the enthusiasts.

The least enthusiastic people on the face of the earth are deputy-surveyors and surveyors-general. They are born so. If not so born, a service incredibly short with line and compass in tamarack swamps and deserts infested with Indians is enough to take all enthusiasm out of them. Therefore it is that we shall to some extent pin our faith on what the deputy-surveyors have to say on this matter. Let us go to the antipodes of the enthusiasts at once. Hard pan cannot be reached too soon. The Hazen desert of sixteen hundred miles in length runs through Dakota, Montana,

5 Governor Stevens did not die in Washington Territory. See page 73, note 4, above.

Idaho, and Washington territories—appraised at less than a penny an acre. Let us see what the official records make of it.

Dakota

What says the Commissioner of the General Land Office in his official reports? "Dakota has as great a variety of surface and as rich a soil as almost any state or territory of the United States" (1870). "In central and eastern Dakota lies a great body of untouched fine agricultural lands, where the farming can be done by the ordinary modes, and where the settlement can be continuous. The North Pacific Railroad will open a large body of them, including the Red River Valley and westward to the Missouri. The products of Dakota vary with its different latitudes, but not very considerably. In the north the smaller grains and potatoes, with a great variety of vegetables, are grown with success. It is not yet fully tested whether the Valley of the Red River will produce and mature *corn* regularly. But for wheat, oats, rye, barley, potatoes, and similar crops, the region is unsurpassed, probably on the continent. The soil is of the finest character, and with proper treatment yields most abundantly" (1871). "The North Pacific Railroad has completed about 120 miles in Dakota, and will have the track laid to the Missouri River within a few weeks. This will open to settlement a rich region along the Red and Dakota rivers, the best part of North Dakota, suitable for a great variety of crops, and comparatively near the lake markets" (1872).

The North Pacific Railroad stops for the present on the Missouri, and the lands on which its present issue of bonds is secured lie chiefly east of meridian 101°, and within the region thus officially described by the resident Surveyor-general of the territory, whose duty it was to know what he affirmed. West of the present terminus at Bismarck to the western boundary of Dakota, there has been no pretense set up by any human being that this country was specially adapted to agriculture; but it has been claimed and with truth that it is well adapted to grazing purposes, and that it is valuable for its deposits of coal. We admit that the agricultural immigrant cannot go far west of meridian 101° except in the valleys, on the borders of the watercourses, and on the fertile table lands that occur at intervals in the mountainous districts. Fortunately the lands are not merely adapted to tillage, because the world is not made up entirely of farmers. There are some miners for gold and silver, some graziers, some delvers for coal, some makers of iron, some hewers of wood, and (for purposes of irrigation) some drawers of water. And therefore it is that we read with much satisfaction the statement of the Surveyor-general of Dakota for 1871, in the exhaustive and excellent report that we have already cited—and in reference to these very penny-an-acre lands, "There is nearly a million square miles of the West not agricultural in character; *but it is rich in untold mineral wealth. The immigrant there should go for gold and silver. In that way lies fortune.*"

Montana

It must be admitted for a country worth less than a penny an acre, Montana makes an extraordinary showing. We will still adhere to the government reports. Thus writes the Surveyor-general of Montana: "The production of this precious metal (gold) steadily maintains itself. The yield was reputed by my predecessor at $12,000,000 last year. Although water has been scarce for mining purposes, I am convinced from the best data I can obtain, the yield will not fall short of that amount for the fiscal year ending June 31, 1871 .... New discoveries are certainly being made all over the country. The real and personal property in Montana [at its taxable valuation] is $15,788,800. This gives an average of a little over $1,082 to each white person, or of over $763 to each enrolled inhabitant. I think no State in the Union can show more wealth to the individual .... The country now is self-sustaining, and presents ample room for millions of settlers of all occupations, who are cordially invited to come and make their homes with us, and grow up in wealth and usefulness, as the country expands its latent productions and power" (1871). In his report of the following year the Surveyor-general estimates that more than one-third of the 92,000,000 acres embraced in Montana could readily be made tillable, by diverting the waters of the abundant streams by means of ditches through the gardens and grain-fields of the farmers. This mode of irrigation he considers preferable to dependence on the varying and uncertain fall of rain. All the vegetables that abound and mature at Fort Buford grow here in great luxuriance, and in some portions of the territory Indian corn is grown and ripened. At an agricultural fair at Helena premiums were awarded to the best acre of wheat, yielding 102 bushels; the best acre of barley, 113½ bushels; the best acre of oats, 101 bushels; the best acre of potatoes, 613 bushels. Besides the gold found in placers and quartz veins, silver, copper, iron, lead, zinc, antimony, and other metals have been discovered in many sections distributed in large and well-defined ledges. "With its fertile valleys and mineral-bearing mountains, with its supply of timber and coal, with its water privileges and healthy climate, all that Montana needs to develop its vast natural resources is capital and railways, and then she will speedily become a great and prosperous State" (1872).

Idaho

In his report of 1871 the Surveyor-general of Idaho speaks of the extensive pasture lands of that territory, the farming lands in the northern portion, and the grazing lands in the centre; the yield of placer gold in three counties averaging $500,000 each; the numerous miners employed on Snake River taking out fine gold, the rich silver district of Altuxas County, and the silver mines of Owyhee County, and a good deal more that creates the impression that the land there must be very cheap at a penny an acre. Northern Idaho, he says, is one-half farming and one-half mineral land; the farming region being prairie covered with most luxuriant grasses, and the lands on the route of the North Pacific Railroad by far the most desirable for farming and grazing purposes. In his report for 1872 the Surveyor-general speaks of the fertile soil and genial climate of Northern Idaho, and the rapidity with which it is filling up with settlers. In addition to continuing good results from the silver and gold crops, he tells us that stock-raising has turned out to be very profitable, and that some parties own thousands of head of cattle and sheep, the extensive grazing lands and mild winters offering inducements which are not found elsewhere.

Washington Territory

We are told by its Surveyor-general in his report of 1872, that this territory has a vast amount of first class agricultural land, and that there is no doubt whatever that in a few years Western Washington in the products of the dairy will compare favorably with the best of the old States and sections. "The crowning glory," he adds "of Washington Territory is the great advantage it offers to the poor man." Of the country lying east of the Cascade Mountains he tells us the broad prairies are ready for the plow with trifling cost of preparation; that they will produce in some parts, in localities capable of irrigation excellent garden vegetables, and everywhere the soil is most desirable for wheat, rye, oats and barley. The territory contains "almost the entire catalogue of minerals, and the more precious metals have been successfully mined in several localities for many years. . . . Immediately along the line of the North Pacific Railroad, between the Columbia River and Puget Sound, there are immense coal fields, not less than 300,000 acres of coal lands, which are likely to be developed at an early day, and which will add millions of dollars of wealth to the country. . . . The greater part of the country traversed by the line of this road is capable of settlement and of the lands being brought under a profitable state of cultivation." And down to this point we have not touched upon the immense forests of merchantable timber, which furnish exports not merely to California and the South American states, but to Australia and to Europe.

Thus far we have cited only official testimony to the value of this 1,600 mile strip. We have quoted the Surveyor-general, whose business it is to know all about it, against the Major-general who knows nothing about it, and who neglects his own business to attend to that of other people. It is not our intention, for we do not think it necessary, to accumulate proof from other quarters. In confirmation of the statements of the Surveyor-general, if they required confirmation, we might refer to the published reports and letters of Mr. W. Milnor Roberts, the engineer in chief of the surveys of the North Pacific Railroad, who has been over the ground and knows whereof he speaks, and who avers that the great bulk of the region traversed by the road beyond the Missouri has great value as a grazing region, from which a very large cattle transportation will be derived, and that its other values will come from mines of gold, silver, copper, and iron in Montana and Idaho, and from agricultural and timber lands in Washington Territory. This is the generalization of what we have given in the details above, and in that view we adopt it. But Mr. Roberts is in the service of the company, it will be said, and has been from an early stage of the enterprise. And it is on this very account that we set the highest value upon his testimony. It was his duty to inform himself in the premises, and equally his duty and interest to report the information he obtained with the most conscientious accuracy. But waiving the testimony of Mr. Roberts, we will further appeal to Mr. Martin Maginnis, the Congressional delegate from Montana, who has resided eight years in that territory, and who has been over the line of the North Pacific Railroad years ago on horseback. There is a wonderful advantage in having a witness who has seen the country. And Mr. Maginnis has behind him a constituency of 20,000 persons,—a most respectable, intelligent and prosperous constituency, whose success in their affairs is the best proof of the wonderful resources of the country.

And then we dare say that General Hancock[6] remembers his remarks on the occasion of his reception at Helena, and is willing to stand by them. General Sheridan is not given to much talking, and we doubt if he ever made so long a speech as he made on a similar occasion, and the burden of it was the laudation of this new Northwest. We may make a similar appeal to General Terry and General Gibbons [*sic*], and to General Hardee if he were not in respect to this country to be numbered among the enthusiasts. We might inquire of General Grant and General Ingalls about

6 See above, page 58n.

Washington Territory, without fear of their disappointing us. And besides all these, we might refer for the confirmation we desire to Reynolds and McClellan, and to many of the young men now distinguished who served under Governor Stevens, and to General Sherman and to one of his favorite brigade commanders —now Governor Potts, but we must stop somewhere, and we will therefore call only one more witness who is as bitter against the managers of the North Pacific Railroad as Major-general Hazen himself.

We refer to Mr. Elizur Wright, who has been pouring out the vials of his indignation against the North Pacific Railroad, not because their lands are worth too little to secure their creditors, but because they are worth too much to put into the hands of any company as a fund for building the road. He has faith in the lands at the two extremities of the route. He thinks the editor of the "Tribune" must have been born since the publication of the thirteen quarto volumes of explorations in this region, and that his geographical education must have been neglected from his birth. "To make out a sufficiently strong case for the practicability and wisdom of the North Pacific Railroad," says Mr. Wright through the columns of the Boston "Daily Advertiser," "indeed to prove that its speedy completion somehow is inevitable . . . . It is quite impossible that the corner of the country best fitted by nature for the production of flesh, fish and wool, to say nothing of its minerals, should escape for many years longer being connected with the rest of it by rail. . . . It is only necessary to look at the map and cull a few facts from perfectly disinterested and scientific explorers in regard to the northwestern corner of the United States."

II. And now with regard to the Bonds. It is rather a delicate matter to advise any man as to the management of his property even when it comes strictly within the adviser's province and duty. But to tender advice of this nature, to volunteer it, to force it upon the parties interested, can only be justified by the possession of information about which there can be no mistake, and of a judgment in which there can be no fallibility. It is not too much to say that Major-general Hazen propounds his dogmas with a confidence that indicates the sublime confidence of occupying just that position. He avers that the bondholders can save themselves from total loss only by following the course that he points out, and that is by changing their bonds into good lands now owned by the road in a named locality. This, it will be observed, is the *only* mode of a partial salvage. This assurance he gives not merely to the large holders who are abundantly able to take care of themselves, who did not consult Major-general Hazen before investing, and have expressed no intention of consulting him since. To such persons the advice is simply impertinence. But to the thousands of petty holders,—to the country clergymen, to the retired officers, to the small farmers, to the widows and orphans, who have invested in bonds of a low denomination as a sort of more convenient savings bank, to all those persons, while the averment is a source of unnecessary apprehension, the advice based on it is of no practical utility. If there are lands by which they can secure their bonds the company will be able to redeem their promises; and the only question is whether the bond-holders will have their landed security managed by the company, under existing guarantees, or whether they will segregate their particular share from the general fund, and employ some other agent to manage and sell it and account for the proceeds.

In his advice about the bonds, Major-general Hazen abandons for a while the *role* of soldier and farmer and appears in the capacity of a financier. It will occur probably to the least interested observer that the valuation of our financier does not apply to an acre of land already accrued to the Company and forming the security of the present issue of bonds. All this land lies to the east of meridian 101, or to the west of the Sierra Nevada. The ten million acres in Minnesota and the valley of the Red River, and the million acres of coal and timber lands in Washington Territory, to which the railroad has already perfected its title,—this is the vast and valuable domain which our financial Mentor compares to a bank account without funds, and represents substantially as a gigantic swindle.

If this imperial domain is managed with the least prudence

and honesty, it will be of itself abundantly able to take care of the principal and interest of all the bonds that have been issued on it. At the prices which these lands have thus far averaged, the Company's grant would yield more than $100,000 for every mile of road constructed. And as far as property is regarded as a security for the bonds, the security will be largely enhanced if it is true, as Major-general Hazen avers, that the whole country west of meridian 101° *"will not produce the fruits and cereals of the East for the want of moisture, and can in no way be artificially irrigated.* If our financier could have had his way of laying down a first-class railroad route that would be sure to pay its bonds, he would have run it all the way through prime agricultural lands. Probably he is impressed with the belief that if he had been consulted in the first seven days he might have suggested some valuable hints for making this globe of ours a far more desirable residence for human beings than it is at present. He would have had the Red River Valley, for instance, protracted to the Pacific coast. He would have guaranteed a sufficient rainfall through the year to irrigate it abundantly, and to keep the atmosphere humid enough to satisfy the most thirsty lover of moisture. He would have taken care that the mercury in the thermometer should never go below the freezing point, and then he could have raised the fruits and cereals of the East without irrigation, and been happy.

It is impossible to say that a Hazen plan for the universe would not have been better than that now existing, but for railroad purposes it is clear enough that it would never answer. What would become of the North Pacific Raliroad, if fruits and cereals were raised along its line and nothing else? There would be nothing to carry, for there would be no market except at the eastern terminus, and no freight except from the Red River Valley to Duluth. Why, the cereals raised on such an expanse of farming land would be enough to feed many worlds like ours, and would be left to perish where they grew. Major-general Hazen may depend upon it that Nature has an eye to these things in laying out her territory, and manages them better than he would even in adapting it to railroads. If there is no soil and climate for cereals

248

west of 101°, what a double inducement is presented to the settler in the valley of the Red River! He will have an outlet for his wheat on the Missouri River as well as on Lake Superior, a market at Bismarck as well as at Duluth, besides a world to the east of Duluth to supply. Through 1,600 miles he will send his wheat to the graziers of Dakota, the graziers and miners of Idaho, the miners and lumbermen of Montana and Washington. His wheat thus sent over the road west will bring cattle and coal and iron and gold and silver to the east of that marvelous meridian of 101°, which is the dividing line between moisture and aridity, between fertility and barrenness.

It strikes us that such a bank account is rather a solid one, and that a company may give a note upon its security without being stigmatized as swindlers. It is so very sufficient, that it is hardly necessary to allude to another item of the assets of the North Pacific Railroad which our financier entirely ignores. The Company has two railroads practically complete, thoroughly equipped, and in successful operation. The line of 452 miles from Duluth on Lake Superior to Bismarck on the Missouri River, is as finished a road, and with as eligible termini, as a line from Albany to Buffalo, or a line connecting the water of Hudson River with the waters of Massachusetts Bay. Equally complete, if another rail is never laid, is the road of 105½ miles from Kalama on the Columbia River to Tacoma on Puget Sound. At Kalama a river navigation of four hundred miles is commanded by means of the Oregon Steam Navigation Company, thus connecting Washington, Oregon and Idaho with the navigable waters of the Pacific. So at Bismarck, the present terminus of the eastern division, there is a steam navigation commanding twelve hundred miles of the Upper Missouri, with the Yellowstone for its confluent, and thus securing the transportation business of western Dakota, and of northern and southern Montana. And all this if the enterprise should stop just where it is. In addition to eleven million acres of land admitted to be valuable, and already earned, the bond-holders of the North Pacific Railroad have the additional security of two completed railroads that will be abundantly able at no remote period to

249

respond to the interest of the bonds already issued, while the land grant is gradually paying off the principal.

We think that it has been demonstrated that the attack of Major-general Hazen on the integrity of the promotors of the North Pacific Railroad is as reckless and wanton as his penny valuation of the territory we have described is preposterous. What motive could have induced him to set up as appraiser of a territory which he has never seen, and to set down half a continent as not worth a penny an acre; or what motive could have induced him to libel men, who to say the least are as well known and as favorably known as himself, we cannot for the life of us imagine. We need not go so far as to seek a motive for the newspapers that indorse his diatribe. Newspapers are printed for profit. Many newspapers are printed for nothing else. When we look at the returns of the Union Pacific and the Central Pacific railroads, we cannot fail to observe that they have ample means for paying the interest on all their securities, land grants, income, and governments, and still to hold in reserve a handsome residue to apply where it will do the most good. A newspaper can afford to be very much appalled and very much inexpressibly shocked, in the interest of two such corporations. And at this point, by way of parenthesis, we should ask the attention of Major-general Hazen to a little table to offset the "statistics" with which he has confirmed his "personal experience" at Fort Buford. The Union Pacific and Central Pacific traverse the Great American Desert—to be known henceforth by the name of Hazen—that 1,600 mile stretch where there is such limited rainfall, and where fruits and cereals can never grow. In the year 1873 the Union Pacific, on ten hundred and thirty-two miles in operation, earned upwards of ten millions of dollars and netted $5,291,242.61. The Central Pacific, on eleven hundred and fifty-eight miles in operation, earned $13,938,969 in gold, and netted nearly eight millions of dollars. The Illinois Central, with eleven hundred and seven miles in operation, running through an agricultural country sufficiently irrigated and tip-top for fruits and cereals, earned in gross $8,628,325 and netted $2,860,741.68. And yet the Illinois Central is esteemed an excellent property. Its stock is above par. It can borrow more money than it wants at five per cent, and buys up its own bonds at a premium as the best investment of its surplus cash. But it will be noted that the net earnings of the road through the desert are already much larger, mile for mile, than the net earnings of the road through the prairies.

I have lived forty years on the frontier. I have probably measured more acres of the Northwest than Major-general Hazen has ever seen. The route of the North Pacific Railroad runs through a region of country adapted to the most important and most diversified industries—from the terminus on Lake Superior to the terminus on Puget Sound. The wheat-growing land of Minnesota is the finest in the world. The grazing lands of Dakota and Idaho are unsurpassed. The mineral lands of Montana are of the most abundant richness. The timber lands of Washington and Oregon are laden with the undisturbed growth of centuries. LUMBER, GOLD and SILVER, COAL, CATTLE and WHEAT—on the broadest areas and in inexhaustible quantities—could not Major-general Hazen reconsider his proposition, and make it a penny better?

15. Postscript

In the years that have intervened since the controversy first flared, it has simmered but never entirely died out. There are many Americans today who think of the region "beyond the wide Missouri" as nothing but a great desert waste, and who cannot be convinced that they are wrong. And statement of that belief brings a chorus of indignant denials from western supporters. Many of the latter are firmly of the counter opinion—that there is no real American civilization east of the ninety-eighth meridian, and that one does not see the real America until the Red River of the North is crossed, going west.

General Hazen's original motive is uncertain. It was probably not entirely due to a desire to protect American investors or settlers against an unwise commitment, nor was it attributable to resentment at the fact that the railroad had refused to carry his baggage free of charge. By 1874 it was a well-matured opinion and was not the result of a temporary irritation. And though Hazen was not averse to publicity, there was more to it than a desire to get his name in the paper. His disposition was contentious and belligerent; he might well have been called "an old curmudgeon" had that phrase then been in common use. Like Custer, he was ambitious, and the pursuit of glory was legitimate for any army officer, particularly one stationed at a frontier outpost. He was perfectly willing to engage in any controversy that would bring his name prominently before the American public. The same was true of Custer, who was probably the more self-seeking of the two, and who was perfectly willing to take up the cudgels against Hazen, towards whom he had a certain amount of hostility. Nor could Custer have been unaware of the exchange of letters between Sheridan and Hazen over the action of the latter in intervening to protect the hostile Kiowa Indians after the battle of the Washita.

The dates in the Hazen-Custer controversy are not without interest. Hazen's original letter to the New York *Tribune* was dated January 1, 1874, but was not published until February 7; Custer's article criticizing Hazen's action in protecting the Kiowas appeared in the January issue of the *Galaxy*. On April 17, Custer's letter, dated April 9, taking issue with Colonel Hazen's appraisal of the western lands, appeared in the Minneapolis *Tribune*. On May 30, 1874, came Hazen's reply to Custer's criticism of his conduct after the Washita. Then the January, 1875, issue of the *North American Review* carried Hazen's article on the great middle region of the United States, which, as I have indicated, was a carefully-thought-out article that must have required some time in preparation. It was later in the spring that he published his pamphlet, *Our Barren Lands*. Thus the two controversies were contemporary, being carried on almost side by side.

In their disagreement over the future possibilities of the area west of the Missouri River and east of the Sierra Mountains, both men overlooked testimony and evidence that would have lent support to their arguments, a common failing of those who criticize. Hazen might have noted that in the decade before the Civil War Lieutenant Gouverneur K. Warren of the Topographical Engineers had made extensive explorations of the American West, including a detailed examination of the Yellowstone Valley from the mouth of that river to a point opposite its confluence with the Powder River.[1] Since the Sioux Indians by this time had become a source of considerable annoyance to the government, his expeditions were for the purpose of acquiring information about the nature of the country and the routes of travel followed by the Indians, and also for locating desirable sites for possible military posts. His reports made it abundantly clear that while there were

[1] *Contributions to the Historical Society of Montana*, X, 297.

exceptions, much of the country was not suitable for agriculture, that in many places the soil was dry and sandy, covered with cactus and sagebrush, and since it was beyond the reach of irrigation, largely unsuitable for settlement.

Similarly, Lieutenant Mullins, who had been with the Raynald's expedition in 1860, had traveled across the region north of the Yellowstone River and left an unflattering picture of what he and his party had experienced. Ordered to march from Fort Benton to Fort Union, keeping as close to the summit of the ridge dividing the Yellowstone and Missouri rivers as the topography of the land would allow, and guided by the veteran Jim Bridger, Lieutenant Mullins left Fort Benton on the twentieth of July. The valleys of the Judith River and its principal tributaries, as well as the valley of the upper Musselshell, were described as fertile and well timbered, with excellent grass; but east of the Big Bend of the Musselshell the nature of the country changed. The land was barren, with little water and less wood, and the scanty grass had been eaten off by the buffalo. These animals were present in large numbers, mute evidence that the country could not be entirely barren. The main stream of the Porcupine was almost dry, the water standing in holes, and the Lieutenant was of the opinion that about one-third of the fluid they dignified by the name of water was buffalo urine. Beyond this stream the country was dry and barren, and there was little wood, water, or grass. In short, it was a region that was "entirely and emphatically worthless." Marching was difficult, the terrain being cut up by dry creeks beds and rock-strewn ravines; but the country gradually improved as they approached the Yellowstone, and the valley of this stream was found to be well timbered, with luxuriant vegetation. Lieutenant Mullins estimated that during the march his detachment had covered nearly four hundred miles over country that was next to worthless, but he considered that it was ideally suited to railroad construction since there were no considerable elevations to be overcome.[2]

Hazen had also included in both his pamphlet and magazine

[2] 40 Cong., 1 sess., *Senate Executive Document No. 77*, 164–67.

article a letter from Colonel Alfred Sully regarding the value of the region lying between the Red River of the North and the Missouri. During the Civil War, Colonel Sully had been in command of a column of troops that had defeated a hostile Indian force at the battle of Kildeer Mountain and then marched across country to the Yellowstone River. This expedition had crossed the Bad Lands of the Little Missouri, and Sully had written a graphic description of the country traversed. After passing through the region that he described as "hell with the fires out," the troops marched through an equally barren area which he described as being very broken and all tumbled to pieces. The grass, not very good in the best of seasons, had been largely eaten off by grasshoppers, while the only water available was heavily impregnated with alkali. Along the Yellowstone River proper, the grass was scarce and scattered, but Sully was of the opinion that this was not usually the case since during the previous winter there had been but little snow, and the rain, when it came, was too late to be of much value. All of this would have been support for Hazen's argument, since the region described was that traversed by the Northern Pacific, but for some reason it was not used.[3]

In 1872, Major J. W. Barlow, who was with a surveying party on the Yellowstone above Pompey's Pillar, described the region between the Yellowstone and the Musselshell River as a dry, alkali country "nearly barren from lack of moisture." It consisted of a vast plateau elevated several hundred feet above the valleys, and while he saw no future possibilities for it, he had been very favorably impressed with the valley of the Musselshell itself, for it consisted of "woody ravines and grassy slopes on which thousands of buffalo were quietly grazing." He commented that this valley was much more inviting than that of the Yellowstone, but of the region east of the Big Bend of the Musselshell, his opinion was distinctly unfavorable. The dry and barren ridges immediately in front presented a very forbidding appearance and behind them were the Bad Lands. He believed that it would be very difficult to force a passage with a heavy wagon train through this region on

[3] *South Dakota Historical Collections*, VIII (1916), 288–324.

account of the rugged nature of the country and the scarcity of water,[4] but it was through this very region that Custer marched the next year on his way back to the base camp near Glendive Creek without the loss of a wagon.

General David Stanley, who had commanded the Yellowstone expeditions of 1872 and 1873—the latter with Custer as a subordinate—had received an unfavorable impression of the country through which his two expeditions had passed. He reported that both grass and water were poor, and he was especially critical of the region around Cabin Creek. The alkaline soil was soft, and there were deep ravines and washouts. He considered the country not only barren but uninteresting, since it was almost destitute of moisture and vegetation.[5]

In February, 1874, General Sherman, testifying before the House Military Affairs Committee, gave aid and comfort to both parties in the controversy. Speaking of "the remote country in Dakota" between the confluence of the Yellowstone and Missouri rivers, which was the location of Fort Buford, and the place where the Northern Pacific Railroad first crosses the Missouri, which was the location of Fort Abraham Lincoln, he expressed the opinion that this section constituted an area that would have to be forever occupied by the army, "for the land is infinitely poor, and there is no chance for any settlement there or thereabouts." At the same time, General Sherman spoke of "the new and very fine territory of Montana" as the "most promising of the new territories," which was rapidly filling up with "a most excellent population, who were occupied in agriculture, the grazing of cattle, and the development of the mines."[6]

Although he was probably not aware of them, Hazen could also have cited in support of his position the experience of the Custers at Fort Abraham Lincoln, where the attempts at cultivating a garden were as unsuccessful as those of Hazen at Fort Buford. Attempts at transplanting cottonwood trees so as to line the parade

[4] 42 Cong., 3 sess., *Senate Executive Document No. 16*, 11–12.
[5] *Personal Memoirs of General D. S. Stanley*, 255–63.
[6] *Army and Navy Journal*, Feb. 4, 1874.

ground, and at growing grass, were alike unsuccessful. The strong, hot summer winds burned out the grass and made impossible the raising of flowers, so that, according to Mrs. Custer, only an occasional blue-bell gave a touch of variety to relieve the arid monotony of the land around the post.[7]

A short time after the publication of Hazen's pamphlet, one of General Crook's officers, writing from the Powder River, gave an unflattering description of the country along the left bank of that stream:

> The region is terribly rough and sterile, and only the narrow river bed running deep in the canyons affords water and pasturage. The country has no attractions for a civilized man, and can offer nothing in mitigation of its general sterility and worthlessness. I most decided agree with General Hazen in his views of the barrenness and utterly valueless character of this whole region of country, in respect to its adaptability to agricultural and pastoral uses.

This officer added, as a final word of condemnation, that only a few wretched Indians were able to live there, and these only by stealing from the frontier settlers and from the agencies. So sterile was the country, and so scarce the animal life that it would have meant starvation to rely on game.[8]

John F. Finerty, a newspaper correspondent with General Crook's column, had not been quite so emphatic. After describing a section of land along Pumpkin Creek as "terrible" he added: "The soil looked like the surface of a non-atmospheric planet, hard, repulsive, sterile. It made one's heart sick to look at the place." He said of the region farther east:

> Beaver Creek is called the Indian branch of the lesser Missouri, and runs through a lovely champaign country. How General Hazen, in his famous report, could call the section from the Powder River to that stream 'a desert' passes comprehension and excited general surprise. A finer locality for either grazing or tillage purposes could hardly be imagined. With few exceptions, the tract indicated is an unbroken meadow-land.

[7] Elizabeth B. Custer, *Boots and Saddles*, 137–39, 156.
[8] *Army and Navy Journal*, April 8, 1876.

257

He had earlier spoken of a portion of the valley of the Rosebud as "the Indian Paradise" and declared that for many miles it truly deserved "that heavenly name." Of the locality of Crook's camp on Goose Creek, he wrote:

> It was a delightfully romantic spot—nothing more beautiful, at least at that season, this side of Paradise. We revelled in the crystal water, and slept beneath the grateful shade of the trees, that fringed the emerald banks of those beautiful tributaries of Tongue River, that winding Daughter of the Snows.[9]

Custer's argument could have been reinforced by his observations and experiences on the Black Hills Expedition of 1874. This expedition although it came after he had written his reply to Hazen, would have furnished him with considerable rebuttal evidence. His account of the Black Hills was almost a rapturous panegyric of unadulterated praise, although he did concede that the country through which his column had passed before reaching "the Hills" and after leaving them left something to be desired. Colonel Forsyth, who was on Custer's staff, described the Hills as "a series of little valleys with plenty of good spring water and and a fine growth of pine timber," and added that it was "about as good a grazing country as he had ever seen," and also that it was well suited to agriculture "rather than being a mass of granite hills as was generally supposed."[10] Captain Ludlow, who had accompanied the expedition as engineering officer, declared that the region between Fort Lincoln and the Belle Fourche River was "rather uninviting," which would seem to have been something of an understatement. But after crossing the Belle Fourche, the expedition had found itself in a new and different country "with an abundance of grass, timber, small flowers and fruits, and what perhaps was the most appreciated of all, an ample supply of pure, cold water." He added that according to his information the valleys on the southern slopes of the hills were ready for the plow,

---

[9] John F. Finerty, *War-Path and Bivouac* (Norman, University of Oklahoma Press, 1961), 103, 157, 167, 176.

[10] *Army and Navy Journal*, Sept. 12, 1874.

and that "the soil was of wonderful fertility as was evidenced by the luxury of the grass."[11]

General John Gibbon, Seventh Infantry, who commanded the Montana Column in the Sioux campaign of 1876, and whose troops had marched over a great deal of the territory under dispute, wrote that

> ... the country visited by the troops is by no means the desert it has been represented. There is, of course, a great deal of barren, worthless land, but there is also much land in the valleys susceptible of cultivation, and an immense region of good grazing country which will in time be available for stock raising. Even where, from the valleys, the appearance of the so called "bad lands" was most forbidding, we found on the plateau above excellent grass in the greatest abundance covering the country for great distances. This was particularly noticeable in the region north of the Powder River, between the Yellowstone and Missouri rivers, and along the Tongue and Rosebud and the country between the two. The country along the Little Big Horn is also a fine grass country, and along the Big Horn itself, immense valleys of fine grass extend.[12]

It is apparent that General Gibbon realized, as so many failed to do, that the region west of the Missouri River was a land of infinite variety, that while there were barren and arid tracts, there also areas of great fertility, and that much of the region that seemed worthless at first glance, was, in reality, superb grazing land. He also realized that the indigenous grasses of the Great Plains, especially the "bunch-grass" which cured on the stalk, that furnished subsistence to millions of head of buffalo, would also furnish pasturage for large herds of cattle. He also knew, what others failed to appreciate, that the American frontiersman was characterized by great adaptability and resourcefulness, and that it would not require too many years for the settler to make himself master of his new environment.

General Hazen was wrong in that his indictment was too sweeping and his general condemnation took in too great an extent of territory. He was also wrong in assuming that the type of agri-

[11] *Ibid.*, Sept. 19, 1874.
[12] *Report of the Secretary of War*, 1876, Section 3A, p. 476.

cultural life which existed east of the Missouri River would have to be transferred, without modification to the territories west of that stream. General Custer was wrong in that he allowed his enthusiasm to run away with his judgment, and he made broad, general deductions from too small a sampling of the territory involved. But if Custer was too much the optimist, Hazen was too much the pessimist, too prone to believe that what had not been done could not be done and too willing to belabor the Northern Pacific. Although not a "glory-hunter" to the extent that Custer was, he was not without ambition. He was also disappointed and embittered, and on this, as on many other occasions, he rushed too precipitately into controversy. Like Custer, he was too anxious to be in the limelight, and Custer was only too willing to "have a go" at Hazen, against whom he held a deep, if apparently unjustified, resentment.

Neither man could foresee the advancements in agricultural science, the development of new methods of cultivation such as "dry farming" that were to transform the business of raising wheat and other grains. Despite these developments, however, there are regions of the American West that are still arid, although worth considerably more than "a penny an acre." That interest in the topic has not entirely died is evident from an article, appropriately enough in *Harper's Magazine* for May, 1957. Entitled "The American West: Perpetual Mirage," and written by the late Walter Prescott Webb, the dean of American western historians, this article repeated many of the familiar arguments and added a few new ones. It drew in subsequent issues of the magazine a chorus of indignant replies from many who resented what they considered an unjustified attack upon their part of the country.

Although the reaction to Hazen's pamphlet was by no means as great as that to his original article, his critics did not forget or forgive. Nor did they overlook any opportunity to remind him of his indiscretion in having called the agricultural potential of the region into question. On Sunday, May 16, 1880, a torrential rainstorm struck the Fort Buford area, and some of the newspapers took delight in mentioning that the rain has not only been so copious as to transform the Colonel's vegetable garden into a duck pond, but that it required the services of a detachment of soldiers long after taps to prevent it from floating away.[13] At that time the Sixth Infantry was under orders for Colorado, and the St. Paul *Pioneer-Press,* on the departure of the regiment, fired its parting salute as Hazen left the country served by the Northern Pacific Railroad.

> As he rides through the waving wheat-fields of Dakota at the rate of twenty miles an hour, his reflections must be unpleasant in view of the report made years ago that Dakota was a desert. The Colonel will perhaps admit that he was mistaken.

But by this time both men and newspapers had had time to reconsider, and to retire somewhat from the advanced positions that they had once occupied. Thus the *Northwest Magazine,* one of the staunchest boosters for the area, summed up the merits and demerits of the region in an article in the October, 1899, issue. Under the heading "Our Arid Lands," this article declared:

> The advancing line of Western settlement has nearly reached the limits of profitable cultivation by rain-fall, and in some localities, such as Kansas, Oklahoma and Texas, the enthusiasm and hopes of the pioneers have carried them beyond the danger line, into regions, which if not classified as arid, are too dry in a majority of seasons for success in farming. Between the area of sufficient rainfall, and that recognized as arid, where no one attempts to farm without irrigation, there is a belt of country about two hundred miles broad, reaching from far up in the British Territory clear down to the Gulf of Mexico which may be termed the sub-arid or sub-humid region, in which a series of years of considerable precipitation of rain and snow are followed by a series of years of scanty moisture. Certain counties in Kansas lying within this belt have been peopled and depopulated three times. . . . No climatic changes are occurring in any part of the American continent. . . .
>
> West of the sub-arid belt lies the vast region acknowledged to be arid, and including all territory lying between the 102nd meridian and the Cascade and Sierra mountains, except certain districts like Palouse and Walla Walla counties in Washington where elevated plateaux receive exceptional moisture from near mountain ranges.

[13] *Army and Navy Journal,* June 19, 1880.

The arid region of the United States contains almost as many square miles as the humid regions. . . . A large amount of its surface is fertile land needing only water to produce crops far greater in yield than can be raised in the rainy regions east of the Mississippi. Great rivers fed by rains, snows and springs of the Rocky Mountains traverse this arid country. . . . The great economic problem of the future in this country is how to utilize these waters for the benefit of the people. It is a problem of national importance appealing to the highest order of statesmanship, for it is indissolubly associated with the development of the Republic for centuries to come.

All the early civilizations were in irrigated regions and when the ancient nations declined it was because their reservoirs and canals were either neglected or were destroyed by enemies.

According to the estimate of the United States Geological Survey, there are in the Yellowstone bottoms 5,000,000 acres of irrigable fertile land.

The Yellowstone Valley, although not too wide, . . . is capable of supporting over half a million prosperous people.

The nation needs its arid lands for the homes for its increasing population and enterprise; capital and statesmanship must now take hold in earnest of the great question of their systematic reclamation.

It must not be overlooked that the greater part of the area of the Great Plains was not suited to the production of the fruits and cereals of the eastern part of the country, which was precisely what General Hazen had maintained. The economic salvation of the settlers of the Northern Plains was to come from the development of the range cattle industry, a development which, as Walter Prescott Webb has pointed out, was a unique American phenomenon, and that the development of the cattle business in Montana coincided almost exactly with the westward building of the Northern Pacific Railroad. Although the greatest period of the industry was still ahead, cattle were being shipped from the Montana ranges down the Yellowstone River by boat at the same time that Bismarck ceased to be the western terminus of the Northern Pacific.

General Hazen was, in the main, correct in his contention, but his estimate of the future value of these barren lands was erroneous in the highest degree. Thus it is somewhat ironic that there is today a Northern Pacific Railroad station in North Dakota named after the irascible infantryman. From this place between three and four thousand carloads of lignite and grain are forwarded annually over the lines of the railroad. This is hardly evidence of a barren land, land not worth "a penny an acre."

Index

agricultural products, 99; attractions
for settlers, 242–43
Mormons: 203
Mount Baker: 199
Mount Lassen: 198n.
Mullan, Lieutenant John: 33, 41 n., 52,
72–73
Mullins, Lieutenant John: 92n., 101, 254
Munson, Lieutenant J. F.: 38, 143, 213
Musselshell River: 29, 91, 175, 197, 254–
55; nature of country, 79
My Life on the Plains, quoted: 12–13

Nation: 210
Nebraska, eastern and western compared: 194
Nevada: 208; hard times in, 204
New Mexico Territory: 208; nature of
country, 187; value of lands, 189;
arable lands in, 192
New York Independent: 28
New York *Tribune*: 15, 55, 57, 61–62, 66,
78, 80, 86, 94, 114, 118, 140, 151, 167,
184, 222, 228
Nineteenth Kansas Volunteer Cavalry:
12
North American Review: 184; Hazen's
article in, 185–219
Northern Boundary Survey: 79, 150
Northern Pacific Railroad: 119, 135,
179–82, 221; land grant to, 24–26, 131,
236; route of, 30–32, 74, 83, 88, 122;
compared with Union Pacific, 45, 74;
financial dealings of, 59, 76, 120, 123,
125, 132–34; nature of country along
route of, 77, 83, 93, 126–27; Custer's
defense of, 78ff.; influence on solution
of Indian question, 112; charter, 121–
22; traffic over, 126–29; Asiatic trade,
129; advertising, 210–11; congressional reports on, 223
"Northern Tropical Belt": 141
Northwest Magazine: 261

One Stab (Indian Chief): 117
Oregon Steam Navigation Company: 249
"Our Arid Lands": 261
Our Barren Lands (pamphlet): 3

"Penny an acre": 3, 53, 69, 72, 75, 239,
243, 263
Phil Sheridan, Kansas: 212 & n.

Platte valley: 193
"Poetry and Philosophy of Indian Sum-
mer": 33, 35
Pompey's Pillar: 29, 79
Porcupine Creek: 254
Porter, H. R.: 156
Post traders, controversy over: 14
Powder River: 51n., 165, 207 & n.;
nature of region, 257
Prickly Pear Valley: 31, 67
Providence *Press*, quoted: 61
Puget Sound: 198, 209, 249

Quaking Ash Creek (Poplar River) : 150
"Question of Fact, A": 64–69

Railroad rings: 221–26; definition of,
221
Rainfall: 213–14; in 1872 and 1873; lack
of, 141, 143; 98th and 100th meridian
compared, 200
Range cattle industry: 262
Rankin, Brevet Colonel John: 20
Raynolds, Captain W. F.: 41n., 73
Red River (of the North) : 195, 216
Red River Valley: 168
Reno, Major Marcus A.: 48, 79, 150
*Report on the Construction of a Military
Road from Fort Walla Walla to Fort
Benton*: 41n.
Reynolds, Lonesome Charley: 114, 116
Roberts, Colonel Thomas P.: 63; criti-
cism of Hazen, 66
Roberts, William Milnor: 245; career of,
70; reply to Hazen, 71; arguments
answered, 164
Rosser, General Thomas L.: 80, 114, 163;
interview with, 47; career summarized,
48–49; controversy with Major Reno,
48; opinion of Hazen, 49–53
Running water, lack of: 165

St. Mary's Mission, Montana Territory:
97n.
Salmon River: 225
Sargeant, George P.: 136
Sargent, George B.: 227
Sargent, John O.: 227
Satanta: 11–12
Schlagintweit, Professor Robert von: 29
Schoolcraft, Henry R.: 233
Selkirk, Lord: 27